本书出版得到《大中华文库》出版经费资助

# 大中华文库

# LIBRARY OF CHINESE CLASSICS

大中华文库

汉英对照

LIBRARY OF CHINESE CLASSICS

Chinese-English

# 吴　子
# WU　ZI
# 司马法
# THE METHODS OF THE SIMA
# 尉缭子
# WEI LIAO ZI

王式金 黄朴民 任力　校释

潘嘉玢　译

*Edited and translated into modern Chinese by*

Wang Shijin, Huang Pumin and Ren Li

*Translated into English by*

Pan Jiabin

军事科学出版社

Military Science Publishing House

First Edition 2004



ISBN 7-80137-721-4


*Published by*
Military Science Publishing House,
Academy of Military Science of
the Chinese People's Liberation Army,
Qinglongqiao, Haidian District,
Beijing 100091,China
*Printed by*
Shenzhen Jiaxinda Printing Co.,Shenzhen,China
*Printed in the People's Republic of China*

# 总　序

杨牧之

《大中华文库》终于出版了。我们为之高兴，为之鼓舞，但也倍感压力。

当此之际，我们愿将郁积在我们心底的话，向读者倾诉。

## 一

中华民族有着悠久的历史和灿烂的文化，系统、准确地将中华民族的文化经典翻译成外文，编辑出版，介绍给全世界，是几代中国人的愿望。早在几十年前，西方一位学者翻译《红楼梦》，书名译成《一个红楼上的梦》，将林黛玉译为“黑色的玉”。我们一方面对外国学者将中国的名著介绍到世界上去表示由衷的感谢，一方面为祖国的名著还不被完全认识，甚而受到曲解，而感到深深的遗憾。还有西方学者翻译《金瓶梅》，专门摘选其中自然主义描述最为突出的篇章加以译介。一时间，西方学者好像发现了奇迹，掀起了《金瓶梅》热，说中国是“性开放的源头”，公开地在报刊上鼓吹中国要“发扬开放之传统”。还有许多资深、友善的汉学家译介中国古代的哲学著作，在把中华民族文化介绍给全世界的工作方面作出了重大贡献，但或囿于理解有误，或缘于对中国文字认识的局限，质量上乘的并不多，常常是隔靴搔痒，说不到点子上。大哲学家黑格尔曾经说过：中国有最完备的国史。但他认为中国古代没有真正意义上的哲学，还处在哲学史前状态。这么了不起的哲学家竟然作出这样大失水准的评论，何其不幸。正如任何哲学家都要受时间、地点、条件的制约一样，黑格尔也离不开这一规律。当时他也只能从上述水平的汉学家译过去的文字去分析、理解，所以，黑格尔先生对中国古代社会的认识水平是什么状态，也就不难想象了。

中国离不开世界，世界也缺少不了中国。中国文化摄取外域的新成分，丰富了自己，又以自己的新成就输送给别人，贡献于世界。从公元5世纪开始到公元15世纪，大约有一千年，中国走在世界的前列。在这一千多年的时间里，她的光辉照耀全世界。人类要前进，怎么能不全面认识中国，怎么能不认真研究中国的历史呢?



二

中华民族是伟大的，曾经辉煌过，蓝天、白云、阳光灿烂，和平而兴旺；也有过黑暗的、想起来就让人战栗的日子，但中华民族从来是充满理想，不断追求，不断学习，渴望和平与友谊的。

中国古代伟大的思想家孔子曾经说过:“三人行，必有我师焉。择其善者而从之，其不善者而改之。”孔子的话就是要人们向别人学习。这段话正是概括了整个中华民族与人交往的原则。人与人之间交往如此，在与周边的国家交往中也是如此。

秦始皇第一个统一了中国，可惜在位只有十几年，来不及作更多的事情。汉朝继秦而继续强大，便开始走出去，了解自己周边的世界。公元前 138 年，汉武帝派张骞出使西域。他带着一万头牛羊，总值一万万钱的金帛货物，作为礼物，开始西行，最远到过“安息”(即波斯)。公元前 36 年，班超又率 36 人出使西域。36 个人按今天的话说，也只有一个排，显然是为了拜访未曾见过面的邻居，是去交朋友。到了西域，班超派遣甘英作为使者继续西行，往更远处的大秦国(即罗马)去访问，“乃抵条支而历安息，临西海以望大秦”(《后汉书·西域传》)。“条支”在“安息”以西，即今天的伊拉克、叙利亚一带，“西海”应是今天的地中海。也就是说甘英已经到达地中海边上，与罗马帝国隔海相望，“临大海欲渡”，却被人劝阻而未成行，这在历史上留下了遗恨。可以想见班超、甘英沟通友谊的无比勇气和强烈愿望。接下来是唐代的玄奘，历经千难万险，到“西天”印度取经，带回了南亚国家的古老文化。归国后，他把带回的佛教经典组织人翻译，到后来很多经典印度失传了，但中国却保存完好，以至于今天，没有玄奘的《大唐西域记》，印度人很难编写印度古代史。明代郑和“七下西洋”，把中华文化传到东南亚一带。鸦片战争以后，一代又一代先进的中国人，为了振兴中华，又前赴后继，向西方国家学习先进的科学思想和文明成果。这中间有我们的领导人朱德、周恩来、邓小平；有许许多多大科学家、文学家、艺术家，如郭沫若、李四光、钱学森、冼星海、徐悲鸿等。他们的追求、奋斗，他们的博大胸怀，兼收并蓄的精神，为人类社会增添了光彩。

中国文化的形成和发展过程，就是一个以众为师，以各国人民为师，不断学习和创造的过程。中华民族曾经向周边国家和民族学习过许多东西，假如没有这些学习，中华民族决不可能创造出昔日的辉煌。回顾历史，我们怎么能够不对伟大的古埃及文明、古希腊文明、古印度文明满怀深深的感激?怎么能够不对伟大的欧洲文明、非洲文明、美洲文明、澳洲文明，以及中国周围的亚洲文明充满温情与敬意?

中华民族为人类社会曾作出过独特的贡献。在15世纪以前，中国的科学技术一直处于世界遥遥领先的地位。英国科学家李约瑟说:“中国在公元3世纪到13世纪之间，保持着一个西方所望尘莫及的科学知识水平。”美国耶鲁大学教授、《大国的兴衰》的作者保罗·肯尼迪坦言:“在近代以前时期的所有文明中，没有一个国家的文明比中国更发达，更先进。”

世界各国的有识之士千里迢迢来中国观光、学习。在这个过程中，中国唐朝的长安城渐渐发展成为国际大都市。西方的波斯、东罗马，东亚的高丽、新罗、百济、南天竺、北天竺，频繁前来。外国的王侯、留学生，在长安供职的外国官员，商贾、乐工和舞士，总有几十个国家，几万人之多。日本派出“遣唐使”更是一批接一批。传为美谈的日本人阿部仲麻吕(晁衡)在长安留学的故事，很能说明外国人与中国的交往。晁衡学成仕于唐朝，前后历时五十余年。晁衡与中国的知识分子结下了深厚的友情。他归国时，传说在海中遇难身亡。大诗人李白作诗哭悼:“日本晁卿辞帝都，征帆一片远蓬壶。明月不归沉碧海，白云愁色满苍梧。”晁衡遇险是误传，但由此可见中外学者之间在中国长安交往的情谊。

后来，不断有外国人到中国来探寻秘密，所见所闻，常常让他们目瞪口呆。《希腊纪事》(希腊人波桑尼阿著)记载公元2世纪时，希腊人在中国的见闻。书中写道:“赛里斯人用小米和青芦喂一种类似蜘蛛的昆虫，喂到第五年，虫肚子胀裂开，便从里面取出丝来。”从这段对中国古代养蚕技术的描述，可见当时欧洲人与中国人的差距。公元9世纪中叶，阿拉伯人来到中国。一位阿拉伯作家在他所著的《中国印度闻见录》中记载了曾旅居中国的阿拉伯商人的见闻：

——一天，一个外商去拜见驻守广州的中国官吏。会见时，外商总盯着官吏的胸部，官吏很奇怪，便问："你好像总盯着我的胸，这是怎么回事？"那位外商回答说："透过你穿的丝绸衣服，我隐约看到你胸口上长着一个黑痣，这是什么丝绸，我感到十分惊奇。"官吏听后，失声大笑，伸出胳膊，说："请你数数吧，看我穿了几件衣服？"那商人数过，竟然穿了五件之多，黑痣正是透过这五层丝绸衣服显现出来的。外商惊得目瞪口呆，官吏说："我穿的丝绸还不算是最好的，总督穿的要更精美。"

——书中关于茶(他们叫干草叶子)的记载，可见阿拉伯国家当时还没有喝茶的习惯。书中记述："中国国王本人的收入主要靠盐税和泡开水喝的一种干草税。在各个城市里，这种干草叶售价都很高，中国人称这种草叶叫'茶'，这种干草叶比苜蓿的叶子还多，也略比它香，稍有苦味，用开水冲喝，治百病。"

——他们对中国的医疗条件十分羡慕，书中记载道："中国人医疗条件很好，穷人可以从国库中得到药费。"还说："城市里，很多地方立一石碑，高10肘，上面刻有各种疾病和药物，写明某种病用某种药医治。"

——关于当时中国的京城，书中作了生动的描述：中国的京城很大，人口众多，一条宽阔的长街把全城分为两半，大街右边的东区，住着皇帝、宰相、禁军及皇家的总管、奴婢。在这个区域，沿街开凿了小河，流水潺潺；路旁，葱茏的树木整然有序，一幢幢宅邸鳞次栉比。大街左边的西区，住着庶民和商人。这里有货栈和商店，每当清晨，人们可以看到，皇室的总管、宫廷的仆役，或骑马或步行，到这里来采购。

此后的史籍对西人来华的记载，渐渐多了起来。13 世纪意大利旅行家马可·波罗，尽管有人对他是否真的到过中国持怀疑态度，但他留下一部记述元代事件的《马可·波罗游记》却是确凿无疑的。这部游记中的一些关于当时中国的描述使得西方人认为是“天方夜谭”。总之，从中西文化交流史来说，这以前的时期还是一个想象和臆测的时代，相互之间充满了好奇与幻想。

从 16 世纪末开始，由于航海技术的发展，东西方航路的开通，随着一批批传教士来华，中国与西方开始了直接的交流。沟通中西的使命在意大利传教士利玛窦那里有了充分的体现。利玛窦于 1582 年来华，1610 年病逝于北京，在华 20 余年。除了传教以外，做了两件具有历史象征意义的事，一是 1594 年前后在韶州用拉丁文翻译《四书》，并作了注释；二是与明代学者徐光启合作，用中文翻译了《几何原本》。

西方传教士对《四书》等中国经典的粗略翻译，以及杜赫德的《中华帝国志》等书对中国的介绍，在西方读者的眼前展现了一个异域文明，在当时及稍后一段时期引起了一场“中国热”，许多西方大思想家的眼光都曾注目中国文化。有的推崇中华文明，如莱布尼兹、伏尔泰、魁奈等，有的对中华文明持批评态度，如孟德斯鸠、黑格尔等。莱布尼兹认识到中国文化的某些思想与他的观念相近，如周易的卦象与他发明的二进制相契合，对中国文化给予了热情的礼赞；黑格尔则从他整个哲学体系的推演出发，认为中国没有真正意义上的哲学，还处在哲学史前的状态。但是，不论是推崇还是批评，是吸纳还是排斥，中西文化的交流产生了巨大的影响。随着先进的中国科学技术的西传，特别是中国的造纸、火药、印刷术和指南针四大发明的问世，大大改变了世界的面貌。马克思说："中国的火药把骑士阶层炸得粉碎，指南针打开了世界市场并建立了殖民地，而印刷术则变成了新教的工具，变成对精神发展创造必要前提的最强大的杠杆。"英国的哲学家培根说：中国的四大发明"改变了全世界的面貌和一切事物的状态"。

## 三

大千世界，潮起潮落。云散云聚，万象更新。中国古代产生了无数伟大科学家：祖冲之、李时珍、孙思邈、张衡、沈括、毕升……，产生了无数科技成果：《齐民要术》、《九章算术》、《伤寒杂病论》、《本草纲目》……，以及保存至今的世界奇迹：浑天仪、地动仪、都江堰、敦煌石窟、大运河、万里长城……。但从15世纪下半叶起，风水似乎从东方转到了西方，落后的欧洲只经过400年便成为世界瞩目的文明中心。英国的牛顿、波兰的哥白尼、德国的伦琴、法国的居里、德国的爱因斯坦、意大利的伽利略、俄国的门捷列夫、美国的费米和爱迪生……，光芒四射，令人敬仰。

中华民族开始思考了。潮起潮落究竟是什么原因？中国人发明的火药，传到欧洲，转眼之间反成为欧洲列强轰击中国大门的炮弹，又是因为什么？

鸦片战争终于催醒了中国人沉睡的迷梦，最先"睁眼看世界"的一代精英林则徐、魏源迈出了威武雄壮的一步。曾国藩、李鸿章搞起了洋务运动。中国的知识分子喊出"民主与科学”的口号。中国是落后了，中国的志士仁人在苦苦探索。但落后中饱含着变革的动力，探索中孕育着崛起的希望。“向科学进军”，中华民族终于又迎来了科学的春天。

今天，世界毕竟来到了21世纪的门槛。分散隔绝的世界，逐渐变成联系为一体的世界。现在，全球一体化趋势日益明显，人类历史也就在愈来愈大的程度上成为全世界的历史。当今，任何一种文化的发展都离不开对其它优秀文化的汲取，都以其它优秀文化的发展为前提。在近现代，西方文化汲取中国文化，不仅是中国文化的传播，更是西方文化自身的创新和发展；正如中国文化对西方文化的汲取一样，既是西方文化在中国的传播，同时也是中国文化在近代的转型和发展。地球上所有的人类文化，都是我们共同的宝贵遗产。既然我们生活的各个大陆，在地球史上曾经是连成一气的“泛大陆”，或者说是一个完整的“地球村”，那么，我们同样可以在这个以知识和学习为特征的网络时代，走上相互学习、共同发展的大路，建设和开拓我们人类崭新的“地球村”。

西学仍在东渐，中学也将西传。各国人民的优秀文化正日益迅速地为中国文化所汲取，而无论西方和东方，也都需要从中国文化中汲取养分。正是基于这一认识，我们组织出版汉英对照版《大中华文库》，全面系统地翻译介绍中国传统文化典籍。我们试图通过《大中华文库》，向全世界展示，中华民族五千年的追求，五千年的梦想，正在新的历史时期重放光芒。中国人民就像火后的凤凰，万众一心，迎接新世纪文明的太阳。

1999年8月

# PREFACE TO THE *LIBRARY OF CHINESE CLASSICS*

Yang Muzhi

The publication of the *Library of Chinese Classics* is a matter of great satisfaction to all of us who have been involved in the production of this monumental work. At the same time, we feel a weighty sense of responsibility, and take this opportunity to explain to our readers the motivation for undertaking this cross-century task.

## 1

The Chinese nation has a long history and a glorious culture, and it has been the aspiration of several generations of Chinese scholars to translate, edit and publish the whole corpus of the Chinese literary classics so that the nation's greatest cultural achievements can be introduced to people all over the world. There have been many translations of the Chinese classics done by foreign scholars. A few dozen years ago, a Western scholar translated the title of *A Dream of Red Mansions* into "A Dream of Red Chambers" and Lin Daiyu, the heroine in the novel, into "Black Jade." But while their endeavours have been laudable, the results of their labours have been less than satisfactory. Lack of knowledge of Chinese culture and an inadequate grasp of the Chinese written language have led the translators into many errors. As a consequence, not only are Chinese classical writings widely misunderstood in the rest of the world, in some cases their content has actually been distorted. At one time, there was a "*Jin Ping Mei* craze" among Western scholars, who thought that they had uncovered a miraculous phenomenon, and published theories claiming that China was the "fountainhead of eroticism," and that a Chinese "tradition of permissiveness" was about to be laid bare. This distorted view came about due to the translators of the *Jin Ping Mei (Plum in the Golden Vase)* putting one-sided stress on the raw elements in that novel, to the neglect of its overall literary value. Meanwhile, there have been many distinguished and well-intentioned Sinologists who have attempted to make the culture of the Chinese nation more widely known by translating works of ancient Chinese philosophy. However, the quality of such work, in many cases, is unsatisfactory, often missing the point entirely. The great philosopher Hegel considered that ancient China had no philosophy in the real sense of the word, being stuck in philosophical "prehistory." For such an eminent authority to make such a colossal error of judgment is truly regrettable. But, of course, Hegel was just as subject to the constraints of time, space and other objective conditions as anyone else, and since he had to rely for his knowledge of Chinese philosophy on inadequate translations it is not difficult to imagine why he went so far off the mark.

China cannot be separated from the rest of the world; and the rest of the world cannot ignore China. Throughout its history, Chinese civilization has enriched itself by absorbing new elements from the outside world, and in turn has contributed to the progress of world civilization as a whole by transmitting to other peoples its own cultural achievements. From the 5th to the 15th centuries, China marched in the front ranks of world civilization. If mankind wishes to advance, how can it afford to ignore China? How can it afford not to make a thoroughgoing study of its history?

## 2

Despite the ups and downs in their fortunes, the Chinese people have always been idealistic, and have never ceased to forge ahead and learn from others, eager to strengthen ties of peace and friendship.

The great ancient Chinese philosopher Confucius once said, "Wherever three persons come together, one of them will surely be able to teach me something. I will pick out his good points and emulate them; his bad points I will reform." Confucius meant by this that we should always be ready to learn from others. This maxim encapsulates the principle the Chinese people have always followed in their dealings with other peoples, not only on an individual basis but also at the level of state-to-state relations.

After generations of internecine strife, China was unified by Emperor

Qin Shi Huang (the First Emperor of the Qin Dynasty) in 221 B.C. The Han Dynasty, which succeeded that of the short-lived Qin, waxed powerful, and for the first time brought China into contact with the outside world. In 138 B.C., Emperor Wu dispatched Zhang Qian to the western regions, i.e. Central Asia. Zhang, who traveled as far as what is now Iran, took with him as presents for the rulers he visited on the way 10,000 head of sheep and cattle, as well as gold and silks worth a fabulous amount. In 36 B.C., Ban Chao headed a 36-man legation to the western regions. These were missions of friendship to visit neighbours the Chinese people had never met before and to learn from them. Ban Chao sent Gan Ying to explore further toward the west. According to the "Western Regions Section" in the *Book of Later Han*, Gan Ying traveled across the territories of present-day Iraq and Syria, and reached the Mediterranean Sea, an expedition which brought him within the confines of the Roman Empire. Later, during the Tang Dynasty, the monk Xuan Zang made a journey fraught with danger to reach India and seek the knowledge of that land. Upon his return, he organized a team of scholars to translate the Buddhist scriptures, which he had brought back with him. As a result, many of these scriptural classics which were later lost in India have been preserved in China. In fact, it would have been difficult for the people of India to reconstruct their own ancient history if it had not been for Xuan Zang's *A Record of a Journey to the West in the Time of the Great Tang Dynasty*. In the Ming Dynasty, Zheng He transmitted Chinese culture to Southeast Asia during his seven voyages. Following the Opium Wars in the mid-19th century, progressive Chinese, generation after generation, went to study the advanced scientific thought and cultural achievements of the Western countries. Their aim was to revive the fortunes of their own country. Among them were people who were later to become leaders of China, including Zhu De, Zhou Enlai and Deng Xiaoping. In addition, there were people who were to become leading scientists, literary figures and artists, such as Guo Moruo, Li Siguang, Qian Xuesen, Xian Xinghai and Xu Beihong. Their spirit of ambition, their struggles and their breadth of vision were an inspiration not only to the Chinese people but to people all over the world.

Indeed, it is true that if the Chinese people had not learned many things from the surrounding countries they would never have been able to produce the splendid achievements of former days. When we look back upon history, how can we not feel profoundly grateful for the legacies of the civilizations of ancient Egypt, Greece and India? How can we not feel fondness and respect for the cultures of Europe, Africa, America and Oceania?

The Chinese nation, in turn, has made unique contributions to the community of mankind. Prior to the 15th century, China led the world in science and technology. The British scientist Joseph Needham once said, "From the third century A.D. to the 13th century A.D. China was far ahead of the West in the level of its scientific knowledge." Paul Kennedy, of Yale University in the U.S., author of *The Rise and Fall of the Great Powers*, said, "Of all the civilizations of the pre-modern period, none was as well-developed or as progressive as that of China."

Foreigners who came to China were often astonished at what they saw and heard. The Greek geographer Pausanias in the second century A.D. gave the first account in the West of the technique of silk production in China: "The Chinese feed a spider-like insect with millet and reeds. After five years the insect's stomach splits open, and silk is extracted therefrom." From this extract, we can see that the Europeans at that time did not know the art of silk manufacture. In the middle of the 9th century A.D., an Arabian writer includes the following anecdote in his *Account of China and India*:

"One day, an Arabian merchant called upon the military governor of Guangzhou. Throughout the meeting, the visitor could not keep his eyes off the governor's chest. Noticing this, the latter asked the Arab merchant what he was staring at. The merchant replied, 'Through the silk robe you are wearing, I can faintly see a black mole on your chest. Your robe must be made out of very fine silk indeed!' The governor burst out laughing, and holding out his sleeve invited the merchant to count how many garments he was wearing. The merchant did so, and discovered that the governor was actually wearing five silk robes, one on top of the other, and they were made of such fine material that a tiny mole could be seen through them all! Moreover, the governor explained that the robes he was wearing were not made of the finest silk at all; silk of the highest grade was reserved for the garments worn by the provincial governor."

The references to tea in this book (the author calls it "dried grass") reveal that the custom of drinking tea was unknown in the Arab countries at that time: "The king of China's revenue comes mainly from taxes on salt and the dry leaves of a kind of grass which is drunk after boiled water is poured on it. This dried grass is sold at a high price in every city in the country. The Chinese call it 'cha.' The bush is like alfalfa, except that it bears more leaves, which are also more fragrant than alfalfa. It has a slightly bitter taste, and when it is infused in boiling water it is said to have medicinal properties."

Foreign visitors showed especial admiration for Chinese medicine. One wrote, "China has very good medical conditions. Poor people are given money to buy medicines by the government."

In this period, when Chinese culture was in full bloom, scholars flocked from all over the world to China for sightseeing and for study. Chang'an, the capital of the Tang Dynasty was host to visitors from as far away as the Byzantine Empire, not to mention the neighboring countries of Asia. Chang'an, at that time the world's greatest metropolis, was packed with thousands of foreign dignitaries, students, diplomats, merchants, artisans and entertainers. Japan especially sent contingent after contingent of envoys to the Tang court. Worthy of note are the accounts of life in Chang'an written by Abeno Nakamaro, a Japanese scholar who studied in China and had close friendships with ministers of the Tang court and many Chinese scholars in a period of over 50 years. The description throws light on the exchanges between Chinese and foreigners in this period. When Abeno was supposedly lost at sea on his way back home, the leading poet of the time, Li Bai, wrote a eulogy for him.

The following centuries saw a steady increase in the accounts of China written by Western visitors. The Italian Marco Polo described conditions in China during the Yuan Dynasty in his *Travels*. However, until advances in the science of navigation led to the opening of east-west shipping routes at the beginning of the 16th century Sino-Western cultural exchanges were coloured by fantasy and conjecture. Concrete progress was made when a contingent of religious missionaries, men well versed in Western science and technology, made their way to China, ushering in an era of direct contacts between China and the West. The experience of this era was embodied in the career of the Italian Jesuit Matteo Ricci. Arriving in China in 1582, Ricci died in Beijing in 1610. Apart from his missionary work, Ricci accomplished two historically symbolic tasks — one was the translation into Latin of the "Four Books," together with annotations, in 1594; the other was the translation into Chinese of Euclid's *Elements*.

The rough translations of the "Four Books" and other Chinese classical works by Western missionaries, and the publication of Père du Halde's *Description Geographique, Historique, Chronologique, Politique, et Physique de l'Empire de la Chine* revealed an exotic culture to Western readers, and sparked a "China fever," during which the eyes of many Western intellectuals were fixed on China. Some of these intellectuals, including Leibniz, held China in high esteem; others, such as Hegel, nursed a critical attitude toward Chinese culture. Leibniz considered that some aspects of Chinese thought were close to his own views, such as the philosophy of the *Book of Changes* and his own binary system. Hegel, on the other hand, as mentioned above, considered that China had developed no proper philosophy of its own. Nevertheless, no matter whether the reaction was one of admiration, criticism, acceptance or rejection, Sino-Western exchanges were of great significance. The transmission of advanced Chinese science and technology to the West, especially the Chinese inventions of paper-making, gunpowder, printing and the compass, greatly changed the face of the whole world. Karl Marx said, "Chinese gunpowder blew the feudal class of knights to smithereens; the compass opened up world markets and built colonies; and printing became an implement of Protestantism and the most powerful lever and necessary precondition for intellectual development and creation." The English philosopher Roger Bacon said that China's four great inventions had "changed the face of the whole world and the state of affairs of everything."

## 3

Ancient China gave birth to a large number of eminent scientists, such as Zu Chongzhi, Li Shizhen, Sun Simiao, Zhang Heng, Shen Kuo and Bi

Sheng. They produced numerous treatises on scientific subjects, including *The Manual of Important Arts for the People's Welfare, Nine Chapters on the Mathematical Art, A Treatise on Febrile Diseases* and *Compendium of Materia Medica*. Their accomplishments included ones whose influence has been felt right down to modern times, such as the armillary sphere, seismograph, Dujiangyan water conservancy project, Dunhuang Grottoes, Grand Canal and Great Wall. But from the latter part of the 15th century, and for the next 400 years, Europe gradually became the cultural centre upon which the world's eyes were fixed. The world's most outstanding scientists then were England's Isaac Newton, Poland's Copernicus, France's Marie Curie, Germany's Rontgen and Einstein, Italy's Galileo, Russia's Mendelev and America's Edison.

The Chinese people then began to think: What is the cause of the rise and fall of nations? Moreover, how did it happen that gunpowder, invented in China and transmitted to the West, in no time at all made Europe powerful enough to batter down the gates of China herself?

It took the Opium War to wake China from its reverie. The first generation to make the bold step of "turning our eyes once again to the rest of the world" was represented by Lin Zexu and Wei Yuan. Zeng Guofan and Li Hongzhang started the Westernization Movement, and later intellectuals raised the slogan of "Democracy and Science." Noble-minded patriots, realizing that China had fallen behind in the race for modernization, set out on a painful quest. But in backwardness lay the motivation for change, and the quest produced the embryo of a towering hope, and the Chinese people finally gathered under a banner proclaiming a "March Toward Science."

On the threshold of the 21st century, the world is moving in the direction of becoming an integrated entity. This trend is becoming clearer by the day. In fact, the history of the various peoples of the world is also becoming the history of mankind as a whole. Today, it is impossible for any nation's culture to develop without absorbing the excellent aspects of the cultures of other peoples. When Western culture absorbs aspects of Chinese culture, this is not just because it has come into contact with Chinese culture, but also because of the active creativity and development of Western culture itself; and vice versa. The various cultures of the world's peoples are a precious heritage which we all share. Mankind no longer lives on different continents, but on one big continent, or in a "global village." And so, in this era characterized by an all-encompassing network of knowledge and information we should learn from each other and march in step along the highway of development to construct a brand-new "global village."

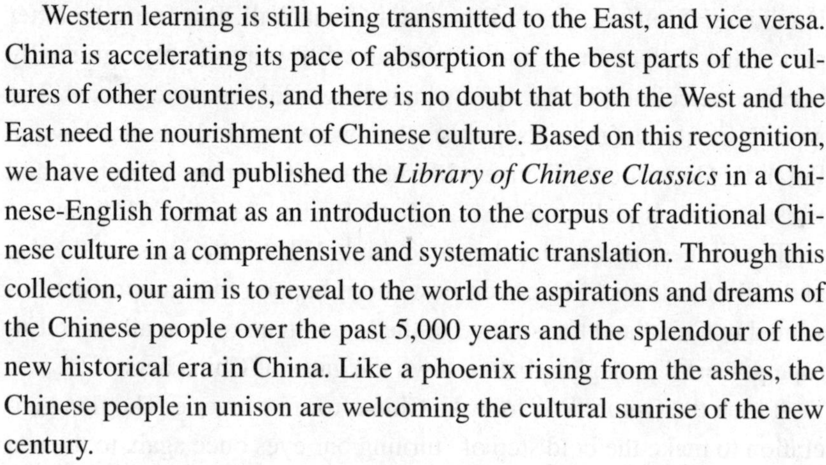

Western learning is still being transmitted to the East, and vice versa. China is accelerating its pace of absorption of the best parts of the cultures of other countries, and there is no doubt that both the West and the East need the nourishment of Chinese culture. Based on this recognition, we have edited and published the *Library of Chinese Classics* in a Chinese-English format as an introduction to the corpus of traditional Chinese culture in a comprehensive and systematic translation. Through this collection, our aim is to reveal to the world the aspirations and dreams of the Chinese people over the past 5,000 years and the splendour of the new historical era in China. Like a phoenix rising from the ashes, the Chinese people in unison are welcoming the cultural sunrise of the new century.

*August 1999*

# 《吴子》简介

《吴子》,中国古代著名兵书,“武经七书”之一。宋代以前称《吴起》或《吴起兵法》,宋以后多以《吴子》称之。作者为战国前期著名的军事家、政治家和改革家吴起(约公元前440年~前381年)。

吴起生于卫国,历任鲁国将军,魏国大将、西河守,楚国苑守、令尹等职。《吴子》一书当修成于吴起仕魏期间。行世后,颇受历代军事家、政治家重视。唐代传入日本,18世纪传入欧洲。现有日、英、法、俄等多种译本流布世界,在世界军事史上占有一定地位。

关于《吴子》最早的文献记载,当属《史记》和《汉书》。据《汉书·艺文志》著录,“《吴起》四十八篇”。惜多佚失。

今本仅存 6 篇，约 5000 字。各篇的主要军事思想是：阐述“内修文德，外治武备”的治国经武方针，对战争的起因和类型进行了可贵探讨；分析了各诸侯国情况和特点，强调要因情制变，战法灵活；提出训练、行军、宿营和驯养役使军马的原则和方法；阐明了将帅在经国治军中的重要性和应具备的条件，判断敌方将领优劣的方法等；并对如何奖功、罚罪和激励士气进行了详细说明。

此次整理时，《吴子》原文以宋版《武经七书》本为底本，并注意吸收前人及当代学者的核勘整理成果，择其善者而从之。对底本中明显的讹夺之处，径将改补文字以圆括孤置于文中，对常见的通假字、异体字，亦是径改未注。现代汉语释文，以军事科学出版社《武经七书鉴赏》(2002 版)为底本，并参以解放军出版社的《武经七书注译》(1986 年版)、《吴子浅说》(1987年版) 等书。英文译文参考了塞缪尔·格里菲思翻译，牛津大学出版社的《孙子兵法》附录一（1963年版）。限于体例，以上诸点，书中未能详加说明。读者见谅。

王显臣

# An Introduction to *Wu Zi*

*Wu Zi,* a well-known military book of ancient China, was one of the *Seven Military Classics of Ancient China.* The title of the book had been *Wu Qi or Wu Qi's Art of War* before the Song Dynasty. Since the Song Dynasty it has been mostly termed *Wu Zi.* The author was Wu Qi (*circa* 440 B.C.—381 B.C.), a famous military scientist, statesman and reformer in the early Warring States Period.

Born in Wei State (卫国), Wu Qi had successively held the posts of General of Lu State, Grand General, and Commandant of the West River region, of Wei State (魏国), and Ling Yin (analogous to prime minister) of Chu State. The book *Wu Zi* might have been completed when he served Wei State. Since it came out, military scientists and statesmen of successive dynasties had paid great attention to it. In the Tang Dynasty the book circulated to Japan. In the 18th century it spread to Europe. Nowadays many translated versions such as Japanese, English, French and Russian have circulated around the world. Hence *Wu Zi* has held a due position in the world' s military history.

The earliest record of *Wu Zi* was made in the *Shi Ji* (Records of the Historian) and the *Han Shu* (History of the Han Dynasty). According to "Bibliography" in the *Han Shu,* "*Wu Qi* had forty-eight chapters." Unfortunately most of them are lost. The extant edition only contains six chapters with about five thousand words. Its main military thought is as follows: *Wu Zi* elaborates on the guidelines of ruling a state and controlling an army to "promote virtue within the state and prepare defense against war from without," and examines the causes of war and its various types. It analyzes the situations and features of all the feudal states in the author's time and stresses dealing with changes in accord with situations and employing flexible methods of combat. It proposes the principles and means of training, marching, encamping, and taming and working war-horses. It dwells on the importance of generals in ruling a state and controlling an army and the qualifications required of them, and on how to judge the merits and demerits of the enemy generals. In addition, it explains in detail the ways and means of giving rewards and punishments and boosting morale.

For this edition, the text of the *Wu Zi* is based on The Seven Military Classics of the Song Dynasty

(960-1279) edition, and we have drawn upon the textual research and collation of contemporary scholars and their predecessors, incorporating their achievements and insights. Corrected and added Chinese characters are enclosed in parentheses where there exist obvious errors and gaps in the original classical Chinese text, while the classical variations of some Chinese characters are not corrected or explained with notes. The text is rendered into modern Chinese based on *Understanding the Seven Military Classics* (2002) published by the Military Science Publishing House and with *The Seven Military Classics with Notes and Translation* (1986) and Introduction to the *Wu Zi* (1987), published by the People's Liberation Army Press, as the reference books. The text is translated into English with the "Appendix I" in *Sun Tzu: The Art of war* tronslated by Samuel B. Griffith, Published by Oxford University Press(1963) as the reference book. The references are not required by the stylistic rules of this edition to be noted one by one, and we sincerely hope readers will excuse us.

By Wang Xianchen

# 《司马法》简介

《司马法》，中国古代著名兵书，“武经七书”之一。又称《司马兵法》、《军礼司马法》、《司马穰苴兵法》。

《汉书·艺文志》著录《军礼司马法》155篇，入“六艺略”礼部。《隋书·经籍志》著录《司马兵法》3卷，司马穰苴撰，入子部兵家类，其后各史志目录书多沿此说。今本3卷，5篇，为《仁本》、《天子之义》、《定爵》、《严位》、《用众》，3400余字。

研究者认为，此书的形成有一个漫长的过程，大约可以从西周初期说起，当时即设有掌管征伐、统御六军、平治邦国的军事长官司马。所谓“司马法”，就是先秦时代司马之官治军用兵的法典条令。到了战国中期，齐威王“使大夫追论古者《司马兵法》，而附《穰苴》于其中，因号曰《司马穰苴兵法》”。

又，古代的礼，是规定社会行为的法

则、规范、仪式的总称，其义通法，故本书又名《军礼司马法》。

此书历来颇受重视。司马迁称其“闳阔深远，虽三代征伐，未能竟其义”。历代学者或是征引其文，考订西周和春秋时期军制及军事思想；或是援引书中观点，作为自己立论的根据。自宋代起，更将其列为“武经七书”之一，颁行武学，教授生员，考选将材。

《司马法》一书，内容相当丰富，既阐述了战争的基本 理论，也论列了重要的治军原则。在论及战争指导和作战原则时，体现出朴素的军事辩证法思想。其中关于古代军制、军令、军礼等“三代遗规，往往于此书见之”，更是弥足珍贵的孑然珍存。但是，它对具体的作战方法则较少论及，或许因本书属于“军法”类兵书使然。

此次整理时，《司马法》原文以宋版《武经七书》本为底本，并注意吸收前人及当代学者的核勘整理成果，择其善者而从之。对底本中明显的讹夺之处，径将改补文字以圆括孤置于文中，对常见的通假字、异体字，亦是径改未注。现代汉语释文，以军事科学出版社《武经七书鉴赏》（2002版）为底本，并参以解放军出版社的《武经七书注译》（1986年版）、《司马法浅说》（1987年版）等书。英文译文参考了拉尔夫·索耶翻译，西景出版社出版的《武经七书》（1993年版）。限于体例，以上诸点，书中未能详加说明。读者见谅。

王显臣

# An Introduction to *The Methods of the Sima*

*The Methods of the Sima*, a well-known military book of ancient China, was one of the Seven Military Classics of Ancient China. The book was also titled *Sima's Art of War, Sima's Methods of Military Rite,and Sima Rangju's Art of War.*

The "Bibliography" in the Han Shu recorded one hundred and fifty-five chapters of *Sima 's Methods of Military Rite* in the Category of Classics of Rites in the "Liuyi Lue" (Summary of the Six classics). The "Bibliography of Classics" in the Sui Shu (the History of Sui Dynasty) recorded three volumes of *Sima's Art of War* written by Sima Rangju in the Category of Philosophical Works, under the sub-category of Military Strategists.Since then most of the catalogs of historical annals had continued to use this record in the *Sui Shu*.The extant edition contains three volumes in five chapters: "Foundation of Benevolence," "Right Conduct of the Son of Heaven," "Determination of Ranks," "Strict Positions," and "Employment of the Masses," numbering approximately three thousand four hundred words.

Researchers held that it had been a long process to complete this book. It might be traced back to the early Western Zhou Dynasty, when the post of sima (war minister or commanding general) who was responsible for directing expeditions, commanding the armed forces, suppressing rebellions and ruling the state was already established. Here, *The Methods of the Sima* refers to codes and regulations whereby the sima in the pre-Qin days directed the armed forces. In the mid-Warring States Period, "When King Wei of Qi was discussing *Sima's Art of War* with his ministers, he added Rangju to the title. Thereby its alternative title was *Sima Rangju' s Art of War.*"

The rite in ancient times was a general term for the rules, standards and rituals of social conduct. Therefore its meaning was equal to the code of conduct. Hence, the book was also termed *Sima 's Methods of Military Rite.*

Importance had always been attached to this book through the ages. The historian Sima Qian said: "Its tenet was profound and far-reaching. Although expeditions had been made during the Three Dynasties (the Xia, Shang and Zhou Dynasties), no one could express its meaning fully." Scholars of successive Dynasties either quoted its contents to make textual research of military institutions and military thought of the Western Zhou Dynasty and the Spring and Autumn Period, or borrowed propositions from the book to support their arguments. Since the Song Dynasty it had further been listed as one of *the Seven Military Classics of Ancient China,* and promulgated by the imperial court as required reading for instructing military cadets and selecting military commanders.

The book is fairly rich in content. It not only explains the fundamental theory of war but also expounds important principles for directing an army. While discussing the principles of directing war and the principles of operations, it displays ideas of military dialectics. What is even more precious, among others, are the ancient military institutions, orders and rites "left behind by the Three Dynasties and often found in the book." However, the book devotes little space to discussing concrete ways of operations, probably because it is a military book in the category of "military laws."

For this edition, the text of the The Methods of the Sima is based on the Seven Military Classics of the Song Dynasty (960-1279) edition, and we have drawn upon the textual research and collation of contemporary scholars and their predecessors, incorporating their achievements and insights. Corrected and added Chinese characters are enclosed in parentheses where there exist obvious errors and gaps in the original classical Chinese text, while the classical variations of some Chinese characters are not corrected or explained with notes. The text is rendered into modern Chinese based on *Understanding the Seven Military Classics* (2002) published by the Military Science Publishing House and with *The Seven Military Classics with Notes and Translation* (1986) and *Introduction to the Sima* (1987), published by the People's Liberation Army Press, as the reference books. The text is translated into English with *The Seven Military Classics of Ancient China* (1993) translated by Ralph D. Sawyer and published by the Westview Press as the reference book. The references are not required by the stylistic rules of this edition to be noted one by one, and we sincerely hope readers will excuse us.

By Wang Xianchen

# 《尉缭子》简介

《尉缭子》,中国古代著名兵书,"武经七书"之一。在《汉书·艺文志》著录中两见,一为"杂家"类《尉缭》29篇,一为"兵形势"类31篇。惜古本已佚。《隋书·经籍志》"杂家"类著录《尉缭子》5卷。按《汉书·艺文志》体例,杂家与兵家本可互见,跨类著录非止一书。传抄各本增删衍夺,致使篇卷有异,古书中实属常见。今本《尉缭子》5卷24篇。

关于本书作者,世有两说,一说战国梁惠王(公元前369~前320年在位)时人,一说秦始皇时人。近年来渐趋一致,多数人主张为前者。

本书内容极为丰富,尤以对军事思想、军事制度的论述和记载占主导地位,同时又杂取诸家之说论兵,在先秦兵书中独显特色。

《尉缭子》以朴素的唯物主义思想为其军事理论奠定了坚实的哲学基础;认为

正确的政治策略和经济措施，是军事胜利的先决条件和根本保证；在战争指导上，认为培养和激励己方士气，削弱和瓦解敌方的士气，是最高明的制胜韬略；认为战争有三种取胜方式："道胜"、"威胜"、"力胜"；在军队管理上，强调"明正赏罚"，依法治军；详尽地讨论了军事训练的方法、内容及其意义。

本书不仅为中国历代论兵者所重，也对其他国家产生较大影响。日本的研究著作多达30余种，朝鲜很早就有了《尉缭子》刊本。18世纪起，传入西方。

此次整理时，《尉缭子》原文以宋版《武经七书》本为底本，并注意吸收前人及当代学者的核勘整理成果，择其善者而从之。对底本中明显的讹夺之处，径将改补文字以圆括孤置于文中，对常见的通假字、异体字，亦是径改未注。现代汉语释文，以军事科学出版社《武经七书鉴赏》（2002版）为底本，并参以解放军出版社的《武经七书注译》（1986年版）、《尉缭子浅说》（1987年版）等书。英文译文参考了拉尔夫·索耶翻译，西景出版社出版的《武经七书》(1993年版)。限于体例,以上诸点,书中未能详加说明。读者见谅。

王显臣

## An Introduction to *Wei Liao Zi*

*Wei Liao Zi,* a well-known military book of ancient China, was one of *the Seven Military Classics of Ancient China.*

It was recorded in the "Bibliography" in the *Han Shu* under two categories: *Wei Liao Zi* of the "Eclectics" category, containing twenty-nine chapters, and *Wei Liao Zi* of the "military" category, containing thirty-one chapters. Unfortunately the ancient edition of the book is lost. The "Eclectics" category in the "Bibliography of Classics" in the Sui Shu recorded *Wei Liao Zi* of five volumes. According to the stylistic rules of the "Bibliography" in the *Sui Shu,* it might be recorded under either of the two categories so the above way of cataloging was not an exceptional case. There were a lot of additions, deletions and omissions as handwritten copies were made of the manuscripts of *Wei Liao Zi,* resulting in the variation in the number of volumes and chapters. Indeed this offen happened to ancient books while they were passed on from generation to generation. The extant edition of *Wei Liao Zi* consists of five volumes in twenty-four chapters.

There used to be two versions about the author's background: One affirmed that he lived in the time of King Hui of Liang (reigned 369 B.C.～320 B.C.) of the Warring States Period, while the other claimed that he lived in the time of the First Emperor of Qin. Recently most of the scholars tend to uphold the former point of view.

The book covers a broad spectrum of subjects, mostly military thought and institutions, coupled with the arguments of different schools on warfare, making it stand apart from military books of the pre-Qin days.

*Wei Liao Zi* with its naive materialist thinking has laid a solid philosophical foundation for its military theory. It holds that correct political tactics and economic measures are a prerequisite and basic guarantee for military victory. With regard to the conduct of war, it holds that building up and boosting the morale of one's own side, and dampening and destroying the enemy's morale were the most intelligent tactic to win victory. It maintains that a war can be won by three ways: "by *Dao* (Right Way)," "by awesomeness," and "by strength." With regard to managing the army, it stresses "fair and strict in meting out punishments," and running military affairs according to law. It also elaborates the ways and means as well as the contents and significance of military training.

The book not only has drawn attention from military scholars of various periods in China, but also has exerted great influence in other countries. In Japan there are well over thirty research works on *Wei Liao Zi,* and in Korea there were printed editions of the book in earlier time. The book circulated to the West in the 18th century.

For this edition, the text of the *Wei Liao Zi* is based on The Seven Military Classics of the Song Dynasty (960-1279) edition, and we have drawn upon the textual research and collation of contemporary scholars and their predecessors, incorporating their achievements and insights. Corrected and added Chinese characters are enclosed in parentheses where there exist obvious errors and gaps in the original classical Chinese text, while the classical variations of some Chinese characters are not corrected or explained with notes. The text is rendered into modern Chinese based on *Understanding the Seven Military Classics* (2002) published by the Military Science Publishing House and with *The Seven Military Classics with Notes and Translation* (1986) and *Introduction to the Wei Liao Zi* (1987), published by the People's Liberation Army Press, as the reference books. The text is translated into English with *The Seven Military Classics of Ancient China* (1993) translated by Ralph D. Sawyer and published by the Westview Press as the reference book. The references are not required by the stylistic rules of this edition to be noted one by one, and we sincerely hope readers will excuse us.

By Wang Xianchen

# 目　录

## 吴　子


图国第一　2

料敌第二　20

治兵第三　36

论将第四　50

应变第五　62

励士第六　76


## 司马法


仁本第一　86

天子之义第二　100

定爵第三　118

严位第四　138

用众第五　154


## 尉缭子


天官第一　162

兵谈第二　168

制谈第三　176

战威第四　190

攻权第五　204

# CONTENTS


**WU ZI**

1. Planning for the State 3
2. Estimation of the Enemy 21
3. Control of the Army 37
4. A Discussion of Generalship 51
5. On Responding to Changing Situations 63
6. Encouragement of Officers 77

**THE METHODS OF THE SIMA**

1. Foundation of Benevolence 87
2. Right Conduct of the Son of Heaven 101
3. Determination of Ranks 119
4. Strict Positions 139
5. Employment of the Masses 155

**WEI LIAO ZI**

1. Omens of Constellations 163
2. On Military Affairs 169
3. On Institutions 177
4. Military Awesomeness 191
5. Strategies of Attacking Cities 205

守权第六 218
十二陵第七 226
武议第八 230
将理第九 248
原官第十 254
治本第十一 260
战权第十二 270
重型令第十三 276
伍制令第十四 280
分塞令第十五 284
束武令第十六 288
经卒令第十七 292
勒卒令第十八 296
将令第十九 304
踵军令第二十 308
兵教上第二十一 314
兵教下第二十二 324
兵令上第二十三 338
兵令下第二十四 346

6. Strategies of Defending Cities 219

7. Twelve Disciplines 227

8. Discussion on Conducting Warfare 231

9. The General as a Law Offcial 249

10. The Source of Offices 255

11. Foundation of Administration 261

12. Combat Tactics 271

13. Orders for Severe Punishments 277

14. Orders for the Squads of Five 281

15. Orders for Division of Encampment Garrison 285

16. Orders for Binding the Squads of Five 289

17. Orders for the Battle Formations of the Troops 293

18. Orders for Restraining the Troops 297

19. Orders for the General 305

20. Orders for the Vanguard 309

21. Military Instructions I 315

22. Military Instructions II 325

23. Military Orders I 339

24. Milirary Orders II 347

# 吴　子
# Wu Zi

# 图国第一

【原文】

吴起儒服以兵机见魏文侯。

文侯曰："寡人不好军旅之事。"

起曰："臣以见占隐，以往察来，主君何言与心违？今君四时使斩离皮革，掩以朱漆，画以丹青，烁以犀象。冬日衣之则不温，夏日衣之则不凉。为长戟二丈四尺，短戟一丈二尺。革车奄户，缦轮笼毂，观之于目则不丽，乘之以田则不轻，不识主君

【今译】

吴起穿着儒生的服装，以用兵的谋略，觐见魏文侯。文侯说："我不喜欢治兵打仗的事情。"

吴起说："我从表面现象推测您内心的想法，从过去观察未来，君主为什么讲的和想的不一致呢？现在君主一年四季派人宰杀兽畜，剥皮制革，涂上红漆，绘上各种颜色，烙上犀牛和大象的图案。冬天穿着它不暖和，夏天穿着它不凉爽。制造的长戟有二丈四尺，短戟一丈二尺。用皮革蒙住战车的车门，车轮和车毂包上皮革，看上去不美观，乘坐打

# 1. Planning for the State

Wu Zi, clad in a Confucian robe, made use of his expertise in military strategies to gain audience with Marquis Wen of Wei (founder of Wei State).

Marquis Wen said: "I am not interested in military affairs."

Wu Zi said: "I can judge what is hidden from the visible indications and by means of the past I can know what great aspiration you have cherished for the future. Why are your words, My Lord, so different from your thoughts? At present, during the four seasons you cause animals to be skinned and lacquer their hides in redness and paint them with various colors, and even draw them with brilliant rhinoceros and elephant pictures. If you wear these in the winter, hey give neither warmth, nor in summer, coolness. You make spears twenty-four feet long, and short halberds of twelve feet long. You cover the doors of the chariots with leather and cap the wheels and naves with hide ornaments. They are

【原文】

安用此也？若以备进战退守，而不求能用者，譬犹伏鸡之搏狸、乳犬之犯虎，虽有斗心，随之死矣。昔承桑氏之君，修德废武，以灭其国。有扈氏之君，恃众好勇，以丧其社稷。明主鉴兹，必内修文德，外治武备。故当敌而不进，无逮于义矣；僵尸而哀之，无逮于仁矣。”

于是文侯身自布席，夫人捧觞，醮吴起于庙，立为大将，守西河。与诸侯大战七十六，全胜六十

【今译】

猎不轻便。不知道君主将干什么用？如果用来准备进攻或防守，但又不去寻求善于使用它的人，那就好像抱窝的母鸡跟野猫搏斗，喂奶的母狗触犯老虎，虽然有拼斗的决心，但很快就会死亡。从前，承桑部落的君主，只讲文德而废弛了武备，国家因而灭亡。有扈部落的君主，依仗兵众而好战，国家因而丧失。贤明的君主鉴察到这些，必须对内修好文德，对外加强武备。所以说，遭到敌军侵犯而不应战，这谈不上义；看见被敌军杀害的尸体而哀怜，这算不了仁。”

于是，魏文侯亲自设宴席，他的夫人捧酒，在祖庙里宴请吴起，任命其为大将，守备河西。此后，吴起率军与各诸侯国大战七十六次，获得全胜的六十四次，其余十二次不分胜负。向魏国的四面开辟

not pleasing to the eyes, and when used for hunting they are not light. I do not understand how you, My Lord, propose to use them. If you are ready to make these available for offensive or defensive operations and seek no competent men to use such equipment, it would be like brooding hens fighting a leopard cat or dogs with young challenging a tiger. Even though they have great fighting spirit for survival they will perish in the end. Anciently the Lord of Cheng Shang tribe cultivated virtue, and put away military affairs. As a result his state was extinguished. There was the Lord of You Hu who put all his trust in numbers and much delighted in war and thereby lost his state. The enlightened ruler who drew lessons from these precedents would assuredly promote virtue in his state and prepare defense against war from without. Hence a ruler who hesitates before the enemy is not worthy of Righteousness and one who looks upon those killed in action and feels remorseful for them is not worthy of Benevolence."

And when Marquis Wen heard these words, he himself spread the mats and his wife offered up a goblet of wine. In the grand banquet held in

【原文】

四，余则钧解。辟土四面，拓地千里，皆起之功也。

吴子曰："昔之图国家者，必先教百姓而亲万民。有四不和：不和于国，不可以出军；不和于军，不可以出陈；不和于陈，不可以进战；不和于战，不可以决胜。是以有道之主，将用其民，先和而造大事。不敢信其私谋，必告于祖庙，启于元龟，参之天时，吉乃后举。民知君之爱其命，惜其死，若

【今译】

领土，扩充土地上千里，这些都是吴起的功劳。

吴起说："从前治理国家的君主，必定首先教诲百姓而且亲近民众。有四种不和谐的情况：国内意志不统一，不能出兵；军队内部不团结，不能上阵；临阵行动不一致，不能作战；战斗动作不协调，不能取得胜利。因此，贤明的君主，要使用他的民众，必先搞好团结而后发动战争。他不敢专信自己计谋的正确，必定向祖庙祭告，用龟甲占卜，观察天时，如果吉利而后行动。民众都知道君主爱护他们的生

the ancestral temple Wu Zi was then designated the Commander-in-Chief. He was responsible for the garrison of the West River region and fought seventy-six battles with different states. Of these he gained complete victory in sixty-four, while the rest were drawn. He opened up lands in every direction and extended the frontiers for a thousand li. All these were the achievements of Wu Zi.

Wu Zi said: "Anciently those who planned state affairs would surely first instruct the hundred clans and then extend their regard to the myriad people. There are four discords: When there is discord or lack of political consensus on war the army cannot be mobilized. When there is discord or lack of team spirit in the army it cannot take the field. When there is discord or lack of harmony in the field the army cannot take the offensive. When there is discord or lack of coordination in battle the army cannot win a decisive victory. Therefore, the enlightened ruler who would employ their subjects in great endeavors for the undertaking of the state should first establish harmony among them. Such a ruler does not presume to place confidence in his own personal plans, but necessarily discuss them

【原文】

此之至，而与之临难，则士以进死为荣，退生为辱矣。”

吴子曰：“夫道者，所以反本复始。义者，所以行事立功。谋者，所以违害就利。要者，所以保业守成。若行不合道，举不合义，而处大居贵，患必及之。是以圣人绥之以道，理之以义，动之以礼，抚之以仁。此四德者，修之则兴，废之则衰。故成

【今译】

命，怜惜他们的死亡，直到无微不至的程度，再率领他们开赴战场，他们就会以前进拼命为光荣，以退却求生为耻辱了。”

吴起说：“所谓‘道’，是用来探求事物本源的。所谓‘义’，是用来创业立功的。所谓‘谋’，是用来避免祸害得到利益的。所谓‘要’，是用来保全国家基业的。如果行为不符合道，举动不符合义，而又掌握大权，身居显贵，祸患就必然临头。所以，圣明的君主安天下用道，治理国家用义，动用民众用礼，抚慰民众用仁。这四种德行，修好它，国家

in the ancestral temple after tortoise divination and reflection upon the suitable season. If the omens are auspicious he then launches the army. If the people know that their lord is careful of their lives, and laments their death to such an extent that he will be together with them in the time of a danger, then all the officers will consider it glorious to advance and die in action and shameful to save their lives by retreat."

Wu Zi said: " Now what is called *Dao* (Right Way) is return to the original and fundamental principles. 'Righteousness' means taking actions to start an undertaking and making achievement and merit 'Stratagem' means avoiding loss and gaining advantage. 'Essentials' means safeguarding the work and protecting achievements. If one's conduct is not in conformity to *Dao* (Right Way) and action not in conformity to 'Righteousness', albeit his position is high-ranking and honorable, disaster will be in store for him. And therefore the Sage maintains order in the state by keeping in *Dao*(Right Way) and governs people with 'Righteousness'. He stimulates people with 'Ritual' and soothes them with 'Benevolence'. If these four virtues should be practiced, there is prosperity; if they be neglect-

【原文】

汤讨桀而夏民喜悦，周武伐纣而殷人不非。举顺天人，故能然矣。”

吴子曰：“凡制国治军，必教之以礼，励之以义，使有耻也。夫人有耻，在大足以战，在小足以守矣。然战胜易，守胜难。故曰，天下战国，五胜者祸，四胜者弊，三胜者霸，二胜者王，一胜者帝。是以数胜得天下者稀，以亡者众。”

【今译】

就振兴;废弃它，国家就衰败。因此，成汤讨伐夏桀而夏朝的民众高兴，周武王讨伐殷纣而商朝的民众不反对。就是因为他们的举动顺从天理合乎人心，所以才能这样。”

吴起说：“凡是管理国家、治理军队，必须用‘礼’教导民众，用‘义’激励民众，使民众懂得羞耻。人们有了羞耻之心，力量强大就可以出战，力量弱小也可以防守。然而打败敌人容易，保持胜利成果困难。所以说，天下相互争战的国家，取得五次战争胜利的会招致灾祸，取得四次战争胜利的会国力疲弊，取得三次战争胜利的可以称霸，取得两次战争胜利的可以称王，取得一次战争胜利的可以成就帝业。所以，经过多次战争胜利得天下的少，而亡国的多。”

ed, there is decline. Hence anciently when Tang of the Shang Dynasty attacked Jie of the Xia Dynasty the people of Xia rejoiced; when Wu of the Zhou Dynasty attacked Zhou of the Yin Dynasty (the later period of the Shang Dynasty) the people of Yin did not oppose him. Both two great ancient Lords acted in accord with Providence and human desire, and thus were able to achieve these things."

Wu Zi said: " Generally in administering a state and controlling an army it is necessary to indoctrinate the people by practice of 'Ritual' and encourage them with 'Righteousness' so as to inculcate them with the sense of shame.If men possess a sense of shame they will be able to campaign when in strength, and they will be able to defend when few in number. To win victory is easy; to preserve its fruits, difficult. Hence it is said that the consequence of continuous fighting between states makes one who gains five victories disastrous; one who gains four exhausted; one who gains three a hegemon; one who gains two a king; one who gains one the Emperor. For those who have gained All Under Heaven by many victories are few; and those who have lost it, many."

【原文】

吴子曰:“凡兵之所起者有五:一曰争名,二曰争利,三曰积恶,四曰内乱,五曰因饥。其名又有五:一曰义兵,二曰强兵,三曰刚兵,四曰暴兵,五曰逆兵。禁暴救乱曰义,恃众以伐曰强,因怒兴师曰刚,弃礼贪利曰暴,国乱人疲、举事动众曰逆。五者之服,各有其道,义必以礼服,强必以谦服,刚必以辞服,暴必以诈服,逆必以权服。”

武侯问曰:“愿闻治兵、料人、固国之道。”

起对曰:“古之明王,必谨君臣之礼,饰上下之

【今译】

吴起说:“引起战争的原因有五种:一是争名位,二是争利益,三是长期有冤仇,四是发生内乱,五是遭受饥荒。战争的名称又有五种:一是义兵,二是强兵,三是刚兵,四是暴兵,五是逆兵。禁除暴虐挽救危亡的叫义兵,依仗兵力众多侵犯别国的叫强兵,因为忿怨而兴兵的叫刚兵,背弃礼义贪图私利的叫暴兵,国乱民疲、兴师动众的叫逆兵。对付这五种战争,各有不同的办法。义兵必须用礼治服它,强兵必须用谦让降服它,刚兵必须用言辞说服它,暴兵必须用诡诈制服它,逆兵必须用权谋慑服它。”

魏武侯问道:“我愿听听治理军队、估量民力、巩固国家的道理。”

吴起回答说:“古代贤明的君主,必定谨守君臣

Wu Zi said: "There are five causes of war: First, struggle for fame; second, struggle for profit; third, accumulation of animosity; fourth, internal disorder; and fifth, famine. Again, there are five natures of war: First, righteous war; second, aggressive war; third, enraged war; fourth, wanton war; and fifth, insurgent war. Wars to crack down violence and quell disturbance are righteous. Those which depend on mighty force are aggressive. When the army is mobilized because rulers are angry, this is enraged war. Those in which all propriety is discarded because of greed are wanton wars. Those which, when the state is in disorder and the people are worn out, set the multitude in motion, cause insurgent war. There is a way to deal with each of these five: A righteous war must be forestalled by propriety and reason; an aggressive war by humbling one's self; an enraged war by dissuading words; a wanton war by deception and treachery; an insurgent war by authority."

Marquis Wu (son of Marquis Wen and his successor) asked: "I wish to know the way to control the troops, to evaluate men and make the state strong and stable."

【原文】

仪，安集吏民，顺俗而教，简募良材，以备不虞。昔齐桓募士五万，以霸诸侯。晋文召为前行四万，以获其志。秦缪置陷陈三万，以服邻敌。故强国之君，必料其民。民有胆勇气力者，聚为一卒。乐以进战效力、以显其忠勇者，聚为一卒。能逾高超远、轻足善走者，聚为一卒。王臣失位而欲见功于上者，聚为一卒。弃城去守、欲除其丑者，聚为一卒。此

【今译】

间的礼法，讲究上下之间的礼仪，安抚团结官吏和民众，按习俗教育他们，选择和招募有才能的人，以防备突然事变。从前，齐桓公召募勇士五万人，因而称霸诸侯。晋文公招募四万人作前锋部队，实现了他的志向。秦穆公建立冲锋陷阵的部队三万人，因而制服邻国。所以，要想使国家强盛的君主，必须估量民众力量。把民众中有胆量、有勇力的人，编为一队；把乐意以决战来显示忠勇的人，编为一队；把能爬高越远、腿脚敏捷能跑路的人，编为一队；把官吏中因过失丢官，而又想立功报效的人，编为一队；把曾经丢城失地，而想洗刷耻辱的人，

Wu Zi replied: "Anciently the enlightened rulers respected propriety between the sovereign and ministers; established etiquette between superiors and subordinates; settled officials and ordinary people in close accord and instructed them in accord with customs; selected and summoned men of ability, and thereby provided against any contingency. Anciently Duke Huan of Qi levied fifty thousand warriors and became the hegemon of the feudal states. Duke Wen of Jin called up forty thousand men for the van army and gained his ambition; Duke Mu of Qin deployed thirty thousand valiant troops and subdued his neighboring foes. Therefore, the ruler of a powerful state must estimate his own people. In such a state those who are bold, spirited and strong will be formed into one detachment.Those who are delighted to attack and exert themselves to show their loyalty and bravery will be gathered into one detachment. Those who are skillful in scaling heights and leaping far with agility will be assembled into one detachment. Princes and ministers who have lost positions and who wish to acquire merit in the eyes of their superiors should be formed into one detachment. Those who abandoned the

【原文】

五者，军之练锐也。有此三千人，内出可以决围，外入可以屠城矣。”

武侯问曰：“愿闻陈必定、守必固、战必胜之道。”

起对曰：“立见且可，岂直闻乎！君能使贤者居上，不肖者处下，则陈已定矣。民安其田宅，亲其有司，则守已固矣。百姓皆是吾君而非邻国，则战已胜矣。”

武侯尝谋事，群臣莫能及，罢朝而有喜色。起

【今译】

编为一队。这五队，都可成为军队中的精锐。有这三千人，由内出击可以突破敌军的重围，从外进攻可以攻克敌人的城池。”

武侯问道：“我愿听听阵势必能隐定，守备必能坚固，作战必能胜利的道理。”

吴起回答说：“立即看到都可以，哪里只是听一听呢！君主能使有贤德的人担任重要职位，平庸的人处于低下位置，那么阵势就会稳定。民众安居乐业，亲近他们的官吏，那么守备就会坚固。百姓都拥护自己的君主而反对邻国，那么作战就能取得胜利。”

魏武侯曾经和群臣商讨国事，大臣们的见解都不如他，退朝以后，他面带喜色。吴起进谏说：

cities they were defending and who wish to rectify their shameful conduct will be gathered into one detachment. These five will form a well-trained and crack army. With three thousand men like this, from within one can strike out and break any encirclement; from without break into any city and slaughter the defenders."

Marquis Wu asked: "I would like to know the way to make my battle array firm, render my defense secure and how in battle to be certain of victory."

Wu Zi replied: "These things can be seen immediately. How is it that you wish to hear of them? If Your Lordship can employ the Worthy in high positions, and the unworthy in inferior positions, then the array will be already firm. If the people are free from anxiety about their farming estates and are friendly with their magistrates, then the defense is already secure. If the hundred clans approve of their own sovereign and disapprove of neighboring states, then the battles are already won."

Marquis Wu once assembled his ministers to discuss state affairs and none of the ministers could equal him in wisdom. When he retired

【原文】

进曰:“昔楚庄王尝谋事，群臣莫能及，退朝而有忧色。申公问曰:‘君有忧色，何也?’曰:‘寡人闻之，世不绝圣，国不乏贤，能得其师者王，得其友者霸。今寡人不才，而群臣莫及者，楚国其殆矣。’此楚庄王之所忧，而君说之，臣窃惧矣。”于是武侯有惭色。

【今译】

“从前楚庄王曾和众臣商讨国事，群臣的见解都不如他，退朝以后却面带忧色。申公问道:‘君王有忧虑的神色，这是为什么呢?’楚庄王说:‘我听说，当今不会没有圣人，国内也不缺少贤能的人，能够得到他们做老师的可以称王，能够得到他们做朋友的可以称霸。如今我没有才能，然而群臣还比不上我，楚国真是危险了。’这是楚庄王所担忧的，而君主却感到高兴，我暗自为您担心受怕呀!”武侯听了，面有羞愧神色。

from court he was looking pleased. Wu Zi advanced and said: "Anciently King Zhuang of Chu once consulted with his ministers on state affairs, and none were equal to him in wisdom. When he left court he was looking worried. Duke Shen asked: 'Why is My Lord troubled?' The Lord replied: 'This humble one has heard that the world never lacks sages and that a state never lacks wise men. One able to get a sage for his teacher will be a king; one able to get a wise man for his friend, a hegemon. Now I have no talent, and still my ministers cannot equal me. Chu is in danger.' This is what worried King Zhuang of Chu, but pleased you. I, your servant, am secretly apprehensive." And hearing this Marquis Wu looked ashamed.

# 料敌第二

【原文】

武侯谓吴起曰："今秦胁吾西，楚带吾南，赵冲吾北，齐临吾东，燕绝吾后，韩据吾前。六国兵四守，势甚不便，忧此奈何？"

起对曰："夫安国家之道，先戒为宝。今君已戒，祸其远矣。臣请论六国之俗：夫齐陈重而不坚，秦陈散而自斗，楚陈整而不久，燕陈守而不走，三晋陈治而不用。

【今译】

魏武侯对吴起说："现在秦国威胁着我国的西面，楚国像衣带一样地横阻在我国的南面，赵国正对着我国的北面，齐国逼近我国的东面，燕国绝断我国的后面，韩国据守在我国的当面。在六国军队的四面包围下，形势对我国极为不利，我为此担忧，怎么办呢？"

吴起回答说："安定国家的办法，预先戒备最为重要。现在君主已经戒备起来，大概可以远离战祸了。我请求谈一谈六国各方面的情况：齐国军队的阵势，兵力部署集中但不坚固；秦国军队的阵势，兵力部署分散但能各自为战；楚国军队的阵势，兵力部署严整但不能持久作战；燕国军队的阵势，兵力部署利于坚守但不善于机动作战；韩国和赵国军队的阵势，兵力部署整齐划一但不实用于作战。

# 2. Estimation of the Enemy

Marquis Wu said to Wu Zi: "Now Qin threatens me from the west; Chu encircles me on the south; Zhao confronts me in the north; Qi overlooks my eastern border; Yan cuts off my rear and Han takes the position to my front. Thus the armies of the six states encompass me on every side, and the strategic posture of our power is extremely disadvantageous. I am anxious of it very much. Can you relieve my worries?"

Wu Zi replied: "Now the way to safeguard the state lies first of all in precaution. Now that My Lord has already taken warning and is aware of the dangers, misfortune is kept at a distance.I beg to discuss the military posture of these six states. Now the Qi army is massive, but not firm. The Qin army is dispersed and each fights for himself. The Chu army is well arrayed but not sustainable. The Yan army defends the position well but without maneuver. The Han and Zhao armies are well governed but can not be used.

【原文】

“夫齐性刚，其国富，君臣骄奢而简于细民，其政宽而禄不均，一陈两心，前重后轻，故重而不坚。击此之道，必三分之，猎其左右，胁而从之，其陈可坏。秦性强，其地险，其政严，其赏罚信，其人不让，皆有斗心，故散而自战。击此之道，必先示之以利而引去之，士贪于得而离其将，乘乖猎散，设伏投机，其将可取。楚性弱，其地广，其政骚，其民疲，故整而不久。击此之道，袭乱其屯，先夺

【今译】

“齐国人性格刚强，国家富饶，君臣骄横奢侈，轻视民众，政令松弛，俸禄不均，齐军阵中人心不齐，前阵兵力强，后阵兵力弱，所以齐阵虽然兵力集中但不坚固。攻击齐阵的战法，必须兵分三路，以两路侧击其左、右翼，一路乘势尾击，它的阵势便可以攻破。秦国人性格倔强，国家地形险要，政令严厉，赏罚有信，士卒临战不退让，都有战斗的决心，所以秦阵虽然兵力部署分散但都能各自为战。攻击秦阵的战法，必须先以利引诱，使其士卒贪图得利而离开指挥他们的将领，尔后乘其阵势混乱之际，攻击分散的队伍，并设置伏兵，待机袭击，他们的将领也可以擒获。楚国人性情柔弱，国家土地广阔，政令紊乱，民众疲困，所以楚阵兵力部署虽

"Now the character of Qi State is stubborn and the state is rich, but the sovereign and ministers are proud and luxurious and neglectful of the common people; the government is loose and rewards are not impartial; in one camp there are two minds; the front is heavy, but the rear is light. Hence it is ponderous without stability.The way to attack the Qi army is this: It must be divided into three parts and its right and left attacked. So you force them to conform to you and their army can be destroyed.

"The character of Qin State is strong; its terrain is rugged and its government firm; rewards and punishments are just; the people indomitable, and all have the fighting spirit.Therefore its formations are dispersed and each fights for himself. The way to attack Qin is first to offer them some apparent gains and allure them to leave. The officers who are greedy of profits will desert their general; then taking advantage of their disobedience, their scattered elements can be chased, ambushes laid, favorable opportunities taken, and their general captured.

"The character of Chu State is weak, its territory is extensive, the government is disturbed, the people are exhausted, and though well or-

【原文】

其气。轻进速退，弊而劳之，勿与战争，其军可败。燕性悫，其民慎，好勇义，寡诈谋，故守而不走。击此之道，触而迫之，陵而远之，驰而后之，则上疑而下惧，谨我车骑必避之路，其将可虏。三晋者，中国也，其性和，其政平，其民疲于战、习于兵、轻其将、薄其禄，士无死志，故治而不用。击此之道，阻陈而压之，众来则拒之，去则追之，以倦其

【今译】

然严整但不能持久作战。攻击楚阵的战法，袭击和扰乱它的驻地，先挫伤其士气。尔后以小部队突然进攻，迅速撤退，消耗和疲劳它，不必与它对阵交战，楚军就可以打败。燕国人性格诚实，民众谨慎，好勇力重义气，军队作战很少运用谋诈，所以燕阵虽然兵力部署利于坚守但不善于机动作战。攻击燕阵的战法，与燕军接触后就胁迫它，袭扰一下就迅速远离它，奔袭它的后方，使它的将领疑惑，士卒恐惧，严密防守我车骑机动时所必经的道路，燕军的将领就可以被我俘获。韩国和赵国地处中原，人性温和，国家政令平稳，民众疲困于战争，厌烦打仗，轻视将领，鄙薄爵禄，士卒没有决死拼斗的意志，所以韩阵和赵阵虽然兵力部署整齐划一但不实用于作战。攻击韩阵、赵阵的战法，必须摆开阵势压制它，如其兵力众多前来攻击就抗住它，若其退

dered the troops are not sustainable. The way to attack Chu is to assault their camp and throw it into confusion. First deprive them of morale.Advance with light troops, withdraw quickly, thus tiring them out. Without contest with them in battle, their armies can be defeated.

"The character of Yan State is straightforward. Its people are cautious, loving courage and righteousness, but lacking in trickery and deception. Therefore they defend but do not make any maneuver. The way to attack Yan is to stir them up and harass their rear, advance upon them and then withdraw to a distance, thus causing bewilderment to their officers and fear in their ranks. Be cautious of our chariots and horsemen,avoiding conflict on the open road and then their generals can be captured.

"The Han and Zhao are states in the Central Plains. The temperament of the people is peaceable. The rule of the governments is gentle.Their people is tired of war. Although well trained for war they despise their generals. Pay is small, and officers have no will to fight to the death. Thus though well governed, they are of little use. The way to attack them is to press upon their formations and keep the pressure on. When their hosts

【原文】

师。

“此其势也。

“然则一军之中，必有虎贲之士；力轻扛鼎，足轻戎马，搴旗斩将，必有能者。若此之等，选而别之，爱而贵之，是谓军命。其有工用五兵、材力健疾、志在吞敌者，必加其爵列，可以决胜。厚其父母妻子，劝赏畏罚，此坚陈之士，可与持久。能审料此，可以击倍。”

武侯曰：“善！”

吴子曰：“凡料敌有不卜而与之战者八：一曰疾

【今译】

却就追击它，以此疲劳它的军队。

“这就是六国的概略形势。

“然而在魏国军队内部，必定有像猛虎那样的勇士，力气大得能把鼎轻松地举起来的，腿脚轻捷跑起来能追上战马的，拔敌军旗斩杀敌将的，一定有这样能干的人。像这样的人，选拔出来分别使用，爱惜和器重他们，这就是三军的命脉。军中擅长使用各种兵器，身强力壮动作敏捷、立志杀敌的人，必须给他们加官晋爵，这样就可以夺取战争的胜利。还要厚待他们的父母妻儿，激励他们立功受奖,使他们害怕受到惩罚,这些都是能坚守阵势的人,可以与敌军持久作战。能够审慎地料理到这些问题，便可以攻击成倍的敌人。”

魏武侯说：“你讲得很好！”

吴起说：“通常判断敌情，不必占卜便可以与敌交战的有八种情况：一是敌军在狂风严寒的天气长

arrive, resist them; when they withdraw, pursue them. So you can tire them out.

"Such is the strategic posture of the six states.

"Naturally in an army there are certain to be some mighty warriors as brave as tigers and strong enough to lift a bronze tripod with ease; swifter of foot than the war horse, they can take the enemy's standard, or slay his general. There are certain to be some who are able. If such men should be selected, valued, cherished and honored, it can be said they are the life of the army. Those who are skilled in using five weapons, who are clever, strong, nimble and ambitious to swallow the enemy, should be given rank and decoration, and used to decide the victory. Their parents and families should be cared for and they should be encouraged by rewards, and kept in fear of punishment. These men can consolidate the formations and endure in battle. If you are able to make a careful estimate of such men they can attack twice their number."

Marquis Wu said: "It is good!"

Wu Zi said: "Now in the estimation of the enemy there are eight conditions in which he may

【原文】

风大寒，早兴寤迁，刊木济水，不惮艰难；二曰盛夏炎热，晏兴无间，行驱饥渴，务于取远；三曰师既淹久，粮食无有，百姓怨怒，妖祥数起，上不能止；四曰军资既竭，薪刍既寡，天多阴雨，欲掠无所；五曰徒众不多，水地不利，人马疾疫，四邻不至；六曰道远日暮，士众劳惧，倦而未食，解甲而

【今译】

途行军，昼夜兼程，还要砍木造筏渡河，不顾部队的艰难困苦；二是在盛夏炎热的天气，休息与行动没有节制，驱使部队长途行军，硬要其走很远的路程；三是敌军长期留驻在外，粮食已经吃完，百姓怨恨和愤怒，怪异的谣言不断发生，将领制止不住；四是军需物资已经耗尽，柴草饲料已经很少，天气又多阴雨，更没有地方去掠夺；五是敌军兵力不多，水土不服，人马患有疫病，四邻的救兵不来；六是长途跋涉已近天晚，士卒疲劳恐惧，又困乏又饥饿，纷纷解甲休息；七是敌军将吏没有威信，军心动摇，

be attacked without recourse to divination. First, in times of strong wind and chilling cold when his men are awakened early to move or shifting campsites in late night, and make rafts by cutting wood to ford the rivers irrespective of stress and hardships. Second, in the height of summer and in scorching heat when they set out late and travel incessantly for a destination far away, and are hungry and thirsty. Third, when his army has already been encamped for a long time and is without provisions; when his people are vexed and indignant and there are many evil omens and portents and the superior officers cannot put a stop to spreading rumors. Fourth, when the army's ordnance is exhausted and firewood and fodder are scare; when the weather has been overcast by long continued rain and the troops wish to plunder but no place to loot. Fifth, when the army's numbers are few, where the terrain and water supply are inconvenient, where both men and horses have contracted infectious diseases and where the neighboring states do not come to their aid. Sixth, when night falls, and the way is yet far; when the officers and men are worn out and fearful, weary and without food, and have laid aside their armor and are resting.

【原文】

息；七曰将薄吏轻，士卒不固，三军数惊，师徒无助；八曰陈而未定，舍而未毕，行坂涉险，半隐半出。诸如此者，击之勿疑。

“有不占而避之者六：一曰土地广大，人民富众；二曰上爱其下，惠施流布；三曰赏信刑察，发必得时；四曰陈功居列，任贤使能；五曰师徒之众，兵甲之精；六曰四邻之助，大国之援。凡此不如敌人，

【今译】

三军数次遭到惊恐，又没有援助；八是阵势没有摆好，宿营尚未完毕，爬山越险，有的隐蔽，有的暴露。凡是遇到这些情况，都可以向敌军攻击，不要有任何迟疑。

“不必占卜便应避免与敌交战的有六种情况：一是敌国土地广大，人民富裕人口众多；二是国君将吏爱护民众和士卒，普遍地施加恩惠；三是赏罚分明，处理及时得当；四是按战功的大小排列爵位，任用有贤德和有才能的人；五是敌军兵力众多，武器装备精良；六是有四周邻国的帮助，有诸侯大国的支援。凡是在这些方面不如敌军，就应避免与它

Seventh, when the general's authority is weak with his incompetent deputies, and the officers and men are not firm in purpose; when their army has been alarmed constantly and no help is forthcoming. Eighth, when his battle formation is not fixed, when his encampment has not yet completed; when he is marching in hilly country, or climbing precipices, when half is hidden and half exposed. In all these conditions, you can attack an enemy without hesitation.

"There are six cases, where, without performing divination, you must avoid attacking the enemy. First, where his state has wide and vast territories, and a large and rich population. Second, where the sovereign and generals love their officers and people, and bestow their benevolence on the grassroots. Third, where rewards are well deserved, punishments accurately apportioned and where these are administered appropriately. Fourth, where those who display merit are given suitable positions, and the Worthy are appointed, and the able employed. Fifth, where the army is large and well-equipped. Sixth, where there is aid from all sides, or from powerful states. Generally when unequal to your enemy in these matters, you must without doubt

【原文】

避之勿疑。所谓见可而进，知难而退也。”

武侯问曰：“吾欲观敌之外以知其内，察其进以知其止，以定胜负，可得闻乎？”

起对曰：“敌人之来，荡荡无虑，旌旗烦乱，人马数顾，一可击十，必使无措。诸侯未会，君臣未和，沟垒未成，禁令未施，三军匈匈，欲前不能，欲去不敢，以半击倍，百战不殆。”

武侯问敌必可击之道。

起对曰：“用兵必须审敌虚实而趋其危。敌人远

【今译】

交战，不要有任何犹疑。这就是说，看到可以取胜就发起进攻，知道难以打败敌人就撤退。”

魏武侯问道：“我想通过观察敌军的外部情况，便能了解它内部的虚实，观察它的行动便可以知道它的企图，以便判定作战的胜负，可有什么方法讲给我听听吗？”

吴起回答说：“敌军的到来，稀稀拉拉，毫无顾忌，军旗凌乱，人马左顾右盼，对这样的军队可以以一击十，必然打得它措手不及。诸侯没有会合，君臣之间不和睦，作战工事没有修好，军令没有宣布施行，三军闹哄哄，要前进不能前进，想后退又不敢后退，对这样的军队可以以半击倍，百战不败。”

魏武侯问判断敌军必定可以攻击的方法。

吴起回答说：“用兵必须审察敌军的虚实，尔后

avoid him. What I mean is that when there is an opportunity, you may advance; when you see things are difficult, withdraw."

Marquis Wu asked : "I wish to know how the interior of the enemy can be examined from his external appearance and when he will stop by observing his advance so as to determine the outcome of the battle. Can I hear how to do so?"

Wu Zi replied: " If the enemy approaches recklessly and carelessly, his flags and banners are confused and disorderly, and the men and horses are frequently looking behind, then ten can be struck with one. Panic will certainly seize him. If the forces of the feudal lords have not yet assembled,if the sovereign and ministers are not in accord, if the moats and ramparts are not yet completed, if the entire army unsettled in noisy disturbance cannot advance or dare not withdraw either, then one may attack an enemy twice his size, and in one hundred battles there will be no peril."

Marquis Wu asked: "Under what conditions may an enemy certainly be attacked? "

Wu Zi replied: "Employment of troops must be in accord with determination of the enemy's strengths and weaknesses, after which you may

【原文】

来新至，行列未定可击，既食未设备可击，奔走可击，勤劳可击，未得地利可击，失时不从可击，旌旗乱动可击，涉长道后行未息可击，涉水半渡可击，险道狭路可击，陈数移动可击，将离士卒可击，心怖可击。凡若此者，选锐冲之，分兵继之，急击勿疑。"

【今译】

攻击它的薄弱要害之处。敌军远来刚到，战斗队形未展开，可以攻击；饭已经吃完，但没有防备，可以攻击；部队慌乱奔走，可以攻击；疲劳过度，可以攻击；敌军所处地形不利，可以攻击；天时不顺，可以攻击；军旗紊乱，可以攻击；经长途行军，后续部队未得休息，可以攻击；敌军涉水渡河，过了一半，可以攻击；在险峻狭隘的道路上，可以攻击；敌军阵势频繁移动，可以攻击；将领脱离士卒，可以攻击；军心动摇恐惧，可以攻击。凡是遇到这些情况，就应选派精锐部队发起冲击，尔后分别派遣后续部队投入战斗，急速攻击，不要迟疑。"

speedily strike his endangered positions. When the enemy approaches from afar and has not yet arrayed his ranks and files, he can be attacked. When his troops have just eaten but have not yet completed their dispositions, they can be attacked. When the enemy is hurrying about, or is busily occupied, or has not made use of the terrain, or has let pass the opportunity, he can be attacked. When his flags and banners are in confusion, he can be attacked. When his troops have come a long distance and those in the rear are late and have not rested, they can be attacked. When the enemy is halfway across waters, or is on a difficult or narrow road, he can be attacked. When his formations frequently move about, they can be attacked. When his general has separated from his officers and men, he can be attacked. When his troops are frightened, they can be attacked. Now, in all such conditions you must employ elite troops to burst into the enemy's ranks; then divide your troops to follow up, and attack with speed and without hesitation."

# 治兵第三

【原文】

武侯问曰："进兵之道何先？"

起对曰："先明四轻、二重、一信。"

曰："何谓也？"

对曰："使地轻马，马轻车，车轻人，人轻战。明知险易，则地轻马。刍秣以时，则马轻车。膏锏有余，则车轻人。锋锐甲坚，则人轻战。进有重赏，

【今译】

魏武侯问道："部队行军作战的方法首先应该掌握什么呢？"

吴起回答说："首先要明确'四轻'、'二重'、'一信'。"

魏武侯问道："这是什么意思呢？"

吴起回答说："四轻就是要选择地形适于战马驰骋，战马驾驶战车跑得轻快，战车使人操纵轻便，士卒能够英勇作战。熟悉地形的险峻平坦，就可以走平坦的道路让战马跑得轻快。适时得当地喂养战马，那么战马驾驶战车就跑得轻松。膏油锏铁备足，人操纵战车就轻便。兵器锋利尖锐，甲胄坚实牢固，士卒就便于作战。二重就是前进要有重赏，后退处

# 3. Control of the Army

Marquis Wu asked: "What is of first importance in employment of troops?"

Wu Zi replied: " First there should be understanding of the four qualities described as 'Easy,' the two described as 'Heavy,' and the one described as 'Reliability.'

Marquis Wu asked: " How do you describe these? What do you mean by them?"

Wu Zi replied: "The ground should be easy for the horses; the horses should pull the chariots with ease; the chariots should carry the men with ease; the men should enter battle with ease. If you know the difficult and easy ground, the ground is easy for the horses. If fodder and grain are provided at the right time, the horses will draw the chariots easily. If there is an abundance of axle grease the chariots can easily carry the men; if their weapons are keen and their armor is strong, the men will fight with ease. Heavy reward is given for an advance, while heavy pun-

【原文】

退有重刑。行之以信。审能达此，胜之主也。”

武侯问曰：“兵何以为胜？”

起对曰：“以治为胜。”

又问曰：“不在众寡？”

对曰：“若法令不明，赏罚不信，金之不止，鼓之不进，虽有百万，何益于用！所谓治者，居则有礼，动则有威，进不可当，退不可追，前却有节，左右应麾，虽绝成陈，虽散成行。与之安，与之危，其众可合而不可离，可用而不可疲。投之所往，天

【今译】

以重罚。一信就是赏罚严守信用。确实做到这些，就具备取胜的主要条件了。”

魏武侯问道：“军队靠什么取胜呢？”

吴起回答说：“靠严格治理取胜。”

魏武侯又问道：“不在于兵力的多少吗？”

吴起回答说：“如果法令不严明，赏罚不讲信用，鸣金而不能收兵，击鼓而不前进，即使有百万大军，又怎能用于作战呢！所谓治理好军队，要求驻扎时守纪律，行动时很威武，进攻时敌人不可抵挡，撤退时敌人追赶不上，前进后退有秩序，向左向右听指挥，队伍虽被隔断，但阵势不乱，队形虽被冲散，但能恢复行列。将领与士卒同安乐，共危难，这些士卒能团结一致而不能使他们分离，能用于作战而不会疲惫。这样的军队不论投入到哪里战

ishment for a retreat. The impartiality in their giving will produce reliability. If you can fully understand these, victory is at hand."

Marquis Wu asked: "By what means an army gains victory?"

Wu Zi answered: "The foundation of victory is proper discipline."

Marquis Wu then asked: "Is it not determined by numbers?"

Wu Zi replied: "If laws and orders are not clear and rewards and punishments not just, troops will not stop at the sound of the gongs nor advance at the roll of drums and even though there be a million of this sort, of what use are they? What is called discipline is that there is propriety at rest, and dignity in motion; none can withstand the attack, and retreat forbids pursuit; advance or retreat is regulated, and movements to the right and left are made in answer to signal. If ranks should be cut off, formation is preserved; if dispersed, their files are retained. In fortune or in danger, there is cohesiveness. They can be assembled and cannot be separated; can be used but not wearied. In whatever situation they are placed, nothing under Heaven can withstand them. An army of this sort is called 'Fa-

**【原文】**

下莫当，名曰父子之兵。”

吴子曰：“凡行军之道，无犯进止之节，无失饮食之适，无绝人马之力。此三者，所以任其上令。任其上令，则治之所由生也。若进止不度，饮食不适，马疲人倦而不解舍，所以不任其上令。上令既废，以居则乱，以战则败。”

吴子曰：“凡兵战之场，立尸之地。必死则生，幸生则死。其善将者，如坐漏船之中，伏烧屋之下，

**【今译】**

斗，任何敌人都不能抵挡，这就叫做‘父子之兵’。”

吴起说：“通常行军的原则，不能违背行进停止的节制，不要忽视饮食的适当，不要使人马疲劳过度。这三条做到了，就能使士卒听从上级的命令。士卒服从上级命令，这是治理好军队的根本。如果行进停止毫无节度，饮食饥渴失宜，人马疲倦而不准解甲住宿，这样士卒就不会听从上级的命令了。上级的命令既然行不通，用这样的军队驻守就会混乱，用他们去作战就会失败。”

吴起说：“凡是两军交锋的战场，是流血战死的地方。抱必死的决心战斗倒可能有生路，如侥幸贪生倒会死亡。善于指挥打仗的将领，就像坐在漏水的船中，躺在着火的房子里面那样情况紧急，有智

ther-Son Army'."

Wu Zi said: "Now the method of conducting the march of an army is this: The established order of advancing and halting is not to be violated; suitable occasions for rationing should not be missed and the strength of the men and horses not exhausted. If these three things should be observed, the commands of superiors can be implemented. If the commands of superiors be implemented, order will be maintained. If advances and halts are not well regulated, if food and drink are not suitable, the horses will be exhausted and the men fatigued and not able to be relaxed and sheltered. In such situations the orders of superiors cannot be obeyed. If the orders are set aside, there will be disorder in the camp and defeat in battle."

Wu Zi said: "Now the battlefield of fierce fighting is a bleeding ground of standing corpses. Those who are determined to die will live; those who hope to escape with their lives will die. A general good at commanding troops is like one sitting in a leaking ship or lying under a burning roof. For there is no time for the wise to offer counsel nor the brave to incite troops in anger. All must come to grips with the enemy.

【原文】

使智者不及谋，勇者不及怒，受敌可也。故曰，用兵之害，犹豫最大；三军之灾，生于狐疑。”

吴子曰：“夫人常死其所不能，败其所不便。故用兵之法，教戒为先。一人学战，教成十人。十人学战，教成百人。百人学战，教成千人。千人学战，教成万人。万人学战，教成三军。以近待远，以佚待劳，以饱待饥。圆而方之，坐而起之，行而止之，左而右之，前而后之，分而合之，结而解之。每变皆习，乃授其兵。是为将事。”

【今译】

谋的人来不及考虑，猛勇的人来不及发怒，就率军迎敌作战。所以说，用兵打仗的最大祸害，是将领的犹豫不决；军队的灾难，往往产生于多疑。”

吴起说：“将士常常战死于没有打仗的本领，军队往往失败于战法不灵活。所以用兵的方法，首先在于教育训练。一个人学会打仗，可以教会十人。十个人学会打仗，可以教会百人。一百个人学会打仗，可以教会千人。一千个人学会打仗，可以教会万人。一万个人学会打仗，可以教会三军。战法要训练以近待远，以逸待劳，以饱待饥。阵法要训练圆阵变方阵，跪姿变立姿，前进变停止，向左转向右，向前转向后，分散变集中，集合变解散。各种战斗队形变换都训练后，于是就给士卒授予兵器。这就是将领的任务。”

Therefore it is said that of all the dangers in employing the troops indecision is the greatest and that the disasters which overwhelm the Three Armies arise from hesitation."

Wu Zi said: "Now men generally die from lack of ability or unskillfulness, and are defeated by unfamiliarity with tactics. Therefore in employing troops, instructing and warning them is of the first importance. If one man studies war he can successfully instruct ten; if ten study they can successfully instruct a hundred, one hundred can successfully instruct one thousand, and one thousand can successfully instruct ten thousand. Ten thousand can successfully instruct the Three Armies.

"In tactics an enemy from a distance should be awaited and struck at short range; an enemy that is tired should be met with fresh troops; a hungry one with well-fed troops. In battle formation the troops must be trained to form squares from circles, to sit down and get up, to move and to stop. They run from the left to the right and the front to the rear; or divide and concentrate or gather and disperse as required in changing formations. All these changes must be learnt, and the weapons distributed. This is the business of

**【原文】**

吴子曰："教战之令，短者持矛戟，长者持弓弩，强者持旌旗，勇者持金鼓，弱者给厮养，智者为谋主。乡里相比，什伍相保。一鼓整兵，二鼓习陈，三鼓趋食，四鼓严办，五鼓就行。闻鼓声合，然后举旗。"

武侯问曰："三军进止，岂有道乎？"

起对曰："无当天灶，无当龙头。天灶者，大谷之口。龙头者，大山之端。必左青龙，右白虎，前朱雀，后玄武，招摇在上，从事于下。将战之时，

**【今译】**

吴起说："教练作战的法令，就是身材矮小的使用矛或戟，个头高大的使用弓和弩，身强力壮的扛大旗，作战勇敢的操金鼓，体质较弱的担负勤杂，有智慧的充当谋士。把同乡同里的人编在一起，使同什同伍的彼此作保。第一次击鼓检查整理兵器，二次击鼓练习阵法，三次击鼓迅速吃饭，四次击鼓急令整装，五次击鼓排好队列。听到鼓声齐响，然后举令旗指挥军队行动。"

魏武侯问道："军队的开进或驻止，难道有什么原则吗？"

吴起回答说："不要对着'天灶'扎营，不要在'龙头'上驻军。所谓天灶，就是大山的谷口。所谓龙头，就是大山的山顶。军队驻守时必须左用青龙旗，右用白虎旗，前用朱雀旗，后用玄武旗，中军用招摇旗在高处指挥，部队在下面按旗号行动。临

the general."

Wu Zi said: "In the teaching of warfare,spears are given to the short; bows and catapults to the tall; flags and banners to the strong; the gong and drum to the bold; fodder and provisions to the feeble and the arrangement of the plan to the wise. Men from the same villages are put together and squads of ten and five will mutually protect one another. At one beat of the drum the ranks are put in order; at two beats of the drum, formation will be made; at three beats of the drum, food will be issued; at four beats of the drum, the men will prepare to march; at five beats of the drum, ranks will be formed. When the drums beat together, then the standards will be raised."

Marquis Wu asked: "What is the way of advancing and halting of an army?"

Wu Zi replied: "Heavenly Ovens or Dragon's Heads should be avoided. Heavenly Ovens are the mouths of large valleys. Dragon's Heads are extremities of large mountains. The green dragons (banner) should be placed on the left, and the white tigers on the right; the sparrows in front; the snakes and tortoises behind; the pole star (standard) above. Under this standard the troops

**【原文】**

审候风所从来。风顺致呼而从之，风逆坚陈以待之。”

武侯问曰：“凡畜卒骑，岂有方乎？”

起对曰：“夫马，必安其处所，适其水草，节其饥饱。冬则温厩，夏则凉庑。刻剔毛鬣，谨落四下。戢其耳目，无令惊骇。习其驰逐，闲其进止。人马相亲，然后可使。车骑之具，鞍、勒、衔、辔，必令完坚。凡马不伤于末，必伤于始。不伤于饥，必

**【今译】**

战的时候，要观测风从哪个方向来。顺风对我有利就乘势呐喊，攻击敌军，逆风对我不利就坚守阵势，待机破敌。”

魏武侯问道：“驯养战马，有什么方法吗？”

吴起回答说：“马匹，必须安置在适宜的处所，适时地给它饮水喂草，节制它的饥饱。冬天要使马厩温暖，夏天要让马棚凉爽。要经常剪刷鬃毛，细心地铲蹄钉掌。要训练战马的听觉和视觉，不要使它受到惊吓。让战马练习奔驰追逐，熟悉前进停止的动作。人和马要相互熟悉，然后就可以使用于作战。战马的装具，马鞍、笼头、嚼子、缰绳，必须完好坚固。通常马不是受伤在跑完长途之后，就是受伤于开始使用之时。不是因为饥饿受伤，就是由于过饱受伤。如天色已晚路程遥远，人就应经常下马走一阵，尔后再上马骑一阵。宁可让人受点劳累，

are assembled for operations. Before the fight begins, the direction of the wind must be studied carefully. If it blows in the direction of the enemy, the troops will march with the wind. If this is a headwind, the position will be strengthened, and a wait made for the wind to change."

Marquis Wu asked: "In what way should horses be treated?"

Wu Zi replied: "Now horses must have peaceful places to rest. Their drink and fodder must be suitable and they must be regularly and properly fed. In winter their stables must be warmed, and in summer sheltered from heat. The hair of their manes and tails must be clipped and their four hooves carefully pared. Their attention to sound and sight must be directed so that they will not be alarmed. They must be practiced in galloping and chasing. Their movements and stops must be leisurely. When mutual affection exists between the rider and his horse they can be used. The equipment of the chariot horse and the cavalry mount consists of saddle, bridle, bit and rein. These must be strong. Now in general horses are harmed either at the end of a march or at the beginning; either by feeding them too little or too much. Toward sunset after a long march

【原文】

伤于饱。日暮道远，必数上下。宁劳于人，慎无劳马。常令有余，备敌覆我。能明此者，横行天下。”

【今译】

也不要使马疲乏。经常使战马保持一定的体力，防备敌军袭击我军。能够明白这些道理，就能无敌于天下。”

the riders must dismount and remount many times, for it is better to tire the men. Take care not to tire the horses! Always see that they have a reserve of strength, and so prepare against the enemy's surprise attacks. One able to understand these things will be unopposed under Heaven."

# 论将第四

【原文】

吴子曰："夫总文武者，军之将也。兼刚柔者，兵之事也。凡人论将，常观于勇。勇之于将，乃数分之一尔。夫勇者必轻合，轻合而不知利，未可也。故将之所慎者五：一曰理，二曰备，三曰果，四曰戒，五曰约。理者，治众如治寡。备者，出门如见

【今译】

吴起说："文武全才的人，才能担任军队的将领。刚柔相兼的人，才能统军作战。人们在评论将领时，常常只着眼于勇敢。勇敢对于将领来说，只是应该具备的若干条件中的一条罢了。仅凭勇敢的将领，必然会轻率与敌交战，轻率与敌交战，就不会考虑利害得失，这是不行的。所以将领必须慎重的有五个方面：一是'理'，二是'备'，三是'果'，四是'戒'，五是'约'。理，就是统率百万大军如同治理兵力很少的小部队一样了如指掌，条

# 4. A Discussion of Generalship

Wu Zi said: "Now the commander of an army is one in whom civil and military perspicacity are combined. To unite resolution with resilience is the business of war. In popular estimation of generals, courage alone is regarded; nevertheless courage is but one of the qualifications of a general. One who has courage alone is reckless in encounter. And rash encounter without regard to the consequences is undesirable. Now there are five matters which a general must carefully consider. The first of these is administration; the second, preparedness; the third, determination; the fourth, prudence; and the fifth, economy. Administration means that a multitude can be controlled like a small number. Preparedness means that when he marches forth from the gates he acts as if he were perceiving the enemy. Determination means that when he approaches the enemy he is not anxious of his own life. Prudence means that although he has conquered, he

【原文】

敌。果者，临敌不怀生。戒者，虽克如始战。约者，法令省而不烦。受命而不辞，敌破而后言返，将之礼也。故师出之日，有死之荣，无生之辱。”

吴子曰：“凡兵有四机：一曰气机，二曰地机，三曰事机，四曰力机。三军之众，百万之师，张设轻重，在于一人，是谓气机。路狭道险，名山大塞，十夫所守，千夫不过，是谓地机。善行间谍，轻兵往来，分散其众，使其君臣相怨，上下相咎，是谓

【今译】

理清晰。备，就是军队一出动如同遇到敌人那样警惕。果，就是临敌作战不考虑个人生死。戒，就是虽然已经打败敌人却如同战斗开始那样戒备。约，就是法令简明而不烦琐。接受命令而不推辞，打败敌军后再提出归返，这都是将领应当遵循的礼法。所以从率师出征的那一天起，就应该下定决心，宁可光荣战死，决不忍辱偷生。”

吴起说：“率军作战有四个关键问题：一是掌握士气，二是利用地形，三是运用谋略，四是增强战斗力。三军人马众多，上百万大军，掌握士气的盛衰，全在于将领一人，这就是掌握士气的关键。道路险狭，高山要塞，十个人防守，千人过不去，这就是利用地形的关键。善于使用间谍，派遣小部队活动，分散敌人的兵力，使其君臣彼此埋怨，上下

acts as if he were just in first encounter. Economy means that laws and regulations are few and concise, not in great numbers and vexatious. It is the proper conduct that he receives the orders without any pretext of denial and talks of return only after the enemy has been defeated. Therefore on the day the army departs he has in mind the glory of death and not the shame of living."

Wu Zi said: "Now in military operations there are four key elements. First, spirit; second, terrain; third, opportunity; fourth, strength. Now as for the multitude of the Three Armies, a host of a million, how to make arrangements rests upon one man. This is called the influence of spirit. When the road is steep and narrow, when there are famous mountains and great bottlenecks where ten men can defend and one thousand cannot pass them by, such is the influence of terrain. When spies have been skillfully employed, and light troops pass to and from the enemy's camp, so that his masses are divided, his sovereign and ministers vexed with each other, and superiors and inferiors mutually censorious, this is the moment of opportunity. When the linchpins of the chariots are secure, the oars and rudders ready for use in the boats, the officers

【原文】

事机。车坚管辖，舟利橹楫，士习战陈，马闲驰逐，是谓力机。

“知此四者，乃可为将。然其威、德、仁、勇，必足以率下安众，怖敌决疑。施令而下不敢犯，所在而寇不敢敌。得之国强，去之国亡。是谓良将。”

“吴子曰：“夫鼙鼓金铎，所以威耳。旌旗麾帜，所以威目。禁令刑罚，所以威心。耳威于声，不可不清。目威于色，不可不明。心威于刑，不可不严。三者不立，虽有其国，必败于敌。故曰，将之所麾，

【今译】

互相责难，这就是运用谋略的关键。战车的轮轴坚固，战船的橹桨轻便，士卒熟练阵法，战马熟悉驰逐，这就是提高部队战斗力的关键。

“把握了这四个关键，才能担任将领。然而将领的威严、品德、仁爱、勇敢，必定要足以统率下属稳定部队，威慑敌军，决断难疑。发布命令部属不敢违犯，所到之处敌军不敢抵挡。得到这样的将领，国家就强盛，失去这样的将领，国家就衰亡。这就是良将。”

吴起说：“军鼓铃铎，是通过听觉来号令部队的行动。旌旗麾帜，是通过视觉来号令部队的行动。禁令刑罚，是靠它来统一军心的。听觉统一行动靠声音，所以金鼓之声不可不清晰。视觉统一行动靠颜色，所以旗帜的颜色不可不鲜艳。军心的统一靠刑罚，所以刑罚不可不严厉。这三条不确立，虽然有国家，也必定会被敌人打败。所以说，将领的令旗挥动所向，部队没有不听从行动的；将领的号令

trained for battle formations and the horses exercised for swift pursuit, this is called the influence of strength.

"He who understands these four matters has the qualifications of a general. Furthermore, dignity, virtue, benevolence and courage are needed to lead the troops, to calm the multitude, to put fear in the enemy, and to remove doubts. When orders are issued, the subordinates do not defy them. Wherever the army is, that place the enemy avoids. If one gets a general like this his state will be strong; if one dismisses one like this his state will perish. This is what is called 'Excellent General'."

Wu Zi said: "The use of drums and gongs is to impress the ears; of banners and standards to impress the eyes; of prohibitory orders and penalties to impress the heart. To impress the ears the sound must be clear; to impress the eyes the colors must be bright. The heart is awed by punishment, therefore punishment must be strict. Now when these three matters are not well established, any state is certain to be defeated. Hence it is said that where the general's banners are, there are none who do not follow; where the general points there are none who will not

【原文】

莫不从移；将之所指，莫不前死。”

吴子曰：“凡战之要，必先占其将而察其才。因形用权，则不劳而功举。其将愚而信人，可诈而诱；贪而忽名，可货而赂；轻变无谋，可劳而困。上富而骄，下贫而怨，可离而间。进退多疑，其众无依，可震而走。士轻其将而有归志，塞易开险，可邀而取。进道易，退道难，可来而前。进道险，退道易，可薄而击。居军下湿，水无所通，霖雨数至，可灌

【今译】

所指，部队没有不拼死向前杀敌的。”

吴起说：“作战中最重要的，必须首先侦知敌将的情况并观察他的才能。根据战场形势采用灵活的权谋，就可以不费多大力量而取胜。敌将愚蠢而轻信于人，可用诈骗手段诱惑他；贪图私利而不顾名誉，可用资财贿赂他；轻易改变主意而无智谋，可以扰乱疲困他。上级富裕而骄奢，下级贫困而怨愤，可以利用矛盾离间他们。将领进退迟疑不决，部队无所适从，可用威势逼跑他们。士卒轻视将领而厌战思归，把大道堵塞，把险路让开，就可以用截击的战法而取胜。敌进路平易，退路困难，就引诱敌人前进而加以歼灭。敌进路艰险，退路平坦，就逼近敌人攻击。敌在低洼潮湿的地方驻扎，无法排除积水，若经常下雨，就可以灌水淹没他。敌在荒芜

advance in the face of death."

Wu Zi said: "Generally it is important in war to know who is the enemy's general and to judge his ability. If the stratagem is used in accord with the enemy's posture then success will be achieved without toil. If the enemy's general is stupid and places his confidence in others, he can be enticed by fraud. If he is covetous and careless of his fame, he can be bribed with gifts. If he is easily changeable and lacks plans, he can be tired out and placed in difficulties. If the superiors are rich and proud and the inferiors poor and resentful, they can be set against each other. If the enemy's general is hesitant in advancing or retreating and his hosts have no trust in him, they would be stampeded and put to flight. If the enemy's officers think lightly of their general and desire to go home, the easy roads should be blocked and the difficult and narrow roads opened. Then they can be intercepted and captured. If the road by which he advances is easy and that by which he would retreat difficult, he can be forced to come forward. If the road by which he advances is dangerous and that by which he would retreat easy, he can be approached and attacked. If he encamps in low-lying

**【原文】**

而沈。居军荒泽，草楚幽秽，风飙数至，可焚而灭。停久不移，将士懈怠，其军不备，可潜而袭。”

武侯问曰：“两军相望，不知其将，我欲相之，其术如何？”

起对曰：“令贱而勇者，将轻锐以尝之。务于北，无务于得，观敌之来，一坐一起，其政以理，其追北佯为不及，其见利佯为不知，如此将者，名为智将，勿与战矣。若其众讙哗，旌旗烦乱，其卒

**【今译】**

的湖沼地带驻扎，那里杂草灌木丛生，若经常刮狂风，可用火攻消灭他。敌久驻一地不转移，将士松懈怠情，部队疏忽戒备，可以偷袭他。”

魏武侯问道：“两军对阵，不知敌将的情况，我想观察他的才能，有什么办法呢？”

吴起回答说：“命令一员级别不高而勇敢的裨将，率轻兵锐卒去试攻，只许败，不准胜，以观察敌军前来的行动，敌军的一举一动，指挥很有条理，向我追击时佯装追不上，看到散于地上的财物假装没看见，像这样的将领，就是智将，不要与他交战。如果敌军之中喧哗嘈杂，军旗纷烦杂乱，士卒自由

damp ground where the water drainage is poor and rainfall is frequent, he can be inundated and drowned. If he encamps in wild marshes covered with dark and overhanging grass and brambles, and swept by frequent high winds, he can be overthrown by fire. If he remains long in one place without moving, and generals and officers become heedless and neglect precautions,he can be approached by stealth and taken by surprise."

Marquis Wu asked: "When the opposing armies confront each other and we know nothing about the enemy's general, and I wish to determine his qualities, what methods are there?"

Wu Zi replied: "Order some brave men to lead a group of lightly but well equipped troops to try him out. Their sole purpose is to flee, not to gain anything but to observe how the enemy reacts. If his actions to start or stop operations are well in order, and when we retreat and he pursues but pretend not to be able to overtake us, sees an advantage but pretends to be not aware of it, then the general is wise, and conflict with him must be avoided. If the enemy host is full of uproar, his flags and banners are disordered, his troops going about or remaining of their own accord and their weapons held sometimes one

【原文】

自行自止，其兵或纵或横，其追北恐不及，见利恐不得，此为愚将，虽众可获。”

【今译】

行动，手中兵器横拿直放，追击时惟恐追不上，见到资财惟恐抢不到，这就是愚将，敌人虽多也可以俘获他。”

way, sometimes another; and when we retreat and they are eager to pursue instantly, and see an advantage which they are desperate to seize,then the general is stupid. Even if there is a host, he can be taken."

# 应变第五

【原文】

武侯问曰："车坚马良，将勇兵强，卒遇敌人，乱而失行，则如之何？"

吴起对曰："凡战之法，昼以旌旗旙麾为节，夜以金鼓笳笛为节。麾左而左，麾右而右。鼓之则进，金之则止。一吹而行，再吹而聚，不从令者诛。三军服威，士卒用命，则战无强敌，攻无坚陈矣。"

【今译】

魏武侯问道："我军战车坚固战马优良，将领勇敢士卒坚强，如果突然遭遇敌人，队伍混乱不成行列，那怎么办呢？"

吴起回答说："通常打仗的方法，白天用旌旗旙麾指挥，夜间用金鼓笳笛指挥。指挥向左部队就向左，指挥向右部队就向右。击鼓部队就前进，鸣金部队就停止。第一次吹笳笛部队就成行列，第二次吹笳笛部队就集合，不听从命令的就要惩罚。三军听从指挥，士卒执行命令，这样就没有打不败的强大敌人，没有攻不破的坚固阵势。"

# 5. On Responding to Changing Situations

Marquis Wu asked: "If strong chariots, good horses, valiant generals and strong troops suddenly meet the enemy, and are thrown into confusion, and ranks broken, what should be done?"

Wu Zi replied: "Now generally the method of fighting is to effect order in daylight by means of flags and banners, streamers and standards; at night by gongs and drums, reed pipes and flutes. When the standards indicate 'Left' the troops move to the left; and when the standards indicate 'Right' the troops move to the right. When the drums beat they advance; when the gongs sound they stop. At one piping they move; at second they rally. Those who disobey are punished to death. If the Three Armies are thus subject to authority and officers and men implement orders, then in battle no enemy will be stronger than you, nor will any defenses remain impregnable to your attack."

**【原文】**

武侯问曰："若敌众我寡，为之奈何？"

起对曰："避之于易，邀之于厄。故曰，以一击十，莫善于厄；以十击百，莫善于险；以千击万，莫善于阻。今有少卒卒起，击金鸣鼓于厄路，虽有大众，莫不惊动。故曰，用众者务易，用少者务隘。"

武侯问曰："有师甚众，既武且勇；背大险阻，右山左水；深沟高垒，守以强弩；退如山移，进如风雨，粮食又多。难与长守，则如之何？"

起对曰："大哉问乎！此非车骑之力，圣人之谋也。能备千乘万骑，兼之徒步，分为五军，各军一

**【今译】**

魏武侯问道："如果遇到敌众我寡的情况，那该怎么办呢？"

吴起回答说："在平坦的地形避开敌人，在险要的地形截击敌人。所以说，以一击十，最好是利用狭隘的地形；以十击百，最好是利用险峻的地形；以千击万，最好是利用险阻的地形。马上派少数士卒突然出现，在狭险的地形上鸣金击鼓，即使敌人众多，也无不惊骇骚动。所以说，使用众多的兵力，务求地形平坦，使用部分兵力，务求地形险要。"

魏武侯问道："敌军兵力众多，训练有素，作战勇敢，背靠高大险阻的地形，右依山，左临水，挖有很深的沟壕，筑有很高的壁垒，防守有强大的弩兵，后退稳如山移，前进疾如风雨，粮食储备又充足。很难与它长期相持，该怎么办呢？"

吴起回答说："这个问题真大呀！这不能单凭车骑的力量，而是要靠圣贤之人的谋略。如果能够配备战车千辆、骑兵万人，加上相应的步兵，编为五

Marquis Wu asked: "What is to be done if the enemy is many and we are few?"

Wu Zi replied: "Avoid such an enemy on open ground, and meet him in a narrow way. For it is said that when one attacks ten, no place is better than a narrow way; for ten to attack a hundred nothing is better than a precipitous place. When one thousand attack ten thousand, nothing is better than a mountain pass. Now when a small force with the beating of gongs and drum suddenly arises in a narrow way, even a host will be upset. Therefore it is said one who has a multitude seeks open ground, and one who has few seeks constricted ground."

Marquis Wu asked: "Suppose there is a mighty army full of valiant and courageous spirit. To its rear are precipitous passes, to its right mountains, to its left a river. It is well protected by deep moats and high ramparts defended by strong crossbow men. In retreat it is like the removal of a mountain; in advance like hurricane. Furthermore, its supplies are in abundance. It is difficult to hold up such an enemy. What should be done in these circumstances?"

Wu Zi replied: "This indeed is a great question. In this situation the outcome does not de-

**【原文】**

衢。夫五军五衢，敌人必惑，莫之所加。敌人若坚守以固其兵，急行间谍以观其虑。彼听吾说，解之而去。不听吾说，斩使焚书，分为五战。战胜勿追，不胜疾归。如是佯北，安行疾斗，一结其前，一绝其后。两军衔枚，或左或右，而袭其处。五军交至，必有其利。此击强之道也。”

武侯问曰：“敌近而薄我，欲去无路，我众甚

**【今译】**

支军队，每军各为一路。五支军队成五路进发，敌人必然疑惑，不知攻击它的什么地方。敌军如果坚守阵势，稳定它的部队，应迅速派出使者，试探它的企图。如果它听从我方劝说，我就撤兵退回。如若不听从我方劝说，必会杀我使者，烧掉我送去的书信，那么五军就分五路与敌交战。打胜了不要追击，不胜就迅速撤回。像这样佯装败阵，要行动慎重迅速反击敌人，一支军队从正面牵制它，一支军队截断它的后路。两支军队隐蔽前进，或者从左侧或者从右侧，袭击它的薄弱处。五支军队全部到达，必然形成强有力的有利态势。这就是攻击强敌的战法。”

魏武侯问道：“敌军临近逼我交战，想撤退没有

pend on the strength of chariots and horses, but on the schemes of a sage. Let one thousand chariots and ten thousand horses be well equipped and with footmen added to them be divided into five columns and a road allotted to each column. Then if there are five columns and each column takes a different road, the enemy is certain to be perplexed and will not know which to deal with. If the enemy has taken up a strong defensive position in order to consolidate his troops, send envoys quickly to him to discover his intention. If he should listen to our advice, he will strike camps and withdraw. But, if he does not listen to our advice and relentlessly executes the envoys and burns their papers, then divide and attack from five quarters. If victorious, do not pursue; if not victorious retreat rapidly. If feigning retreat, proceed slowly to attract enemy to be engaged. One column ties up his front while another cuts off his rear. Then two columns with gags in their mouths should silently and swiftly attack his weak point, whether on the right or on the left. If the five columns coordinate their attacks, it will certainly be advantageous. This is the way to attack a strong enemy."

Marquis Wu asked: "If the enemy draws near

【原文】

惧，为之奈何？”

起对曰：“为此之术，若我众彼寡，各分而乘之。彼众我寡，以方从之。从之无息，虽众可服。”

武侯问曰：“若遇敌于谿谷之间，傍多险阻，彼众我寡，为之奈何？”

起对曰：“遇诸丘陵、林谷、深山、大泽，疾行亟去，勿得从容。若高山深谷，卒然相遇，必先鼓噪而乘之，进弓与弩，且射且虏。审察其政，乱则击之勿疑。”

武侯问曰：“左右高山，地甚狭迫，卒遇敌人，

【今译】

去路，部队甚为畏惧，这有什么办法呢？”

吴起回答说：“对付这种情况的战法，如果我众敌寡，就分兵几路合击它。如敌众我寡,就集中兵力攻击它，不断地袭扰它,敌军虽众也能被制服。”

魏武侯问道：“如果与敌军遭遇在溪涧峡谷之间，两傍地形险峻，而且敌众我寡，那该怎么办呢？”

吴起回答说：“遇到丘陵、森林、谷地、深山、大泽等不利地形，必须急速通过，不能从容不迫。如果在高山深谷之间，突然与敌遭遇，必须首先击鼓呐喊乘势攻击敌军，指挥弓、弩手向前推进，一面射箭一面俘虏敌人。观察敌军指挥行动，如果混乱惊恐，就立刻攻击，不要迟疑。”

魏武侯问道：“左右都是高山，地形十分狭窄，

and presses upon us and we would retreat but there is no way and in our host there is fear,what is to be done?"

Wu Zi replied: "The methods to use in such a case are as follows: If we are many and the enemy is few we divide our forces and charge. If the enemy is many and we are few we concentrate our force to harass him. By harassing him increasingly his host, however large, can be overcome."

Marquis Wu asked: "If we unexpectedly meet the enemy in a narrow valley with steep places on either side, and he is many and we are few, what should be done?"

Wu Zi replied: "In all cases you must march swiftly to get away from such places as hills, forests, valleys, and marshlands. You cannot march leisurely. If the enemy is suddenly met among high mountains or deep valleys, you must first beat the drums with shouting and fall upon him. Let bows and crossbows advance, shoot and capture. Carefully observe the state of his array and if he falls into confusion, strike without hesitation."

Marquis Wu asked: "If the enemy is unexpectedly met in a narrow place with high moun-

【原文】

击之不敢，去之不得，为之奈何？”

起对曰：“此谓谷战，虽众不用。募吾材士与敌相当，轻足利兵以为前行，分车列骑隐于四旁，相去数里，无见其兵，敌必坚陈，进退不敢。于是出旌列旆，行出山外营之，敌人必惧。车骑挑之，勿令得休。此谷战之法也。”

武侯问曰：“吾与敌相遇大水之泽，倾轮没辕，水薄车骑，舟楫不设，进退不得，为之奈何？”

【今译】

与敌突然遭遇，进攻不敢，撤退又不行，这该怎么办呢？”

吴起回答说：“这叫做谷战，兵力虽多也用不上。我军应挑选精锐士卒与敌对阵，以轻捷善走、使用锋利兵器的士卒为前队，把车兵骑兵分别隐蔽在四周，彼此相距数里，不能暴露自己的兵力，敌军必然固守阵势，不敢进也不敢退。我军便突然亮出排列整齐的旌旗，整队走出山外安营，敌军必然惧怕。尔后派车兵骑兵向敌挑战，不让它得到休息。这就是谷战的战法。”

魏武侯问道：“我军在大的湖沼地带与敌遭遇，车轮倾陷，车辕淹没，大水逼近车兵骑兵，没有准备船只，进退两难，这该怎么办呢？”

tains on either side, and advance and retreat alike are impossible, what should be done in such a case?"

Wu Zi replied: "This is called fighting in valleys where numbers are of no avail. Talented men should be collected, and set against the enemy. Well-armed light troops should be deployed in front; the chariots divided; the horsemen drawn up and placed in ambush on four sides with several li in between and without showing themselves. Then the enemy will certainly make his defense firm and will not venture either to advance or retreat. Whereupon raise your standards and show the ranks of banners, march out of the mountains and pitch camps in the plain. The enemy will certainly be apprehensive. Challenge him with your chariots and horsemen and allow him no rest. Such is the method of fighting in valleys."

Marquis Wu asked: "If the enemy is suddenly encountered in a marsh where the water is out, so that the chariot wheels are sunk in, and the shafts are covered, and the chariots and horsemen overcome by the waters, and if there are no boats or oars, and it is impossible either to advance or retreat, what should be done in these circumstances?"

【原文】

起对曰："此谓水战，无用车骑，且留其傍。登高四望，必得水情。知其广狭，尽其浅深，乃可为奇以胜之。敌若绝水，半渡而薄之。"

武侯问曰："天久连雨，马陷车止，四面受敌，三军惊骇，为之奈何？"

起对曰："凡用车者，阴湿则停，阳燥则起；贵高贱下，驰其强车；若进若止，必从其道。敌人若起，必逐其迹。"

武侯问曰："暴寇卒来，掠吾田野，取吾牛羊，则如之何？"

【今译】

吴起回答说："这叫做水战，不要使用车兵骑兵，暂时把它们留在湖沼的傍边。登上高处四面瞭望，必定要掌握水情。确知水域的宽窄，查清水的深浅，就可以出奇制胜。敌军如果渡水，就乘它渡过一半靠近攻击它。"

魏武侯问道："天气长期不断下雨，车马被陷不能行动，四面受敌威胁，三军惊慌恐惧，这该怎么办呢？"

吴起回答说："通常使用战车作战，阴雨泥泞就停下来，天晴地干就行动；选择高地避开洼地，让强固的战车驰行；或者前进或者停止，必须顺着道路走。敌军战车如果行动，必须追踪它的车辙马迹。"

魏武侯问道："凶暴的敌寇突然来袭，掠夺我的田野，抢劫我的牛羊，那该如何对付呢？"

Wu Zi replied: "This is called water fighting, where chariots and horsemen cannot be used, and must be put aside for a time. Go up to the top of a high place and look out to four quarters. The state of the waters will certainly be seen; their extent and depth fully ascertained. Then by using unorthodox tactics the enemy can be defeated. If the enemy should cross the waters, strike him when he is half over."

Marquis Wu asked: "If there has been long continued rain so that the horses sink and the chariots cannot move, if the enemy appear from four quarters, and the forces are frightened, what is to be done in such a case?"

Wu Zi replied: "Generally chariots halt when the weather is cloudy and damp, but can be set in motion when it is bright and dry. High ground is to be preferred; low ground to be shunned. Drive your strong chariots and choose well the road on which to advance or halt. If the enemy's chariots move, immediately pursue them following their tracks."

Marquis Wu asked: "If the brutal enemy suddenly arrives to pillage our fields and pastures and carry off our oxen and sheep. What should be done?"

【原文】

起对曰："暴寇之来，必虑其强，善守勿应。彼将暮去，其装必重，其心必恐，还退务速，必有不属。追而击之，其兵可覆。"

吴子曰："凡攻敌围城之道，城邑既破，各入其宫。御其禄秩，收其器物。军之所至，无刊其木、发其屋、取其粟、杀其六畜、燔其积聚，示民无残心。其有请降，许而安之。"

【今译】

吴起回答说："凶暴的敌寇来袭，必须想到它的来势凶猛，要好好坚守不与应战。敌将会在天黑撤走，它的装载必然沉重，军心必然恐惧，只想尽快撤走，队伍必定互不统属。这个时候追击它，敌军便可覆灭。"

吴起说："通常攻城作战的原则，就是城邑攻破后，部队分别进驻敌人的宫、府。控制他们有俸禄爵秩的官吏、贵族，没收他们的器皿和财物。军队所到之处，不准砍伐树木、折毁房屋、抢夺粮食、宰杀牲畜、焚烧储存的财物，向民众表示没有残害之心。敌军请求投降的，要予以准许并且安抚他们。"

Wu Zi replied: "When the brutal enemy comes you must take precautions against his brutality and lawlessness. You had better stand on the defensive and not meet him. When at dusk he is about to depart and encumbered with loots he is certain to be apprehensive, for his withdrawal is by distant routes and he must travel fast. The connection of the enemy troops will be lost and some of them will certainly lag behind. Pursue and attack them, and they can be overthrown."

Wu Zi said: "Generally the way of attacking the enemy and besieging his walled cities is as follows: When the cities and towns have been broken into, enter all his offices, and make use of his officials and take over his public property. Where the troops encamp let none of them fell trees, dismantle houses, take away crops, slaughter the six domestic animals, or burn the barns. Thus you show the people that there is no cruel desire. Those who wish to surrender should be received and freed from anxiety."

# 励士第六

【原文】

武侯问曰:“严刑明赏,足以胜乎?”

起对曰:“严明之事,臣不能悉。虽然,非所恃也。夫发号布令而人乐闻,兴师动众而人乐战,交兵接刃而人乐死。此三者,人主之所恃也。”

武侯曰:“致之奈何?”

对曰:“君举有功而进飨之,无功而励之。”

于是武侯设坐庙廷,为三行飨士大夫。上功坐

【今译】

魏武侯问道:“严明刑赏,就能够打胜仗吗?”

吴起回答说:“严明刑赏之事,我不能详尽说明。即使能够打胜仗,也不能完全依靠它。发号施令而人们乐意听从,出兵打仗而军队乐意作战,两军交战而将士乐意拼死。这三条,才是君主可以依靠的。”

魏武侯问道:“怎样才能做到这三条呢?”

吴起回答说:“君主挑选有功的人而宴请他们,对没有立功的人就激励他们。”

魏武侯便立即在宫廷设宴,分前、中、后三排

# 6. Encouragement of Officers

Marquis Wu asked: "Are just punishments and impartial rewards sufficient to gain victory?"

Wu Zi replied: "I cannot speak of all the things that concern justice and impartiality, but on these alone dependence cannot be placed. Now to issue orders and make known commands which the troops happily obey, to raise the army and mobilize the people in such a way that men are happy to fight, and when they cross swords, happy to face death, are the three matters in which the ruler of the people can place trust."

Marquis Wu asked: "How can this be brought about?"

Wu Zi replied: "When the ruler raises up those who are meritorious and entertains them and when he encourages those who lack merit."

Accordingly Marquis Wu set seats in the

【原文】

前行，肴席兼重器、上牢。次功坐中行，肴席器差减。无功坐后行，肴席无重器。飨毕而出，又颁赐有功者父母妻子于庙门外，亦以功为差。有死事之家，岁遣使者劳赐其父母，著不忘于心。

行之三年，秦人兴师，临于西河，魏士闻之，不待吏令，介胄而奋击之者以万数。

武侯召吴起而谓曰："子前日之教行矣。"

【今译】

席位款待将士。立上等功的坐在前排，荤菜席位，并使用贵重的器皿和有整只的牛、羊、猪三牲。立二等功的坐中排，荤菜席位，使用的器皿次一等。没有立功的坐后排，荤菜席位，没有贵重器皿。宴席结束后武侯就出来，在宫门外颁发赏赐有功人员的父母妻儿，也按战功大小而有所差别。对阵亡将士的家庭，每年派使者慰劳和赏赐死者的父母，表示没有忘记他们。

这个办法实行了三年，秦国出兵，临近西河，魏国的士卒听到这个消息，不等待将吏的命令，自动穿戴盔甲奋起抗敌的有上万人。

魏武侯召见吴起，并对他说："你以前的指教，如今已行之有效了。"

吴起回答说："我听说人有短长，士气也有盛

ancestral temple hall in three rows, and entertained the nobles and great officers at a banquet. Those of chief merit sat in the first row and on the table were placed the best meats in the precious utensils. Those of medium merit sat in the middle row and the utensils on the table were fewer in number. Those without merit sat in the last row,and utensils of no value were put before them.When the banquet was over, and the guests had departed, the parents, wives, and children of those with merit were given presents outside the temple gates, and the same discrimination was applied as previously. Furthermore messengers were sent yearly with gifts to condole with the parents of those who had lost a son in the service of the state and to show that they were held in remembrance.

After this was carried out for three years, the people of Qin set forth with their army and approached the West River region. When the troops of Wei heard of this, without waiting orders from their officials, tens of thousands of them donned their armors and attacked the Qin vigorously .

Marquis Wu summoned Wu Zi and said to him: "Your previous teachings have been effected."

【原文】

起对曰："臣闻人有短长，气有盛衰。君试发无功者五万人，臣请率以当之。脱其不胜，取笑于诸侯，失权于天下矣。今使一死贼伏于旷野，千人追之，莫不枭视狼顾。何者？忌其暴起而害己。是以一人投命，足惧千夫。今臣以五万之众，而为一死贼，率以讨之，固难敌矣。"

于是武侯从之，兼车五百乘，骑三千匹，而破秦五十万众，此励士之功也。

先战一日，吴起令三军曰："诸吏士当从受敌。

【今译】

衰。君主可试派没有立战功的五万人，我请求率领他们去抵抗秦军。如果不能取胜，就会被诸侯耻笑，在天下诸侯中失去权威。譬如，现有一亡命之徒隐伏在旷野里，上千人追捕他，没有一个不瞻前顾后的。这是什么原因呢？因为怕他突然出来伤害自己。所以一人拼命，能使上千人害怕。现在我用五万人，使每个人都像一个亡命之徒，率领他们征讨敌人，必定使敌人难以抵挡。"

魏武侯听从了他的意见，并给他加派了战车五百辆、战马三千匹，打败了秦军五十万人。这是激励士气的功效。

在作战的前一天，吴起向三军发布命令说："各位将士都要跟着我去迎击敌军。不论车兵、骑兵

Wu Zi replied: "I heard that men have strengths and weaknesses and that sometimes their spirits may be flourishing or depressed. Now if Your Lord is willing to send forth fifty thousand men of no merit, I beg to lead them to engage the enemy. If we fail, the state will be the laughing stock among the feudal lords, and its power under Heaven will be lost. Now suppose there is a desperate bandit lurking in the fields and one thousand men are pursuing him, their glances will be furtive like the owl, looking backward like the wolf. Why? The reason is that they are in fear of harm from a sudden onslaught. Consequently one man willing to throw away his life can terrorize a thousand. Now if I use a host of fifty thousand and all are like this one desperate bandit and I lead them to attack the enemy, they cannot be matched."

On hearing these words Marquis Wu agreed and granted him another five hundred chariots and three thousand horses. They defeated a Qin army of half a million. This is all due to the encouragement of the officers.

On the day before the battle Wu Zi gave orders to the Three Armies, saying: "All officials and officers should follow up and fight against

【原文】

车骑与徒，若车不得车，骑不得骑，徒不得徒，虽破军皆无功。”故战之日，其令不烦而威震天下。

【今译】

还是步兵，如果车战的不能缴获敌人的战车，骑战的不能擒获敌人的骑兵，步战的不能俘获敌人的步兵，即使打败敌军，都不算立下战功。”所以在作战的那一天，他发布的命令不多，而能威名震撼天下。

the enemy's chariots, horsemen and infantrymen. If the chariots do not capture chariots, the cavalry does not capture the horsemen and the dismounted do not capture the infantrymen, even if the enemy army is destroyed, no merit will be gained." Therefore on the day of battle his orders were not vexatiously numerous, but his prestige shook All Under Heaven.

# 司马法

# THE METHODS OF THE SIMA

# 仁本第一

【原文】

古者以仁为本，以义治之之谓正。正不获意则权。权出于战，不出于中人。是故杀人安人，杀之可也；攻其国，爱其民，攻之可也；以战止战，虽战可也。故仁见亲，义见说，智见恃，勇见(身)〔方〕，信见信。内得爱焉，所以守也；外得威焉，所以战也。

【今译】

上古时候，人们以仁爱为根本，用合乎情理的方法治理国家，这是正常的途径。用正常的方法达不到目的，那么就采取特殊的手段。特殊的手段表现为战争，而不是表现为中和与仁爱。因此，如果杀掉坏人而使好人得到安宁，那么杀人是可以的。如果进攻别国是出于爱护该国民众的目的，那么攻打是可以的。如果用战争的手段来制止战争，那么从事战争也是可以的。所以要施仁爱以获得人们的亲近，行正义以获得人们的悦服，凭智慧来赢得人们的钦仰，靠勇敢以争取人们的效法，用诚实以博取人们的信任。这样，对内就能得到民众的爱戴，从而可以守土卫国；对外就能保持强大的威慑，从而可以战胜敌人。

# 1. Foundation of Benevolence

Anciently Benevolence was taken as the foundation and Righteousness as a method to govern. This was referred to as a normal and reasonable way. If this normal way was not feasible, weighing of power must be used. Weighing of power was represented by warfare, not harmony among the people. Thus if killing men can pacify the people, the killing is permissible. If attacking a state is out of love for the people, the attack is permissible. If war must be stopped by means of war, though it is war the means is permissible. Therefore Benevolence attains the love of the people; Righteousness renders happiness to the people; wisdom is respected by the people; courage is worth of people's emulation; credibility produces people's trust. Within a state if its government gets people's love, it is able to defend the state. Outside a state if its government has established awesomeness, it is able to conduct warfare.

【原文】

战道：不违时，不历民病，所以爱吾民也；不加丧，不因凶，所以爱夫其民也；冬夏不兴师，所以兼爱民也。故国虽大，好战必亡，天下虽安，忘战必危。天下既平，天(下)〔子〕大恺，春蒐秋狝，诸侯春振旅，秋治兵，所以不忘战也。

古者，逐奔不过百步，纵绥不过三舍，是以明其礼也；不穷不能而哀怜伤病，是以明其(义)〔仁〕也；成列而鼓，是以明其信也；争义不争利，是以

【今译】

用兵的原则是：不要违背农时，不要让民众遭受苦难，这样做是为了爱护自己的民众；不乘敌人有国丧时前去进攻，也不趁敌国发生灾害时起兵征伐，这样做是为了爱护敌国的民众；在严寒冬季和酷热夏季不兴师出征，这样做是为了爱护敌我双方的民众。所以，国家虽然强大，乐兵好战就必定灭亡；天下虽然太平，安恬忘战则必有危险。即使天下已经太平，天子也大功凯旋，但仍然要在每年春秋两季进行田猎以操练部队，演习战阵。各国诸侯也要在春天整顿军队，在秋天训练部队，这样做就是为了让人们不忘战备。

古代作战，追逐败退的敌人不超过一百步，追击主动退却的敌人不超过九十里，这是为了表明礼让的精神；不过分逼迫已经丧失战斗力的敌人，同时哀怜敌方的伤病人员，这是为了表明仁慈的原则；等待敌人布阵就绪再发动攻击，这是为了表明诚信

The way of conducting warfare is not contravening the seasons nor forcing the people to experience sufferings and scourge of war. This is the means to love our people. Neither attacking a state in its national mourning nor in its facing disaster is out of love for its people. In the winter and summer seasons, no army is raised. This is the means to love both our people and the enemy's people. Therefore even though a state is vast, those who indulge in warfare are certain to perish. Even though it is peaceful under Heaven those who forget warfare are certainly endangered. When peace prevails under Heaven, the Son of Heaven orders to perform the Great Peace music in rejoicing celebrations. Then in spring and autumn he insists on hunting to make military exercise. In spring the feudal lords regroup their troops and in autumn they train their soldiers. Thus they do not forget warfare.

Anciently they did not pursue the fleeing enemy more than one hun dred paces nor did they follow the actively retreating enemy more than ninety li, thereby making clear their observance of Rite. They did not press hard the disabled enemy and treated well his wounded and

**【原文】**

明其义也；又能舍服，是以明其勇也；知终知始，是以明其智也。六德以时合教，以为民纪之道也，自古之政也。

先王之治，顺天之道，设地之宜，官民之德，而正名治物，立国辨职，以爵分禄，诸侯说怀，海

**【今译】**

的态度：恪守大义而不追逐小利，这是为了表明崇高的正义；赦免已经降服的敌人，这是为了表明真正的勇敢；洞察掌握战争的起因和结局，这是为了表明超人的智慧。根据以上六德按时进行综合教育，作为民众行动的规范准则，这是自古以来的为政之道。

从前的圣王治理天下，能顺应自然变化的规律，因地制宜，任用民众中有德行的人担任官职，并确定官职名分，以治理各项事务，分封诸侯，区分其职权，按照爵位的高低给予数额不等的俸禄。这样，诸侯就都心悦诚服，海外的邦国也就倾心归附，讼

sick men, thereby making evident their observance of Benevolence. They waited the completion of the enemy's deployment of formations then beat drums to fight, thereby making clear their observance of credibility. They contended for Righteousness not for profits, thereby making clear their observance of Righteousness. They were also able to pardon the surrendered enemy, thereby making evident their courage. They had foreknowledge of the outcome of war and knew its beginning, thereby making clear their wisdom. The above-mentioned six virtues were taught together at any time, being taken as the code of conduct to govern people. This has been the rule from ancient times.

The governing methods of the former Sage Kings' rule: They complied with the laws of nature; they established what was appropriate on earth; they selected virtuous people into office; they set up the names of official posts and designated terms of reference for each named post respectively. They established the states, defined the hierarchy of feudal positions, and apportioned emoluments according to rank. The feudal lords were pleased and completely convinced by them and those beyond the seas

【原文】

外来服，狱弭而兵寝，圣德之治也。

其次，贤王制礼乐法度，乃作五刑，兴甲兵以讨不义，巡狩(者)〔省〕方，会诸侯，考不同。其有失命乱常、背德逆天之时， 而危有功之君，遍告

【今译】

狱停止，兵革不起，这乃是最为完美的圣王之治。

次圣王一等的政治是这样的：贤王制定礼乐法度来管教人民，设置五等刑罚来惩治罪犯，动用军队来讨伐不义。君王亲自巡视诸侯各国领地，察访地方，会合诸侯考核其政治得失。如发现诸侯国君中有违抗命令、破坏纪律、亵渎道德、逆天行事、嫉功害贤这样的人，便通告于各国诸侯，公布他的罪状，并且上告于皇天上帝日月星辰，祈祷于后土四海等地下神灵，诉述于宗庙祖先。然后由冢宰向各诸侯国发布征调军队的命令：“某某诸侯国暴虐无道，现在决定出兵征讨它。各诸侯国的军队应于某年某月某日抵达某地，随同天子对犯罪的诸侯明

bowed to their authority. Punishments were eliminated and causes of war removed. This was the rule of Sagely Virtue.

Next to the Sage Kings were the Worthy Kings. They ordered the rites, music, laws and regulations and then established the five punishments, raising armored troops to attack the unrighteous. They made inspection tours of the feudal lands, investigated the customs, rallied the feudal lords and observed the differences. If they found any of the feudal lords who had disobeyed the order, violated laws and disciplines, degraded the Virtue or contravened the seasons of Heaven so as to endanger the meritorious rulers, they would publicize it among all the feudal lords, making it clear that he had committed crime. Then they announced it to August Heaven and to the sun, moon, planets, and constellations. They prayed to the Gods of Earth, the spirits of the Four Seas, mountains, and rivers and the state altar. Then they made calculations in the ancestral temple of the Sage Kings. Only thereafter would the Prime Minister order the feudal lords to assemble troops, saying: "A certain state has acted against *Dao*. You will take part in the rectification campaign on such and

【原文】

于诸侯，彰明有罪。乃告于皇天上帝日月星辰，祷于后土四海神祇山川冢社，乃造于先王。然后冢宰征师于诸侯曰："某国为不道，征之，以某年月日师至于某国，会天子正刑。"冢宰与百官布令于军曰："入罪人之地，无暴神祇，无行田猎，无毁土功，无燔墙屋，无伐林木，无取六畜、禾黍、器械。见其老幼，奉归勿伤；虽遇壮者，不校勿敌；敌若伤之，医药归之。"既诛有罪，王及诸侯修正其国，举贤立明，正复厥职。

王霸之所以治诸侯者六：以土地形诸侯，以政

【今译】

正典刑。"然后冢宰又与百官向全军宣布作战原则以及战场纪律："大军进入罪犯辖境后，不许亵渎神灵，不许举行围猎，不许破坏建筑，不许焚烧房舍，不许砍伐林木，不许擅自掠取牲畜、粮食和器具，见到老幼者要护送回家，不得加以伤害；即使遇到青壮之人 只要他们不进行抵抗，就不以敌人对待。对受伤的敌人，应给予医药治疗，然后将他们释放回去。"在惩治了罪犯后，贤王和诸侯还要帮助整顿那个国家，选用贤能，册立明君，调整恢复其各级官职。

王霸统辖管理诸侯的方法有六种：通过封疆裂土的途径来控制诸侯；依靠政策法令来约束诸侯；

such a year, month, and day. On that date the army will reach the offending state and rendezvous with the Son of Heaven to apply "the punishment of rectification." The Prime Minister and other high officials issued an order to the army, saying: "When you enter the offending state, do not commit any sacrilege; do not hunt in the fields; do not destroy any public buildings; do not set fire to houses; do not make deforestation; do not take away the six domestic animals, grains and implements. When you see the old and the very young, advise them to return without hurting them. Even though meeting the strong adults, unless they fight against you do not treat them as enemy. If the enemy's soldiers are wounded, provide them with medical treatment and allow them to go home." When those who had committed crimes were already punished to death, the King and feudal lords rectified the state, recommended the Worthy, supported the enlightened ruler and restored its original feudal position.

There were six means by which the kings and hegemons controlled the feudal lords:

With location area and territorial boundaries they constrained the feudal lords. With govern-

**【原文】**

令平诸侯，以礼信亲诸侯，以材力说诸侯，以谋人维诸侯，以兵革服诸侯。同患共利以合诸侯，比小事大以和诸侯。

会之以发禁者九：凭弱犯寡则眚之，贼贤害民则伐之，暴内凌外则坛之，野荒民散则削之，负固

**【今译】**

凭借礼仪诚信使诸侯亲近自己；借助任贤使能而让诸侯悦服自己；重用深谋远虑的智士以维系诸侯间的关系；依赖强大的军事力量慑服诸侯。要与众诸侯共患同利合为一体；大国亲近小国，小国奉事大国，做到和衷共济和睦相处。

会合诸侯颁布以下九条禁令：恃强欺弱以众凌寡的，就限制削弱他；虐杀贤良残害民众的，就用兵讨伐他；对内暴虐对外侵凌的，就坚决废除他；使田野荒芜民众逃散的，就削贬其诸侯的爵位；仗恃险固不服从王命的，就出兵打击他；背逆人伦残杀骨肉至亲的，就坚决惩罚他；驱逐或弑杀国君的，

ment directives they pacified the feudal lords. With the rites and credibility they were on intimate terms with the feudal lords. With men of wisdom and strength they pleased the feudal lords. With strategists they assembled the feudal lords. With armed forces they forced the submission of the feudal lords.

By showing misfortune with them, by showing profits with them, they brought the feudal lords together. They made the larger states have closer relations with the smaller ones, and the smaller states serve the larger ones in order to bring the feudal lords into harmony.

They rallied the feudal lords in order to announce nine prohibitions:

Those who bully the weak states or encroach on the less populated states will have their borders reduced on all sides. Those who cruelly murder the Worthy and harm the innocent people will be suppressed. Those who are brutal within their state and encroach on others outside it will be purged. Those whose fields become desolated and whose people displaced will be reduced. Those who depend on firmness of precipitous positions to disobey orders will be invaded. Those who cruelly kill their relatives will be

【原文】

不服则侵之，贼杀其亲则正之，放弑其君则残之，犯令陵政则杜之，外内乱、禽兽行则灭之。

【今译】

就严厉处置他；违抗命令、凌侮王政的，就孤立制裁他；内外淫乱，厚颜无耻，行同禽兽的，就彻底诛灭他。

punished. Those who depose or murder their ruler will be exterminated. Those who violate orders and resist government will be sanctioned and isolated. Those who are hectically rebellious both within and without their borders, who act as savagely as animals, will be extinguished.

# 天子之义第二

【原文】

天子之义，必纯取法天地，而观于先圣。士庶之义，必奉于父母而正于君长。故虽有明君，士不先教，不可用也。

古之教民，必立贵贱之伦经，使不相陵。德义不相逾，材技不相掩，勇力不相犯，故力同而意和也。

古者，国容不入军，军容不入国，故德义不相

【今译】

天子正确的行为准则，必须严格按照天地运行的规律，并垂鉴古代圣王的法度。士民们正确的行为准则，必须是敬从父母的教诲，并遵循君主长辈的规诫和指导。所以，即使世上有贤明的君主，但假如对普通民众不先加以教育训练，也是无法使用的。

古代对民众的教育，必定是先确立制定贵贱上下的伦常规范，以确保贵贱尊卑之间不相侵凌。德和义两者互不逾越，有材技的人不致被埋没，勇武刚强的人不敢违犯命令。这样，大家就会力往一处使，心往一处想了。

古时候，朝廷的礼仪法度不用于军队，军队的规章制度也不用于朝廷，所以德和义两者就不会互

# 2. Right Conduct of the Son of Heaven

The right conduct of the Son of Heaven must follow the example of Heaven and Earth and observe the trace of the former Sage Kings. The right conduct of officers and men must be in conformity to the teachings of their parents and instructions of their sovereign and superiors. Hence even though there is an enlightened sovereign, the officers cannot be employed if they are not first instructed.

Anciently people were taught to establish and comply with the ethics in making distinction between the noble and the humble in order that they would not encroach on each other. Thereby the virtuous and righteous would not transgress each other; the talented and technically skilled would not block each other; the brave and strong would not clash with each other. Thus they worked in full cooperation and with unity of purpose.

Anciently protocols and moral standards in

【原文】

逾。上贵不伐之士，不伐之士，上之器也。苟不伐则无求，无求则不争。国中之听，必得其情；军旅之听，必得其宜；故材技不相掩。从命为士上赏，犯命为士上戮，故勇力不相犯。既致教其民，然后谨选而使之。事极修，则百官给矣。教极省，则民兴良矣。习惯成，则民体俗矣。教化之至也。

【今译】

相逾越了。君主敬重任用不自我夸耀的人，因为不自我夸耀的人，正是君主所需的宝贵人才。如果一个人能做到不自我夸炫，就表明他本身没有奢求，而没有奢求就肯定不会争名夺利。朝廷大事上如听取他们的意见，就一定能掌握真实情况；军队事务上如听取他们的意见，就一定能妥善处理好各种问题。所以，有才技的人就不致被埋没了。以服从命令为军人的最高奖赏，以违抗命令为军人的最重惩罚，因此，有勇力的人就不敢违犯命令了。在对民众进行了这些教育之后，再慎重地选择任用他们。如将各项事务都处理妥善适宜，那么各级官吏也就恪尽职责了。教育内容简明易学，那么民众就会欣然好学，积极向上。习惯一经养成，那么民众就会依照习俗行事。这就是教育上的最佳效果。

the court did not apply to the military; the military rules and regulations did not apply to the court. Thus the virtuous and righteous would not transgress each other. Superiors valued those officers who had not boasted themselves for they were the greatest talents. If they did not boast they were not self-seeking, and if they were not self-seeking they would not be contentious. Within the state the court would be certain to listen to the truth of facts. Within the army the commanding generals would be certain to handle the military affairs appropriately. Thus the talented and technically skilled would not block each other. The officers obeying orders would receive the highest rewards; those disobeying orders would receive the most severe punishments. Then the brave and strong would not contend with each other.

When the people have already been instructed effectively, then they can be carefully selected and employed by the state. When everything is kept in order, all the high officials will strictly observe their duties. If the process of instructions is greatly simplified, people will be glad to study hard. As the habit has been established, people will put it into practice in accord with

【原文】

古者，逐奔不远，纵绥(绥)不及。不远则难诱，不及则难陷。以礼为固，以仁为胜。既胜之后，其教可复，是以君子贵之也。

有虞氏戒于国中，欲民体其命也。夏后氏誓于军中，欲民先成其虑也。殷誓于军门之外，欲民先意以行事也。周将交刃而誓之，以致民志也。

夏后氏正其德也，未用兵之刃，故其兵不杂。殷义也，始用兵之刃矣。周力也，尽用兵之刃矣。

【今译】

古代作战，追击败溃的敌人不过远，追逐主动退却的敌人不逼近。不过远就不易为敌人所诱骗，不逼近就不易陷入敌人的埋伏。以礼制为规范，军队就能得到巩固；以仁爱为宗旨，就能够战胜敌人。战争取得胜利之后，对民众的教化就可以推行。因此，贤德之君十分重视这种方法。

虞舜时代在国都中举行誓师，这是想让民众理解支持君主的决定；夏代在军中举行誓师仪式，这是想让部队上下事先在思想上有所准备；殷商时期在军门外举行誓师，这是想让部队事先了解作战意图以便展开行动；周代在两军交锋前夕举行誓师，这是为了激励士卒的战斗意志。

夏代的君主依靠仁德匡正天下，未曾使用武力，所以当时的兵器种类并不复杂；殷商用义取得天下，开始使用武力；周代凭借武力夺取天下，于是就使用各种各样的兵器。

customs. This is the best result of instructions.

Anciently they did not pursue a fleeing enemy too far or follow a retreating enemy too closely. By pursuing not too far it would be difficult to entice them into a trap. By following not too closely it would be difficult to ambush them. They regarded Rite as the foundation of conduct and Benevolence as the source of victory. After they gained victory their teachings could again be employed. For this reason the men of noble character valued them.

Yu Shun made warning within the state in order to persuade the people to understand his orders. Xia Qi swore oath within the army in order to have his troops first psychologically prepared. Shang Tang swore oath outside the gate of army encampments in order to have his troops know his intention before taking action. King Wu of Zhou waited until the weapons were about to clash and then took oath in order to stimulate his men's will to fight.

Xia Qi rectified his Virtue and did not employ the sharp blades of weapons, thus his weapons were not intermixed. Shang Tang relied on righteousness and began to employ the sharp blades of weapons. King Wu of Zhou resorted to force

【原文】

夏赏于朝，贵善也。殷戮于市，威不善也。周赏于朝，戮于市，劝君子惧小人也。三王彰其德一也。

兵不杂则不利。长兵以卫，短兵以守。太长则难犯，太短则不及；太轻则锐，锐则易乱；太重则钝，钝则不济。戎车：夏后氏曰钩车，先正也；殷

【今译】

夏代在朝堂上行施奖赏，这是为了鼓励好人。商代在集市上行施诛戮，这是为了警惧坏人。周代在朝堂上行施奖赏，在集市上行施杀戮，这是为了劝勉君子，惧骇小人。三王鼓励人们改恶为善的精神实质是完全一致的。

兵器不掺杂使用就没有威力。长兵器是用来掩护短兵器的，而短兵器则是用来近身格斗抵御的。兵器过长则不便使用，太短就打击不到敌人。太轻就脆弱，脆弱就容易折断；太厚重就不锋利，不锋利就派不上用场。

兵车，在夏代称作为钩车，注重行驶的平稳；在殷代称作为寅车，注重行动的迅疾；在周代称作

and employed the sharp blades of all the weapons.

The Xia Dynasty bestowed rewards in the court in order to encourage the good. The Shang Dynasty made executions in the marketplaces in order to overawe the evil. The Zhou Dynasty bestowed rewards in the court and made executions in the marketplaces in order to encourage the men of noble character and frighten the persons of low positions. All kings of the three dynasties publicized Virtue in the same way.

If the weapons are not intermixed, they will not be advantageous. Long weapons are for protection of the short ones; short weapons are for defending of the long ones. If the weapons are too long they will be difficult to wield against others. If they are too short they will not reach the enemy. If they are too light they will be fragile and the fragility will tend to break. If they are too heavy they will be clumsy, and clumsiness will render them impotent. As for the war chariots, those of the Xia Dynasty were called "hook chariots" (one "hook chariot" consists of one chariot, four horses and fifty-one men) for they put uprightness first. Those of the Shang Dynasty were called "Yin chariots" (one "Yin

【原文】

曰寅车，先疾也；周曰元戎，先良也。旂，夏后氏玄，首人之势也；殷白，天之义也；周黄，地之道也。章，夏后氏以日月，尚明也；殷以虎，白(尚)戎(威)也；周以龙，尚文也。

师多务威则民诎，少威则民不胜。上使民不得其义，百姓不得其叙，技用不得其利，牛马不得其任，有司陵之，此谓多威。多威则民诎。上不尊德

【今译】

为元戎，注重结构的精良。旗帜，夏代用黑色，取其像手持人头那样的威武；殷代用白色，取其像天穹那样的洁白；周代用黄色，取其像大地那样的深厚。徽章，夏代以日月为标志，表示光明；殷代以猛虎为标志，象征威武；周代以蛟龙为标志，体现文采。

治军上过于威严，士气就会受到压抑；如果缺乏威信，就难以指挥士卒克敌制胜。君主使用民力不得当，任用官吏不适宜，有技能的人士无法发挥作用，牛马等物资不能合理使用，主管者又盛气凌人强迫人们服从，这就叫做滥施权威。滥施权威，

chariot" consists of one chariot, four horses and seventy-five men) for they put speed first. Those of the Zhou Dynasty were called "Yuan Yong" (one "Yuan Yong" consists of one chariot, four horses and seventy-five men, with one additional ox cart for logistic support) for they put excellence first. For flags those of the Xia Dynasty were black signifying a head clutched by hands; those of the Shang Dynasty were white signifying Righteousness of Heaven; those of the Zhou Dynasty were yellow signifying *Dao* of Earth. For emblems the Xia Dynasty used the sun and moon esteeming brightness; the Shang Dynasty used tiger valuing awesomeness; the Zhou Dynasty used dragon valuing culture.

If the army pays too much attention to awe-inspiring it will inhibit the troops' morale. If it is lacking in awe-inspiring the troops will not win victory. When superiors are not able to employ the troops appropriately, nor arrange the officials in accord with their positions, nor employ the skilled to their advantage, nor use the oxen and horses in a reasonable way, the responsible commander will be arrogant to force the troops to obey orders. This is referred to as "too much awe-inspiring" and the over-awesomeness tends

【原文】

而任诈慝，不尊道而任勇力，不贵用命而贵犯命，不贵善行而贵暴行，陵之有司，此谓少威。少威则民不胜。

军旅以舒为主，舒则民力足。虽交兵致刃，徒不趋，车不驰，逐奔不逾列，是以不乱。军旅之固，不失行列之政，不绝人马之力，迟速不过诫命。

古者，国容不入库，军容不入国。军容入国，

【今译】

士气就会受到压抑。君主不敬重有德行之人而信任奸邪之徒，不尊道敬义而任意恃勇逞强，不推重服从命令而默许违抗命令，不赞许善行而放任残暴行径，这必然导致坏人侵凌官吏，这叫做缺乏威信。缺乏威信，那就不能约束和指挥士卒去战胜敌人。

军队行动，注重的是从容不迫，从容不迫就能保持战斗力旺盛。即便是在战场交锋厮杀之际，也要做到步兵不奔跑，兵车不疾驰，追击敌人不逾越行列，这样才不至于扰乱战斗队形。军队的强大和稳固，在于不打乱行列的部署，不用尽人员、马匹的力量，行动的快慢节奏不超出上级的指令要求。

古代，朝廷的礼仪法度不应用于军队，军队的规章制度也不应用于朝廷。把军队的规章制度应用于朝廷，那么民众的礼让风气就会废弛；将朝廷的

to inhibit the troops' morale. When superiors do not respect the Virtuous but rely on the evil, do not esteem the Righteous but rely on the brave and strong, do not value those who obey orders but value those who disobey, do not value the Kind but value the brutal, the responsible commander will be encroached on. This is referred to as "less awe-inspiring," and the less awesomeness will make the troops gain no victory. When an army on the move focuses on a relaxed pace, then the relaxation will make the strength of the troops sufficient. Even though in hand-to-hand fight with clash of the blades, the infantrymen will not advance at a quick pace and the chariots will not run fast. Their pursuit will not break formation, thereby avoiding chaos. The firmness of the army lies in not disrupting the order of ranks of the formation, not exhausting the strength of men and horses, not exceeding the measure of the command whether in slow motion or rapid action.

Anciently protocols and moral standards in the court did not apply to the military, and military rules and regulations did not apply to the court. If the military rules and regulations are applied in the court, the virtue of the people will

【原文】

则民德废；国容入军，则民德弱。故在国言文而语温，在朝恭以逊，修己以待人，不召不至，不问不言，难进易退。在军抗而立，在行遂而果，介者不拜，兵车不式，城上不趋，危事不齿。故礼与法，表里也；文与武，左右也。

古者贤王，明民之德，尽民之善，故无废德，无简民。赏无所生，罚无所试。有虞氏不赏不罚而

【今译】

礼仪法度应用于军队，那么部队的士气就会涣散削弱。所以，在朝廷上，要言词文雅，语气温和。在朝廷做事应是恭敬谦逊，严以律己，宽以待人。君主不召见就不来，不问话就不发言。入朝晋见时礼节隆重，下朝辞退时礼节简单。而在军队中，则要做到昂首直立，在战阵上，要做到行动果断。穿着铠甲时遇尊者毋需跪拜，身乘兵车时见上级不必行礼，在城上值更时用不着小步急走以示恭敬，遇有危险时都可挺身而出而无须讲究长幼尊卑。所以说，礼和法两者互为表里，文与武如同人的左右手。

古代圣明贤德的君主，总是显彰民众的美德，鼓励民众的善行。所以没有败坏道德的事情，也没有不遵守法度的奸民，奖赏用不着推行，惩罚也无需实施。虞舜时代既不用赏也不施罚，而民众乐于

decline. If the court protocols and moral standards are applied in the military, the morale of the troops will be weakened. For this reason in the court words are cultivated and speaking is gentle. In audience one is courteous and submissive, strict with himself and generous to others. Unsummoned, he does not step forth; unquestioned, he does not speak. It is difficult to advance but easy to retire. In the army one speaks straightforward and stands firm. In battle formation one devotes himself to service and acts resolutely. Those wearing armor do not kneel; those in war chariots need not observe the forms of propriety; those manning fortifications do not move swiftly. In times of danger one stands up to the threat without paying attention to seniority. Therefore civilian proprieties and military regulations are like inside and outside; the civil and the military are like left and right.

Anciently the Worthy Kings publicized Virtue among the people and encouraged the people to conduct themselves well. Thus there was no degradation of Virtue, nor any one defying the orders and regulations. Rewards were not bestowed, and punishments were never even tried. Yu Shun neither bestowed rewards nor imposed

【原文】

民可用，至德也。夏赏而不罚，至教也。殷罚而不赏，至威也。周以赏罚，德衰也。赏不逾时，欲民速得为善之利也。罚不迁列，欲民速睹为不善之害也。大捷不赏，上下皆不伐善。上苟不伐善，则不骄矣；下苟不伐善，必亡等矣。上下不伐善若此，让之至也。大败不诛，上下皆以不善在己。上苟以不善在己，必悔其过；下苟以不善在己，必远其罪。

【今译】

为君主所用，这是最高尚的德治。夏代用赏而不行罚，这乃是最美妙的教化。商代仅仅施罚而不用赏，这乃是最强大的威严。周代赏罚一并使用，这表明在当时道德已经走向衰微。行赏不要拖延时日，这是为了使民众迅速得到做好事的利益；施罚要就地执行，这是为了使民众立即看到做坏事的害处。大胜之后不颁施奖赏，这样，上下各级就不会夸耀战功了。如果君主不夸功，也就不会骄傲；如果官兵不夸功，也就不会相互攀比。上上下下不像这样矜夸争功，可谓是谦让到了极致。打了大败仗后不行诛戮，这样，上下各级就会把过失往自己的身上揽。君主如果认为过失在自己身上，必定痛加悔改，改正错误；下属如果认为过失在自己身上，必定下决

punishments and the people could still be employed. This was the pinnacle of Virtue. The Shang imposed punishments but did not bestow rewards. This was the pinnacle of awesomeness. The Zhou employed both rewards and punishments, and Virtue declined. Rewards must not be delayed beyond the appropriate time in order that people can immediately gain profits from their good conduct. Punishments must not be imposed out of the scene of misconduct in order that people can see immediately the harm of doing what is not good. If there is no bestowal of rewards after a great victory, the superiors and inferiors will not boast themselves. When the superiors do not boast, they will not be arrogant. When the inferiors do not boast, they will not contend with each other for fame or fortune. If both the superiors and inferiors do not boast themselves to such an extent, this is the pinnacle of comity. If no punishments are imposed after a crushing defeat, the superiors and inferiors will feel guilty for the cause of the defeat. When the superiors feel guilty themselves, they will be certain to feel remorseful for their mistakes. When the inferiors feel guilty themselves, they will be certain to avoid repeating their mistakes.

【原文】

上下分恶若此，让之至也。

古者戍军，三年不兴，睹民之劳也；上下相报若此，和之至也。得意则凯歌，示喜也。偃伯灵台，答民之劳，示休也。

【今译】

心不再犯类似错误。上下各级像这样勇于承担错误，也称得上是最好的谦让风气了。

古代对于戍守边防的士兵，(服役一年后) 三年之内不再征调，这是看到了他们的辛苦。上下之间像这样的互相体恤和爱护，就是最和睦的表现。打了胜仗就高奏凯歌，这是表达喜庆。结束战争后高筑灵台，慰劳民众，这是表示休养生息从此开始。

If both the superiors and inferiors share responsibilities for the defeat to such an extent, this is the pinnacle of comity.

Anciently those who had completed one-year border duty were not required to serve labor for three years thereafter, and the sovereign would personally observe the people's labor. When the superiors and inferiors recompensed each other in such a manner, this was the height of harmony. When achievements were attained, triumphal trumpets would be sounded to show pleasantness. When war was over, the Spirit Terrace would be set up for the sovereign to respond to the labors of the people. This indicated the beginning of rehabilitation.

# 定爵第三

【原文】

凡战，定爵位，著功罪，收游士，申教诏，讯厥众，求厥技，方虑极物，变嫌推疑，养力索巧，因心之动。

凡战，固众相利，治乱进止，服正成耻，约法省罚，小罪乃杀，小罪胜，大罪因。

顺天，阜财，怿众，利地，右兵，是谓五虑。

【今译】

大凡用兵打仗，首先要做到：确定军职爵位，明确赏罚规定，收用各方游士，申明军队教令，征询民众的意见，募求有技能的人才。反复思虑，摸清事情的来龙去脉，分辨是非，推究疑问，积蓄力量，索求巧计，依据民众的心愿来采取行动。

凡是作战，要做到稳固军心，明辨利害，整治混乱，申明进退原则，服膺正义，激发廉耻之心，简约法令，慎省刑罚。小罪就要加以制止，如果让小罪得逞，那么大罪恶也就会随之而来了。

要顺应天时，广殖财富，取悦民心，利用地利，重视武器装备的建设，这就是作战所必须考虑的五

# 3. Determination of Ranks

Generally in conducting warfar rst determine rank and position; then record merits and demerits; retain mendicant knights; announce instructions and edicts; solicit people's opinions; seek out the skilled; consider all the options and thoroughly study them to grasp the substance; remove people's rancor and suspicions; nourish strength and search out the intelligent; and take action in accord with people's wish.

Generally in warfare: Consolidate the masses; analyze the advantages of terrain; control the confused situations; regulate advancing and stopping; bear righteousness in mind; stimulate a sense of shame; simplify the rules and regulations; investigate punishments. Minor offense should be prevented. If minor offense has its way, major offense will follow.

Comply with Heaven; broaden the source of finance, bring happiness to the people, take advantage of terrain, and value the weapons. These

【原文】

顺天奉时。阜财因敌。怿众勉若。利地，守隘险阻。右兵，弓矢御，殳矛守，戈戟助。凡五兵五当，长以卫短，短以救长。迭战则久，皆战则强。见物与侔，是谓两之。

主固勉若，视敌而举。将心，心也；众心，心

【今译】

件事情。顺应天时，就是要巧妙利用天候季节；广殖财富，就是要善于利用敌人的资财；取悦人心，就是要顺应大众的意志；利用地形，就是要占领狭隘险要的地域；重视兵器，就是要在作战中用弓矢御敌，用殳矛守阵，戈戟等兵器配合使用，互为辅助。五种兵器有五种用途，长兵器是用来掩护短兵器的，短兵器则是用来弥补长兵器的不足的。五种兵器轮番作战可以持久，一齐使用就能发挥强大的威力。发现敌人使用新式兵器，就要仿效制造，从而同敌人保持力量的平衡。

主将既要顺应众人意志，巩固军心，又要观察敌情，随机行事。将军的心是心，士卒的心也是心，

are referred to as "Five Considerations." To comply with Heaven means observing the seasons; broadening the source of finance relies on capturing the enemy's properties; bringing happiness to people is to encourage the troops to fight in accord with people's wish; taking advantage of terrain means defending the passes and precipices; valuing the weapons means bows and arrows for withstanding attacks, maces and spears for defense, and halberds and spear-tipped halberds for support. Now each of these five weapons has its appropriate use respectively. The long protect the short, the short rescue the long. When they are employed in turn, the battle can be sustained. When they are used together, the fighting force will be strengthened. When you see the enemy's new weapon, you can imitate and match for it. This is termed "Balancing."

The defending army should consolidate its positions and encourage the troops to keep unity.It moves in accord with the enemy's situations. The mind of the generals is sensible, the mind of the masses is sensible, and they will be of one mind. Horses, oxen, chariots, weapons, relaxation and an adequate diet all together are the

【原文】

也。马牛车兵佚饱，力也。教惟豫，战惟节。将军，身也；卒，支也；伍，指拇也。

凡战，智也。斗，勇也。陈，巧也。用其所欲，行其所能，废其不欲不能。于敌反是。

凡战，有天，有财，有善。时日不迁，龟胜微行，是谓有天。众有有，因生美，是谓有财。人习陈利，极物以豫，是谓有善。

人勉及任，是谓乐人。大军以固，多力以烦，堪物简治，见物应卒，是谓行豫。轻车轻徒，弓矢

【今译】

应该同心协力。马、牛、战车、兵器，休整良好，供应充足，合在一起，就构成军队的战斗力。教育训练重在平时，作战打仗重在指挥。军队中，将军好比是人的躯干，卒恰似人的四肢，伍如同是人的手指(彼此间必须协调一致)。

大凡指挥作战，讲究的是智谋韬略；近敌格斗，注重的是勇敢顽强；布列阵势，推重的是巧妙灵活。要努力去实现自己的意图，同时要在力所能及的前提下行动，不要去做违背自己意图和力所不及的事情。对于敌人，则要反其道而行之。

大凡作战，应该具备“有天”、“有财”、“有善”诸项条件。遇上好时机不要错过，占卜到胜利的预兆就要机密行动，这就叫做“有天”。民众富足，国力充实，这就叫做“有财”。士卒训练有素，阵形优势明显，武器装备精良预有准备，这就叫做“有善”。

人人都能够勉力去完成战斗任务，这叫做“乐人”。军队强大而阵势巩固，兵员充足而训练有素，

strength of the army. Instructions focus on the peacetime training; warfare focuses on regulating the strategies. The commanding general is like the body of a man, companies are like a man's limbs and squads of five like his thumb and fingers.

Generally warfare is a question of wisdom; fighting is a matter of courage; deployment of formations is a matter of skill. Do your utmost to realize what your men want, and effect what they are capable of; put an end to what they do not want and are incapable of. Do the opposite of this to the enemy.

Generally warfare depends on having Heaven, resources and good preparedness. Do not change the favorable date and time. When tortoise divination presages victory, take stealth actions immediately. This is termed "having Heaven." When the masses have material resources and thereby turn favorably to profits, it is termed "having resources." Men are well trained to be familiar with the advantages of the deployed formations; matériel and implements are in combat readiness. This is termed "having good preparedness."

When the people are encouraged to fulfill

【原文】

固御，是谓大军。密静多内力，是谓固陈。因是进退，是谓多力。上暇人教，是谓烦陈。然有以职，是谓堪物。因是辨物，是谓简治。

称众，因地，因敌令陈；攻战守，进退止，前

【今译】

选拔各种人才以管理各类事务，洞察种种情况以应付突然事变，这叫做预有准备。兵车轻捷，步兵精锐，弓箭足以固守坚御，这就是强大的军队。兵力集中，军心稳定，力量充实，这就是巩固的阵势。在这样的情况下做到进退有序，就叫做富有战斗力。主将从容不迫，士卒操练娴熟，这就是训练有素。各项事务都有专人负责，这就叫做事有所司。在这样的基础上分辨清事物的轻重缓急，这就是简明而实用的管理。

正确衡量兵力，巧妙利用地形，根据敌情部署

their responsibilities, they are referred to as "men who are happy in warfare." Strengthening the army to consolidate the positions, enhancing the fighting capability to reduce complexities, selecting the competent to take simplified governance, and investigating the situations to respond to comtingencies are what is referred to as "effecting preparedness." Fast chariots and elite infantrymen, bows and arrows, and a strong defense are what is referred to as "strengthening the army." Concentration, calmness and the great internal strength are what is referred to as "enhancing the fighting capability." Generals being calm and leisurely and troops receiving instructions are termed "being well trained through frequent exercises." Posts being set up to bear responsibilities for various businesses is termed "selecting the competent." On this basis, being able to differentiate between what is important and what is unimportant is termed "simplifying governance."

Weigh the masses of the army in accord with the terrain; deploy the formations in accord with the enemy's situations. When attacking, waging battle, defending, advancing, withdrawing, and stopping, the front and the rear are kept in order,

【原文】

后序，车徒因，是谓战参。

不服、不信、不和、怠、疑、厌、慑、枝、拄、诎、顿、肆、崩、缓，是谓战患。

骄骄、慑慑、吟旷、虞惧、事悔，是谓毁折。

大小、坚柔、参伍、众寡、凡两，是谓战权。

凡战，间远、观迩、因时、因财、贵信、恶疑。

【今译】

阵势，掌握攻战、守的不同要领，把握进、退、止的时机，注意前后的配合和战车步兵的协同，这些都是临战时应该考虑的事情。

对上级不服从，不信任，彼此间不和睦，怠忽职守，猜疑丛生，骄傲自满，畏惧敌人，军心涣散，互相拆台，丧失斗志，疲劳困顿，肆意妄为，分崩离析，军纪松弛，所有这些都是作战的祸患。

骄傲自大，畏葸恐惧，士卒呻吟吵闹，部队忧虞自扰，临事不审而事后反悔，这些都是导致军队覆灭的原因。

制造声势或大或小，采用战法或刚或柔，实行编组或参或伍，投入兵力或多或少，都必须衡量利害得失而适当处置，这就是作战上的权变之道。

大凡作战，要侦知远方的敌情，观察近处的事态。要利用天时，凭藉财力；要崇尚诚信，杜绝猜

and the chariots and infantrymen in coordination, it is termed "essentials to warfare."

If the troops disobey orders, do not trust their officers, are not in harmony, are lax, skeptical, weary, frightened, loose, frustrated, wronged, troubled, unrestrained, deflated or dilatory, it is termed "disastrous warfare."

When they suffer extreme arrogance, abject terror, groaning and grumbling, worry and fear, or frequent regrets over actions being taken, they are termed "destroyed and broken."

Being able to be large or small, or firm or flexible, to scatter in teams of three or squads of five, and to employ the masses or small groups —— in all respects being a match for the enemy —— is termed "weighing of power in warfare."

Generally in conducting warfare: Use spies for reconnaissance of the distant; observe the near with the naked eyes; act in accord with the seasons; take advantage of the enemy's material resources; adore good faith; abhor skepticism. Mobilize troops with enthusiasm of Righteousness. Undertake affairs at the appropriate time. Employ the people with profits. When you see the enemy, remain calm; when you see turmoil,

**【原文】**

作兵义，作事时，使人惠，见敌静，见乱暇，见危难无忘其众。居国惠以信，在军广以武，刃上果以敏。居国和，在军法，刃上察。居国见好，在军见方，刃上见信。

凡陈，行惟疏，战惟密，兵惟杂。人教厚，静乃治。威利章，相守义，则人勉。虑多成则人服，

**【今译】**

疑。兴兵要合乎正义，做事要把握时机，用人要施以恩惠。遇见敌人必须镇静，面对混乱必须从容，碰到危难不要忘掉部众。治国要广施恩惠讲究信用，治军既要宽厚又要威严，面临战阵则要果断敏捷。治理国家务求和睦相安，管理军队务求严明法纪，临阵对敌务求明察敌情。治国要能为民众所爱戴，治军要能为士卒所敬重，临阵要能为大家所信赖。

大凡布阵，行列要疏散，接敌作战时队形要密集，兵器要掺杂配合使用。士卒训练有素，沉着冷静，就能保持阵形严整。威令鲜明准确，上下恪守

do not be hasty to respond; when you see dangers and hardships, do not forget the masses. Within the state be generous and secure confidence; within the army be magnanimous and militant. When the blades clash, be decisive and agile. Within the state there should be harmony; within the army there should be rules and regulations. When the blades clash, investigate the situations in battle. Within the state display solidarity; within the army display fairness; in battle display trust.

Generally in deploying formations: When advancing the first priority for the ranks is to keep space in between; when engaged in battle, it is to be concentrated and for the weapons to be intermixed. When people are frequently instructed, they will be calm under control. The edge of awesome orders lies in clarity and publicity. When people preserve each other according to righteousness, they will be encouraged to devote themselves to service. If the planning is always successful, people will be convinced. When they are convinced in time, affairs will be managed one by one. When flags and emblems are easily identified, people will have good eyesight. When plans have already been conceived, decision-making

【原文】

时中服厥次治。物既章，目乃明。虑既定，心乃强。进退无疑，见敌无谋，听诛。无谁(诳)其名，无变其旗。

凡事善则长，因古则行。誓作章，人乃强，灭厉祥。灭厉之道，一曰义：被之以信，临之以强，成基一天下之形，人莫不说，是谓兼用其人。一曰权：成其溢，夺其好，我自其外，使自其内。

一曰人，二曰正，三曰辞，四曰巧，五曰火，六曰水，七曰兵，是谓七政。荣、利、耻、死，是

【今译】

信义，就能使人人奋勉杀敌。谋划屡次取得成功就能使部众信服，人们心悦诚服，事情就可以逐次办妥。旗帜鲜明，部众就能够看得清楚；谋略既经确定，信心就会增强。对那些进退行动中冒冒失失，遇上敌人无谋辱师的人，要给予惩罚。不要随意乱用金鼓。不要轻易变换旗帜。

凡是从事正义事业就能够长久，遵循古法就能够顺利。战斗誓词鲜明有力，士气就会振作旺盛，从而消灭一切敌人。消灭敌人的方法，一是依靠道义，即用诚信感化敌人，用武力慑服敌人，造成一统天下的形势，民久无不高兴，这叫做争取敌国之人为己所用。一是利用权谋，即设法促成敌人的骄傲自满，夺取敌人的要害，用兵力从外部打击它，并促使敌人自掘坟墓、自我毁灭。

一是广罗人才，二是遵奉正义，三是注重宣传，四是讲求技巧，五是善用火攻，六是擅长水战，七

will be firm and powerful. Those who are rash to advance or retreat and on seeing the enemy have no tactics to cope with him will be punished. Their gongs and drums should not be beaten at random, and their flags should not be changed.

Generally good things persist, and they will be feasible with ancient methods. When the general swears oath clearly, the troops will be strong with high morale and all the evil will be exterminated. The way to extinguish the evil: One is called Rghteousness. When you persuade the enemy with good faith and impose awesomeness on him to complete the cause of reunification under Heaven, there will not be any men who are not pleased. It is termed "concurrently employing the enemy." The other is called weighing of power. Excite his arrogance, and seize what he values. Then use our troops from without, and employ the spies from within.

The first is called men; the second, discipline; the third, language; the fourth, skill; the fifth, fire; the sixth, water; the seventh, weapons. They are termed "Seven Administrative Affairs." Glory, benefit, shame and death are termed "Four Preservations." Being tolerant and kind and ac-

【原文】

谓四守。容色积威，不过改意，凡此道也。

唯仁有亲，有仁无信，反败厥身。人人，正正，辞辞，火火。

凡战之道，既作其气，因发其政。假之以色，道之以辞。因惧而戒，因欲而事，蹈敌制地，以职命之，是谓战法。

凡人之形，由众之求，试以名行，必善行之。

【今译】

是改善兵器，这就是七项军政大事。荣誉、利禄、耻辱、死亡，这是四种约束人们遵纪守法的手段。或是和颜悦色，或是严厉冷酷，两者的目的都不过是为了让人改恶从善。所有这些都是治军的方法。

只有仁慈爱人，才能使人们亲近拥戴自己。但是如果光讲究仁爱而不注重信义，就反而会祸及自身。要做到知人善任，正己正人，审以辞令，疾恶如仇。

通常的作战原则是，既然已经激励起士气，就要跟着颁布纪律。对待士卒，要和颜悦色；教导士卒，要言辞恳切，要针对其畏惧心理而加以告诫，利用其名利欲望而加以驱使。进入敌境后要控制住有利地形，并按照将士的职位给他们分别指派任务。这就是通常的战法。

凡是要求人们执行的规章制度，应当来源于人们的共同要求，同时要通过一段时间的试行来考察它是否名实相符，一经制定，一定要妥善地予以执

cumulating awesomeness are for the purpose of avoiding transgressions and changing evil intentions. In general this is the *Dao* (Right Way) to control the troops.

Only Benevolence can lead to kindness. Being benevolent yet without good faith, one will vanquish himself. Appoint right men to right positions; rectify yourself then rectify others; speak with appropriate language; attack by fire where firing is essential.

The general principles of warfare: When the troops' morale has already been boosted, announce the rules and regulations. Treat the troops with a kind and pleasant countenance, and instruct them with what you have said. Take advantage of their fear to warn them, and make use of their desire to employ them. When you have crossed the enemy's borders and taken control of his territory, appoint men to appropriate tasks of government. These are termed "methods of warfare."

All human qualities must be sought among the masses. Test and evaluate them in terms of name and action to see if they match, for they must choose and follow what is good. If they are to perform some action but do not, then you your-

【原文】

若行不行，身以将之。若行而行，因使勿忘。三乃成章。人生之宜，谓之法。

凡治乱之道：一曰仁，二曰信，三曰直，四曰一，五曰义，六曰变，七曰尊(专)。

立法，一曰受，二曰法，三曰立，四曰疾，五曰御其服，六曰等其色，七曰百官宜无淫服。

凡军，使法在己曰专，与下畏法曰法。军无小

【今译】

行。如果应该执行而没有能做到，将帅就要去身体力行。如果一切都做到了，就要让部众牢记这些准则。经过多次反复执行，就能形成为制度。凡是符合人们要求的规章制度，就叫做“法”。

大凡治理纷乱的方法，一是仁爱，二是信用，三是正直，四是统一，五是道义，六是权变，七是集权。

建立法制，一要人人遵守，二要法度严明，三要不可动摇，四要雷厉风行，五要规定各级服制，六要用颜色区别不同等级，七要使百官按规定着装，不得随意混淆。

治军上，凡是法令出于将帅个人好恶的，称做为专制；主将和部众一样畏法受其约束的，才能称做为法。在军队中不能传播小道消息，作战时不能

self should lead them. If they are to perform some action and do so, then ensure them not to forget it. If you test them three times successfully, then make their good qualities evident. What is appropriate to human life is referred to as "the law."

Generally the way to control chaos: The first is called Benevolence; the second, credibility; the third, uprightness; the fourth, unity; the fifth, Righteousness; the sixth, change; the seventh, centralized command.

As for formulation of the laws, the first is called acceptability; the second, the laws; the third, the establishment; the fourth, urgency; the fifth, wearing the uniforms; the sixth, ordering colors; the seventh, no nonstandard uniforms among the officers.

Generally in control of the army, if the authority to carry out laws lies solely with oneself,it is termed "centralized command." If the generals and their subordinates all fear the law, it is termed "law." When the army does not believe the grapevine, when in battle it does not concern itself with minor advantages, and when progress has been made everyday and actions have been taken in a subtle fashion, it is termed "the way to

【原文】

听，战无小利，日成，行微曰道。

凡战，正不符(行)则事专，不服则法，不相信则一，若怠则动之，若疑则变之，若人不信上，则行其不复。自古之政也。

【今译】

贪图眼前利益，制定计划要能够克日成功，行动时要求做到隐蔽莫测，这些都是治军的原则。

作战中，正常的办法行不通就要采取专断手段，拒绝服从就要绳之以法，互不信任就要统一认识，如果军心懈怠就要加以鼓舞，如果士卒心存疑虑就要设法加以改变，如果士卒不信任上级，更要使命令得到坚决贯彻而不轻易改变。所有这一切，都是自古以来治军作战的方法。

govern the army."

Generally in conduct of warfare, when normal methods do not prove effective, the centralized control of affairs must be undertaken. If the people do not submit, laws must be enforced. If they do not trust each other, they must be unified. If they are dilatory, move them. If they are skeptical, change their skepticism. If the people do not trust the sovereign, then the promulgated orders must be carried out to the end without any revision. This has been the administrative rule from ancient times.

# 严位第四

【原文】

凡战之道，位欲严，政欲栗，力欲窕，气欲闲，心欲一。

凡战之道，等道义，立卒伍，定行列，正纵横，察名实。立进俯，坐进跪。畏则密，危则坐。远者视之则不畏，迩者勿视则不散。位，下左右，下甲

【今译】

通常的作战原则是，职责要分明，号令要严明，行动要敏捷，士气要镇静，意志要尽可能统一。

通常的作战原则是，要区分战争是否符合道义，制定各级编制，确定行列次序，调正纵横队列，核查名实是否相符。

士卒立而前的进必俯其身，坐而进者必跪其膝。部队存有畏惧心理时，队形要密集；遇上危急情况时，要采用坐阵。远处的敌人一经观察清楚，就不至于心怀畏惧；对近处的敌人则当视而不见，以便集中精力进行战斗。士卒在阵中的位置，应按左右序列排列。屯兵集结时当采用坐阵。从容地下达命

# 4. Strict Positions

Generally the way to wage war: The positions should be strict; the discipline, awesome; the fighting force, agile; the morale, stable; the minds of officers and men, unified.

Generally in conducting warfare: Appoint men to right positions in accord with their moral and righteous influence. Establish the companies and the squads of five. Order rows and files. Regulate the spacing between the vertical and the horizontal. Investigate if names and actions cohere. When the troops in a standing position advance, they should crouch down. When in a sitting position advance, they should kneel. If they are frightened, their ranks should be close. If there is danger they should assume a sitting position. When they see the distant clearly, they will not be frightened; when they do not see the near meticulously, they will not divert their attention. The squad leaders deploy the men to the left and right; all below the commander wearing

【原文】

坐，誓徐行之，位逮徒甲，筹以轻重。振马噪，徒甲畏亦密之，跪坐，坐伏，则膝行而宽誓之。起，噪，鼓而进，则以铎止之。衔枚，誓，糗，坐，膝行而推之。执戮禁顾，噪以先之。若畏太甚，则勿戮杀，示以颜色，告之以所生，循省其职。

凡三军，人(卒)戒分日；人禁不息，不可以分

【今译】

令，规定好每个甲士和徒卒的具体位置，并妥善兼顾各类兵器的轻重配置。如果车震马躁，士卒畏惧，亦应当使队形靠拢密集，采用跪、坐、卧等各种不同的姿势。而做将领的则应当膝行前去温和地告诫士卒。如果要起身投入进攻，就高声呼喊，擂鼓前进；如果要停止行动，就鸣金铎。当衔枚、誓师、吃饭之时，均采用坐阵，必须移动时，则用膝挪动。执行诛戮来严禁临阵畏葸、顾盼不前，大声命令士卒冲锋向前。假如士卒畏惧太严重，就不要再行施杀戮，而应该和颜悦色地告诉他们杀敌求生的方法，促使他们各尽其职，完成任务。

大凡统辖军队，对小部队下达命令，半天以内就要执行；对个别人下达禁令，要立即执行，甚至

armor sit; the oath is sworn; then the army slowly advances. Deployment of infantrymen and armored soldiers should be appropriate and priorities of using weapons should be considered. With the whipping of the horses to action, the infantrymen and armored soldiers advance amid the clamor. When they are frightened, they should be deployed in dense formations. Those who are kneeling should squat down; those who are squatting should lie down. They should crawl forward on their knees and then be ordered to keep at ease. They stand up, shout, and advance to the drums. Then the gongs are sounded to halt them. When the soldiers with a gag in each one's mouth carry the minimal dry rations, they should crouch down in the sitting position and use the knees to move when necessary. Execute any deserters to stop the others from looking about for desertion. Shout loudly in order to lead them. If they are too fearful of the enemy, do not threaten them with more executions but show a kind countenance. Tell them how to survive and supervise them to perform their duties.

Within the Three Armies the disciplinary action against men should not be performed for

【原文】

食。方其疑惑，可师可服。

凡战，以力久，以气胜。以固久，以危胜。本心固，新气胜。以甲固，以兵胜。凡车以密固，徒以坐固，甲以重固，兵以轻胜。

人有胜心，惟敌之视；人有畏心，惟畏之视。两心交定，两利若一。两为之职，惟权视之。

凡战，以轻行轻则危，以重行重则无功，以轻

【今译】

不等吃饭就要落实。要理解部众们的忧虑和困惑，从而确保部队整治，士卒服从。

通常作战，依靠力量持久，凭借士气取胜；依靠阵形坚固持久，凭借经受危险取胜。真心求战就稳固，朝气蓬勃就取胜。用盔甲防护自己，用兵器战胜敌人。大凡车战稳固取胜在于阵形密集，步战稳固取胜在于采用坐阵。铠甲坚固在于厚重，兵器胜敌在于轻锐。

士卒具有胜敌的信心，这时就观察敌情是否可打；士卒怀有畏敌的心理，这时就了解他们畏惧的原因。把求胜之心和畏惧心理都考察清楚，通盘考虑两方面的利弊得失。而对这两方面情况的全面把握，关键在于做将帅的权衡机宜。

一般作战，用小部队对付敌军小部队会有危险，

more than half a day. Confinement should not be imposed for more than a rest period and reduction of their food is not allowed. Dispel their doubts and puzzlement, and they can be led, can be made to submit to orders.

Generally in warfare: The troops endure through strength; gain victory through high morale; sustain fighting capability through consolidation; achieve victory through being endangered; consolidate positions through firm resolve; win victory through vigor and vitality; make firm defense through armors; attain victory through weapons. In general, the chariots are solid through concentration; the infantrymen are solid through the squatting position; the armors are solid through weight; victory is achieved through lightness of the weapons.

When men have a mind to gain victory, all they see is the enemy. When men have a mind full of fear, all they see is their fear. When these two minds are compared to determine action, the advantages of both minds can be turned to make up their mind. The duty to make this defermination is up to the commander's weighing of power.

Generally in warfare: If you advance with a

【原文】

行重则败，以重行轻则战，故战相为轻重。

舍谨甲兵，行阵'慎'行列，战谨进止。

凡战，敬则慊，率则服。上烦轻，上暇重。奏鼓轻，舒鼓重。服肤轻，服美重。

凡马车坚，甲兵利，轻乃重。

【今译】

用大部队对付敌军大部队就难以成功，用小部队去对付敌人大部队就会导致失败，用大部队对付敌人小部队就可以决战。所以说，作战是双方兵力的对比和较量。

屯驻时应注意戒备严整，行军时应注意行列整齐，战场交锋时应注意进退有节。

一般作战，将帅谨慎恭敬就能让士卒尊重，以身作则就能使士卒服从。将帅急躁烦乱就会行事轻率，雍容沉着就会遇事持重。鼓点急是让士卒轻捷向前，鼓点缓是让士卒徐缓前进。服装简陋则军容萎靡，服装华丽则军容壮观。

只要兵车坚固，甲胄兵器精良，那么劣势也就可以转化为优势。

light force into the light ground (enemy's area near borders), you will be endangered. If you advance with a heavy force into the heavy ground (enemy's area in depth), you will not make achievements. If you advance with a light force into the heavy ground, you will be defeated. If you advance with a heavy force into the light ground, you will engage in a decisive battle. Thus in warfare the light and heavy are mutually related. When encamping be careful of armors and weapons; when marching be cautious about rows and files; when engaging in battle be careful about advancing and halting.

Generally in warfare: If you are respectful, the troops will be satisfied. When you lead in person, they will follow. If the commanding general is agitated, the troops will act rashly; if he keeps a leisurely manner, they will act steadily.When drums are beaten rapidly they will move quickly; when drums are rolled slowly they will move at a measured pace. When their uniforms are light they will feel quick; when their uniforms are gorgeous they will feel stalwart.

Generally if horses and chariots are sturdy, and armors and weapons strong, the light force will become a heavy one. If the commanding

【原文】

上同无获，上专多死，上生多疑，上死不胜。

凡人，死爱，死怒，死威，死义，死利。凡战之道，教约人轻死，道约人死正。

凡战，若胜，若否，若天，若人。

凡战，三军之戒，无过三日；一卒之警，无过分日；一人之禁，无过皆(瞬)息。

凡大善用本，其次用末。执略守微，本末惟权，

【今译】

将领热衷于下属随声附和，就会一事无成；将领热衷于个人专横武断，作战就必多死伤。将领一味贪生怕死，就会疑虑重重。将领仅仅知道死打硬拼，就不能够克敌制胜。

士卒拼死效命的情况，有出于感恩戴德的，有出于一腔激怒的，有出于受胁被逼的，有出于依仗正义的，有出于贪图利益的。作战的规律是，法令约束士卒不惧怕战死，而道义感化士卒为正义而献身。

一般作战，无论胜败与否，都取决于是否顺应天时，符合民心。

作战中，对全军下达的号令，三天之内就要执行；对百人小部队下达的号令，半天之内就要执行；对个别人下达的禁令，必须立即执行。

进行战争，最佳的途径是用谋略取胜，而战胜攻取，斩将搴旗则为下策。要掌握全局，抓住细节，通过权衡比较，来决定是用谋略取胜，还是用攻战

general echoes what others say, no achievements will be attained. If he acts arbitrarily, many soldiers will die. If he cravenly clings to life, then there will be a lot of suspicions. If he acts desperately, no victory will be gained. Generally men will die for love, out of indignation, out of fear or awesomeness, for righteousness, and for profits. Generally the way to wage war: When instructions constrain, men will regard death lightly. When moral influence constrains, men will of their own accord die for uprightness.

Generally in warfare, whether victory or defeat ensues depends upon your compliance with Heaven and people's wish.

Generally combat readiness of the Three Armies should not be completed more than three days; alertness of a single company should not be completed more than half a day; sentry duty of a man should not be completed more than a moment.

Generally the best is to use strategy; the next is to employ force. Have the overall situations under control and pay attention to the details simultaneously. Whether to use strategy or to employ force, it is a question of weighing of power. This is a fundamental principle of warfare.

【原文】

战也。

凡胜，三军一人，胜。

凡鼓，鼓旌旗，鼓车，鼓马，鼓徒，鼓兵，鼓首，鼓足。"七"鼓兼齐。

凡战，既固勿重，重进勿尽，凡尽危。

凡战，非陈之难，使人可陈难；非使可陈难，使人可用难；非知之难，行之难。

人方有性，性州异，教成俗，俗州异，道化俗。

【今译】

破敌。这就是驾驭战争的高明艺术，作战的胜利，是由于全军上下团结一致如同一人的缘故。

通常的作战鼓点，有指挥旌旗的，有指挥兵车的，有指挥战马的，有指挥步兵的，有指挥兵器使用的，有指挥队形的，有指挥起坐行动的。这七种鼓点都应当规定齐全。

通常作战，兵力强大厚实就不必过于谨慎。即使是兵力雄厚，实施进攻时也不要一次性投入全部的力量，力量用尽会带来危险。

一般作战，不是布阵困难，而是让官兵们熟习阵法困难；不是让官兵们熟习阵法困难，而是让他们真正掌握灵活运用阵法的奥秘困难。不在于懂得了阵法难，而在于实际运用阵法难。

不同地方的人具有不同的气质秉赋，秉性气质各州自有其差异，教化可以造成一定的风俗，习俗也是各州有所不同，而道德的教化则可以改变各地的风俗习惯。

As for victory, when the Three Armies are united as one man they will be victorious.

For the drums: Drums are beaten for the motions of flags, chariots, horses, infantrymen, weapons, heads, and feet. For the motions of all these seven drums should be properly beaten together.

Generally in waging war: When deployment has already been strengthened, no reinforcements are needed. When the reinforcements advance, do not exhaust them for the exhaustion of reinforcements is dangerous.

Generally in conducting warfare: It is not deploying formation that is difficult; it is reaching the point that men can be familiar with the formation that is hard. It is not instructing men to be familiar with the formations that is difficult; it is reaching the point of being able to fully employ the formation that is hard. It is not knowing what should be done that is difficult; it is putting it in practice that is hard.

Men living in different quarters have different indigenous characters. Men's character also varies with administrative divisions. Instructions cultivate customs; customs vary with administrative divisions. Moral influence unifies the customs.

【原文】

凡众寡，既胜若否。兵不告利，甲不告坚，车不告固，马不告良，众不自多，未获道。

凡战，胜则与众分善。若将复战，则重赏罚。若使不胜，取过在己。复战，则誓以居前，无复先术。胜否勿反，是谓正则。

凡民，以仁救，以义战，以智决，以勇斗，以信专，以利劝，以功胜。故心中仁，行中义，堪物

【今译】

不论兵力多少，打了胜仗要像未曾打胜仗一样。不讲求兵器锋利，不讲求盔甲坚韧，不讲求战车牢固，不讲求马匹优良，不努力扩充军队的，那就意味着没有掌握用兵的要领。

凡是作战，打了胜仗就应该同大家分享荣誉。如果还要再次进行战斗，就应该重申赏罚规定。如果作战失利，就要自己主动承担过错。再次作战时，要举行誓师激励部众，并且做到身先士卒，不重复运用先前的战法。无论胜败都不要违反这个做法，这就是正确的原则。

对待民众，应当以仁爱解救他们的危难，以道义激励他们去参战，以智慧判断他们的是非，以勇敢统率他们去战斗，以诚信使他们团结一致，要用利益勉励他们去奋战，用功爵鼓舞他们去取胜。因此，思想要合乎仁爱，行为要合乎正义，能够以智

Generally whether large or small in numerical strength, when you have already gained victory, do not regard that you have been victorious. If you do not pay attention to the sharpness of the weapons, nor the stoutness of the armors, nor the sturdiness of the chariots, nor the agility of the horses, nor your endeavor to increase the numbers of the masses themselves, you have not attained the realization of final victory.

Generally in warfare: When victory is gained, mete out merits to the masses. If you will restart the battle, put stress on rewards and punishments. If the battle is lost, blame yourself only. If you must fight again, swear oath and lead in person. Do not repeat the previous tactics. Whether you have gained victory or not, do not contravene this method. This is what is referred to as "the normal code of conduct."

Generally with regard to people: Rescue them with Benevolence; encourage them to fight with Righteousness; judge them by wisdom; lead them in battle with courage; cultivate their loyalty through credibility; persuade them by profits; stimulate them to win victory through achievements. Thus the mind must set on Benevolence; the action must correspond to

【原文】

智也，堪大勇也，堪久信也。让以和，人以洽，自子(予)以不循，争贤以为人，说其心，效其力。

凡战，击其微静，避其强静；击其倦劳，避其闲窕；击其大惧，避其小惧。自古之政也。

【今译】

慧判断事物的是非，以勇气担当大任，以诚信长久地赢得人心。谦让和蔼，上下关系融洽。把过错归于自己，把贤名让给他人，这样就能使部属心悦诚服，乐于为自己效力。

作战的一般原则是，进攻兵力弱小而故作镇静的敌人，避开兵力强大而沉着冷静的敌人；进攻疲劳困顿的敌人，避开休整良好的敌人；进攻畏惧惊恐的敌人，避开已作戒备的敌人。这是自古以来治军作战的方法。

Righteousness. It is wisdom that you can fully make use of resources; it is bravery that you can cherish and realize the great aspiration; it is credibility that you can win the people's hearts permanently. Yield results in harmony, and the relationship between the officers and men will be congenial.If men attribute failings to themselves, they will compete to be worthy and make their contributions. When men are pleased in their hearts, they will not spare their efforts.

Generally to wage war: Attack where the enemy is vulnerable in silence; avoid where he is strong in calmness. Attack when he is tired; avoid when he has refreshed in leisure. Attack what he fears most; avoid what he fears least. This has been the rule for controlling the army from ancient times.

# 用众第五

【原文】

凡战之道，用寡固，用众治，寡利烦，众利正。用众进止，用寡进退。众以合寡，则远裹而阙之，若分而迭击。寡以待众，若众疑之，则自用之。擅利则释旗迎而反之。敌若众，则相众而受裹；敌若

【今译】

大凡作战的规律是，用小部队作战，要注重营阵的巩固；用大部队作战，要讲求整治不乱。兵力寡少利于战术多变出奇制胜，兵力众多利于正面交战。兵力强大要能进能止；兵力弱小要能进能退。用优势兵力同劣势之敌交战，就对其实施包围并虚留缺口，同时分兵轮番进行攻击。用劣势兵力对付优势之敌，则要虚张声势迷惑敌人，并用权变诡诈的战法打击敌人。如果敌人已占领有利的地形，就卷起旌旗，佯装败退以诱敌出击，然后再予以反击。如果敌人兵力众多，就当明察情况并准备在被围条件下作战。如果敌人兵力寡少而行动谨慎，就先行

# 5. Employment of the Masses

Generally in warfare: When you employ a small force, it must be solid. When you employ a large mass it must be well ordered. A small force is advantageous to take unorthodox tactics in raiding the enemy. A large mass is advantageous to take orthodox tactics. When you employ a large mass, advance and halt steadily. When you employ a small force, advance and withdraw easily. If your large mass engages a small enemy force, envelope them at a distance but leave one side open, or divide your mass to attack them in turn. When your small force withstands the enemy's masses, and if the masses are upset by uncertainty, take advantage of it. When the enemy has already occupied the favorable terrain, abandon your flags as if in flight, and when he attacks turn around to launch a counterattack. If the enemy is greater in number, investigate his masses and prepare to be surrounded by them. If the enemy is fewer and fear-

【原文】

寡若畏，则避之开之。

凡战，背风背高，右高左险，历沛历圮，兼舍环龟。

凡战，设而观其作，视敌而举。待则循而勿鼓，待众之作。攻则屯而伺之。

凡战，众寡以观其变，进退以观其固，危而观其惧，静而观其怠，动而观其疑，袭而观其治。击其疑，加其卒，致其屈，袭其规，因其不避，阻其

【今译】

避开它，为其虚留生路，然后乘隙消灭它。

用兵打仗，要背对风向背靠高地，右边倚托高地左边依恃险阻，遇上沼泽地带和崩陷地段宜迅速离开，选择外低内高、有险可守的地形驻屯军队。

大凡作战，要事先摆好阵势以便观察敌人的反应，并根据敌情变化，采取相应的行动。发现敌人已经做好战斗准备，我们就要按兵勒卒，暂不发起进攻，而等待敌人的下一步行动。敌人主动发起进攻，就要集结兵力寻求破敌的机会。

通常作战，应用数量不等的兵力去试探敌人，以观察其不同的反应；应用忽进忽退的行动，来观察其阵势是否稳固；通过逼近威胁的手段，观察敌人是否恐惧；通过按兵不动的方式，观察敌人是否懈怠；进行佯动，看敌人是否疑惑；进行袭击，看敌人是否整治。在敌人犹豫不决情况下发起打击，乘敌人仓猝无备的时候实施进攻，从而使敌人陷于困境。要通过袭击打乱敌人的部署，并利用敌人冒

ful, avoid him and leave a path open.

Generally in warfare: Deploy your troops to keep the wind to their back, the mountains behind them, the heights on the right and the precipices on the left. Pass through the marshland and cross over the destroyed roads. March at a doubly normal speed before encamping. Select a raised ground like a turtle's back for encamping.

Generally in warfare: Deploy your troops first and observe the enemy's actions closely, then launch the attack in accord with the enemy's situations. If he is waiting for your attack, demonstrate to act accordingly. Do not drum the advance, but wait for the moment when his masses arise. If he attacks, concentrate your troops and seize the opportunity to mount a counterattack.

Generally in warfare: Employ large and small force to observe the variations of the enemy's tactics. Advance and retreat to probe the solidity of his formations. Threaten him to see if he is frightened. Keep silence to observe his laxity. Move to observe his doubts. Strike to see his discipline. Attack when he is doubtful. Reinforce your attacking troops when he is in haste. Impel him to constrict his deployments. Attack

【原文】

图，夺其虑，乘其惧。

凡从奔勿息，敌人或止于路则虑之。

凡近敌都，必有进路；退，必有反虑。

凡战，先则弊，后则慑，息则怠，不息亦弊，息久亦反其慑。

书亲绝，是谓绝顾之虑。选良次兵，是谓益人之强。弃任节食，是谓开人之意。自古之政也。

【今译】

险轻进的错误，粉碎它的企图，制止它的计划，并乘其军心恐惧不稳之际一举加以聚歼。

凡是追击溃败的敌人，不要松懈停止。敌人有时在中途上停留下来，那就要考虑它的企图。

凡是在迫近敌人都邑的时候，一定要预先研究好进军的路线。退却的时候，也一定要事前考虑好后撤的方案。

一般作战，过早行动会使得军队疲惫，过迟行动会使得军心畏怯，只注意休整会使军队懈怠，总不休整则会导致军队疲困。一味休整，反而会产生怯战心理。

要禁止所有的亲友间书信往来，这样就能断绝士卒思家的念头。选拔勇敢善战的人才，准备好精良的兵器，这样就能提高军队的战斗力。舍弃笨重的装备，少携带粮食，这样就能激发士卒死战的决心。这些，是自古以来治军作战的方法。

in surprise on his order of formations. Take advantage of his arrogance. Obstruct his strategy. Deprive him of realizing his planning. Capitalize on his fear.

When you pursue a fleeing enemy, do not rest. If the enemy halts on the way, discreetly investigate his attempt.

When you press forward near an enemy's capital, you must have an approach road to it. When about to withdraw, you must plan the return route.

Generally in warfare: If you take action too early, the troops will be tired out. If too late, they will be afraid. If the troops take rest, they will be lax. If they do not take rest, they will also be tired out. If they take a long rest, on the contrary, they will also be afraid.

Writing no letters home is termed "breaking off homesickness." Selecting the elite and distributing weapons to them are termed "enhancing the strength of men." Casting aside the ponderous implements and carrying the minimal dry rations are termed "boosting the fighting spirit of men." From ancient times all these have been the rule of controlling the army.

# 尉缭子

# WEI LIAO ZI

# 天官第一

**【原文】**

梁惠王问尉缭子曰："黄帝刑德，可以百胜，有之乎？"

尉缭子对曰："刑以伐之，德以守之，非所谓天官、时日、阴阳、向背也。黄帝者，人事而已矣。何者？今有城，东西攻不能取，南北攻不能取，四方岂无顺时乘之者邪？然不能取者，城高池深，兵

**【今译】**

梁惠王问尉缭子说："黄帝的刑德之术，可以百战百胜，有这回事吗？"

尉缭子回答说："刑是讲讨伐敌人的，德是讲治理国家的，并不是世间有些人所说的天象、时日、阴阳、向背那一套东西。黄帝的刑德之术，只是讲处理好人事罢了。为什么这样说呢？比如现在有一座城，从东面、西面进攻攻不下来，从南面、北面进攻也攻不下来，难道四个方向中就没有顺应时辰的方向吗？之所以不能攻取，是城墙高大、护城河深、武器齐备、物资粮食积蓄充裕、豪杰之士齐心协力啊。如果城墙低，护城城河线，守备力量弱，那么就可以攻取了。由此看来，天官、时日（这些

# 1. Omens of Constellations

King Hui of Liang asked Wei Liao Zi: "The Yellow Emperor's doctrine of violence and virtue can win a hundred victories without peril. Is it true?"

Wei Liao Zi replied: "Violence was used to conquer the enemy, and virtue used to control the state. This is not what is referred to as 'omens of constellations, auspicious timing, ying and yang, positive or negative.' The Yellow Emperor's victories were all due to human endeavor. Why was that? For instance,now there is a walled city and one attacks it from the east and west but cannot take it, and attacks from the south and north but cannot take it either, can it be that all quarters have no auspicious moment to be exploited? The reason why it cannot be taken is that the walls are high, the moats deep, the weapons and ordnance fully prepared, food and supplies adequately accumulated and the nobles and officers unison in planning defense. If the walls are

【原文】

器备具，财谷多积，豪士一谋者也。若城下、池浅、守弱，则取之矣。由是观之，天官、时日，不若人事也。按《天官》曰：‘背水陈为绝纪(地)，向阪陈为废军。’武王伐纣，背济水向山阪而陈，以二万二千五百人，击纣之亿万而灭商，岂纣不得《天官》之陈哉？楚将公子心与齐人战，时有彗星出，柄在齐。柄所在胜，不可击。公子心曰：‘彗星何知！

【今译】

条件)，不及人事重要。按《天官》一书中的说法：‘背水布阵就是自处绝地，向山列阵就会断送部队。’但周武王讨伐商纣王时，背靠济水，面对山坡而设阵，率领二万二千五百名士兵，打败了商纣王的数十万大军，灭亡了商朝。这难道是因为商纣王没有得到《天官》中所说的布阵之法吗？楚国将领公子心与齐人作战，当时有彗星出现，星柄在齐国一方。(按《天官》的说法）彗柄所在的一方胜，是不能攻击的。公子心说：‘彗星哪有知觉！用扫帚打架的

low, the moats shallow and the defense is weak, then it can be taken.Therefore, from this perspective, the omens of constell- ations and timings are not as important as human endeavor. According to the Book of Omens of Constellations (Tian Guan), 'Deploying troops with water to the rear istantamount to placing them in the desperate ground; and deploying troops facing a mountain slope is tantamount to abandoning them in the 'doomed ground.' When King Wu of the Zhou attacked King Zhou of the Shang Dynasty, he deployed his troops with the Qi River behind him, facing a mountain slope. With his twenty-two thousand and five hundred men he attacked King Zhou's hundreds of thousands and overthrew the Shang Dynasty. Yet, had not King Zhou deployed in line with the omens of constellations? When the Chu general Gongzi Xin was about to fight against Qi, a comet appeared with its tail over Qi. According to the Book of Omens of Constellations, wherever the tail pointed there would be victorie, and Qi could not be attacked.Gongzi Xin said: 'What does a comet know? If we fight by means of a " broom star" (comet traditionally nicknamed "broom star" in China),conversely we point its

【原文】

以彗斗者，固倒而胜焉。’明日与齐战，大破之。黄帝曰：‘先神先鬼，先稽我智。’谓之天时，人事而已。”

【今译】

话，就是要倒转帚柄才能取胜啊。’第二天与齐人交战，大败齐军。黄帝说：‘先去求神问鬼，不如先考察自己的智慧。’这里所说的天官，不过是强调发挥人的作用罢了。”

handle or comet's tail to the enemy and hit him, then he will be defeated.' On the next day Chu engaged Qi in battle and inflicted severe blows on Qi's army.The Yellow Emperor said: "Instead of attaching the first importance to spirits and ghosts, I examine my own knowledge first.' This means that the omens ofconstellations are nothing but human endeavor."

# 兵谈第二

【原文】

量土地肥垗而立邑。建城称地，以城称人，以人称粟。三相称，则内可以固守，外可以战胜。战胜于外，备生于内，胜备相应犹合符节，无异故也。

治兵者，若秘于地，若邃于天，生于无。故开之，大不窕，小不恢。明乎禁舍开塞，民流者亲之，

【今译】

应该根据土地的肥瘠来确定设置都邑。都邑的兴建要与土地的广狭相称，都邑的大小要与人口的多少相称，人口的多少要与粮食的产量相称。三者相称，那么自卫时就可以稳固防守，进攻时就可以取得胜利。能在国外战胜敌人，在于国内有充分的准备。胜利和准备的相互对应，就像符节的两半相吻合一样，是由于没有差异的缘故呀。

统兵的将帅 (指挥部队)，犹如深藏于大地，犹如运行于高天，产生于无形之中。所以用兵作战时，战斗规模再大也不会感到兵力不足，规模再小也不会感到兵力过多。明了禁绝坏事、赦免小错、广开财源、杜绝浪费之术，人民流离失所的招徕亲抚他

# 2. On Military Affairs

Survey the fertility and sterility of the soil and then erect cities and towns. The establishment of a city must be commensurate to the size of the surveyed land. The area of the city must be commensurate to the number of the population, and the number of the population must be commensurate to the quantities of food supplies. When these three are in conformity with each other, then internally one can set up a solid defense, and externally gain victory in battle. Moreover, the external victory is gained on the basis of the internal preparations. Hence victory is closely connected with preparation, and they are like the halves of a tally exactly matching each other.

Controlling the army is as secretive as the deep recesses of Earth, as remote as the topmost space of Heaven, and derives from the invisible nonexistence. Hence it must be opened to apply in military operations. When the troops disperse

【原文】

地不任者任之。夫土广而任则国富，民众而制则国治。富治者，民(车)不发轫，车不暴出(甲不出橐)，而威制天下。故曰：“兵胜于朝廷。”不暴甲而胜者，主胜也。陈而胜者，将胜也。

兵起，非可以忿也。见胜则与(兴)，不见胜则止。患在百里之内，不起一日之师；患在千里之内，

【今译】

们，土地荒芜闲置的开垦利用起来。土地广阔而能利用，国家就富庶；人民众多而管理有序，国家就安定。富庶安定的国家，战车不必出动，盔甲不必启封，就能凭威势而制服天下。所以说：“军事的胜利取决于朝廷的决策。”不动用军队而获胜，是君主的胜利；两军对阵而后取胜，是将领的胜利。

出兵作战，不可只凭一时的意气。有取胜的把握就出兵，没有取胜的把握就不要出兵。祸患在百里之内，部队不可只作一天的准备；祸患在千里之

in the field, they will not be out of control for its vastness, and when they concentrate they will not be congested for its narrowness. All measures of prohibitions, pardons, enlightenments, and putting an end to extravagance must be taken in public. The displaced persons should be treated kindly, and the unworked lands be cultivated. When land is vast and under cultivation, the state will be prosperous; when the people are in great numbers and well ordered, the state will be governed in good condition. When a state is well governed and moreover wealthy, even though it does not remove the blocks from the chariots, nor is the armor taken out from the bags, its awesomeness will cause All Under Heaven to submit. Therefore, it is said: 'Military victory depends upon the court.' When one is victorious without using the army, it is the sovereign's victory; when victory comes after deploying the army to confront the enemy, it is a general's victory.

The army cannot be deployed to engage in war by an enraged general. If it is sure in winning, the army will be mobilized; if not, the mobilization of the army will be stopped. If trouble arises within a hundred *li*, do not make just one

【原文】

不起一月之师；患在四海之内，不起一岁之师。

将者，上不制于天，下不制于地，中不制于人。宽不可激而怒，清不可事以财。夫心狂、目盲、耳聋，以三悖率人者，难矣。

兵之所及，羊肠亦胜，锯齿亦胜，缘山亦胜，入谷亦胜，方亦胜，圆亦胜。重者如山如林，如江如河；轻者如炮如燔，如垣压之，如云覆之。令之聚不得以散，散不得以聚，左不得以右，右不得以

【今译】

内，部队不可只作一个月的准备；祸患在遥远的区域，部队不可只作一年的准备。

作为大将，应上不受制于天，下不受制于地，中不受制于人。心胸豁达，不会一受刺激就发怒；清明廉洁，不会被财物所收买。内心狂妄、眼睛不明、耳朵不灵，有这三种缺点的人去统率军队，是很难取胜的。

军队所到之处，在羊肠小道上能取胜，在崎岖的山路上也能取胜；攀山而上能取胜，深入狭谷也能取胜；设置方阵能取胜，设置圆阵也能取胜。部队稳重时就像高山深林、长江大河，轻捷时就像煨烤的袅袅文火、渗泄的涓涓细流。要像城垣倒塌那样将敌人压倒，像乌云蔽日那样将敌人吞没。使敌人集结时无法分散，分散时又无法集中；左边的部队无法调到右边，右边的部队也无法调到左边。我

day's preparation. If trouble arises within a thousand *li*, do not make merely a month's preparation. If trouble lies within the Four Seas, do not make only one year's preparation.

Now as for the general: Above he is not controlled by Heaven, below he is not restricted by Earth, in the middle he is not influenced by men. He should be broad-minded so that he cannot be irritated to indignation. He should be honest and bright so that he cannot be bribed with wealth. Generally if one's mind is upset to madness, and his eyes are blind, and his ears deaf, he is difficult to lead men with these three aberrations.

Wherever the army maneuvers, it will be victorious along the narrow winding trails, and it will be victorious too along the most rugged paths. Its venture to climb mountains and step down to valleys will be victorious, and its deployment in square formation or round formation will be victorious too. When the heavy army attacks, it is like mountains, like forests, like rivers and great streams. When the light troops attack, it is like blazing flames, like the collapse of city walls pressing upon the enemy and like clouds covering him. They cause

【原文】

左。(兵)如总木，弩如羊角。人人无不腾陵张胆，绝乎疑虑，堂堂决而去。

【今译】

军刀枪并举如丛林，弓弩齐发如旋风，人人无不奋发踊跃、放胆直前，毫不犹豫，勇敢果决地冲向敌人。

the enemy to be unable to disperse out of concentration, nor to be concentrated from dispersal. The enemy troops on the left are unable to rescue the right, and those on the right unable to rescue the left. The massive weapons are like forests, and catapulting crossbows are like whirlwinds. Every man, without exception, plucks up in high spirit. Casting off all doubts, they press forward decisively with an indomitable will.

# 制谈第三

【原文】

凡兵，制必先定。制先定，则士不乱；士不乱，则刑乃明。金鼓所指，则百人尽斗。陷行乱阵，则千人尽斗。覆军杀将，则万人齐刃。天下莫能当其战矣。

古者，士有什伍，车有偏列。鼓鸣旗麾，先登者未尝非多力国士也，先死者亦未尝非多力国士也。损敌一人而损我百人，此资敌而伤我甚焉，世将不

【今译】

凡是军队，必须先定好制度。制度先定好了，士卒就不会散乱。士卒不散乱，刑罚才能分明。进攻令一下，百人就勇猛作战，冲锋陷阵。千人就奋勇当先。消灭敌军、擒杀敌将，万人就齐心向前。这样的军队天下无敌。

古时候，士卒有什伍的编制，战车有偏列的编制。当战鼓擂响，旌旗挥动，率先登上敌城的，未尝不是为国尽力的勇士；先战死的，也未尝不是以身殉国的勇士。但是，杀死敌方一人，而我方伤亡百人，这实际是帮助敌人而严重损伤自己，现在的

# 3. On Institutions

Generally in military affairs, institutions must be set up first. As the institutions are set up, the men will not be disordered. As the men are not disordered, punishments will be clear. Wherever the gongs and drums direct them, a hundred men will all devote themselves to fighting and breaking in the enemy's ranks; a thousand men will all press forward to overturn the enemy's army and kill his generals; a ten thousand men will raise their weapons in unison, and no one under Heaven can withstand them in battle.

Anciently soldiers were organized into squads of five and ten, and chariots into convoys of five and twenty-five. When the drums are rolling and the standards are waving, those who first climb the enemy's wall might not be unworthy of the outstanding state warriors; those who first die in action also might not be unworthy of the outstanding state warriors. If one enemy is killed at

【原文】

能禁。征役分军而逃归，或临战自北，则逃伤甚焉，世将不能禁。杀人于百步之外者，弓矢也；杀人于五十步之内者，矛戟也。将已鼓，而士卒相嚣，拗矢、折矛、抱戟，利后发。战有此数者，内自败也，世将不能禁。士失什伍，车失偏列，奇兵捐将而走，大众亦走，世将不能禁。夫将能禁此四者，则高山

【今译】

将领无法杜绝这种情况。应征入伍而又逃归，或临战自行溃逃，会造成部队严重的逃亡和伤亡，现在的将领无法杜绝这种现象。能在百步之外取人性命的武器是弓和箭，能在五十步以内取人性命的武器是矛和戟。指挥员已擂鼓发令，而士兵却在喧哗吵闹，折箭、断矛、抛戟，都想走在最后。作战中出现这几种现象，部队自己就溃败了，现在的将领不能杜绝这种情况。士卒混乱，失去了什和伍的编制；战车混乱，失去了偏和列的编制；奇袭的部队弃将而逃，正面的大部队也跟着逃散，现在的将领不能杜绝这种情况。如果将领能杜绝上述这四种现象，

the cost of our own one hundred lives, it is not only helping the enemy in reality, but also doing great harm to us. However, the contemporary generals cannot prevent it. If those enlisted in military service run off to their native places, or escape of their own accord when they approach a battle, the result will be an exodus of the deserters and a great deal of casualties. However, the contemporary generals cannot prevent it. What can kill men beyond one hundred paces are bows and arrows. What can kill men within fifty paces are spears and halberds. When the general's drums are already beaten but the officers and soldiers yell at each other, twist the arrows to break them, smash the spears, abandon the halberds and find it advantageous to lag behind, and when all these have happened in battle, it is self-defeating. However, the contemporary generals cannot prevent it. The officers losing the squads of five and ten, the chariots losing the convoys of five and twenty-five, the unorthodox force abandoning its generals to flee, and the main body of the army running off too — these are things which the contemporary generals cannot prevent. Now if a general can prevent these four, he can lead his army to traverse the moun-

【原文】

陵之，深水绝之，坚陈犯之。不能禁此四者，犹亡舟楫绝江河，不可得也。

民非乐死而恶生也，号令明，法制审，故能使之前。明赏于前，决罚于后，是以发能中利，动则有功。

令百人一卒，千人一司马，万人一将，以少诛众，以弱诛强。试听臣言其术，足使三军之众诛一人无失刑。父不敢舍子，子不敢舍父，况国人乎！

一贼杖剑击于市，万人无不避之者，臣谓非一

【今译】

那么多高的山也能翻越，多深的水也能横渡，多坚固的敌阵也能攻克。不能杜绝这些现象，那就像欲渡河而没有船和桨一样，是不可能成功的。

人并非乐死而厌生。只有号令严明、制度健全，才能使士兵勇往直前。明确对进攻者的赏赐，坚决执行对退缩者的惩罚，才能出兵就获胜，行动就立功。

使百人听从一卒长的指挥，千人听从一司马的指挥，万人听从一将军的指挥，就能以少胜多、以弱胜强。若能采纳我的办法，就足以使全军上下不错杀一人，使父亲不敢袒护儿子，儿子不敢袒护父亲，更何况一般的人呢？

一个亡命之徒持剑在闹市中挥舞，众人没有不躲避他的。我认为这并不是只有这一个人勇敢，整

tains, ford the deep water and attack the strong formations. If he cannot prevent these four, he is like being about to cross a river without any boat and oar, and cannot succeed.

People are not delighted to die nor have an aversion to life. Only when the commands and orders are clear, and the laws and regulations carefully examined, can the troops go forward with courage. Only when rewards are clearly bestowed on those who advance and punishments decisively given to those who lag behind can the troops gain advantage upon launching attacks and be successful in maneuvers.

Now one hundred men are commanded by a company leader, one thousand men by a Sima, and ten thousand men by a general. Thereby a mass can be controlled by a small number, and the strong can be controlled by the weak. I beg to hear my advice on the tactics that it is sufficient for the massive Three Armies to punish only one to death without losing the awesomeness of penalty. Even a father dare not cover up his son, and a son does not dare to cover up his father, let alone the citizens of the state!

When a bandit is brandishing his sword to strike people in the marketplace, among ten

【原文】

人之独勇，万人皆不肖也。何则？必死与必生，固不侔也。听臣之术，足使三军之众为一死贼，莫当其前，莫随其后，而能独出独入焉。独出独入者，王霸之兵也。

有提十万之众而天下莫当者谁？曰桓公也。有提七万之众而天下莫当者谁？曰吴起也。有提三万之众而天下莫当者谁？曰武子也。今天下诸国士所率，无不及二十万之众者，然不能济功名者，不明乎禁舍开塞也。明其制，一人胜之，则十人亦以胜之也；十人胜之，则百、千、万人亦以胜之也。故

【今译】

个集市上的人都胆怯。那为什么大家都躲着他呢？这是因为一人敢死而众人求生，所以这是根本不同的两回事。若能采纳我的办法，就足以使三军之众人像亡命徒那样不怕死，无人敢在前面阻挡，也无人敢在后面追逐，能独往独来，如入无人之境。独往独来的军队，正是能成王霸之业的军队。

有谁能统率十万军队纵横天下呢？是齐桓公啊。有谁能统率七万军队纵横天下呢？是吴起啊。有谁能统率三万军队纵横天下呢？是孙武子啊。现在天下各国的将领，所率领的军队没有少于二十万的，然而不能成就功名，这是因为不懂得禁止奸邪之心、赦免小的过失、开启养生之道、杜绝奢靡风气这些治国之道啊。明白了这些治国良策，一人能取胜，十人也能取胜；十人能取胜，那么千百万个人也能

thousand people there will not be anyone who does not avoid him. I say this is not because of the single one's bravery and less courage of all the ten thousand people. The reason is that the one who is determined to die and those who are committed in seeking life are not comparable. I beg to hear my advice on the tactics that it is sufficient for the massive Three Armies to act as a desperate bandit, and no one in front can withstand him nor in rear can follow him. He can come and go alone. If one is able to come and go alone, it is the army of a king or hegemon.

Who was able to lead a host of one hundred thousand and no one under Heaven could oppose him? Lord Huan of Qi. Who was able to lead a host of seventy thousand and no one could oppose him? Wu Zi. Who was able to lead a host of thirty thousand and no one could oppose him? Sun Zi. Today the commanders from the feudal states under Heaven lead the mass of armies not less than two hundred thousand, but they are unable to make any meritorious achievements, because they do not understand the institutions of prohibitions, pardons, enlightenments and putting an end to extravagance. Having understood the institutions, one is victorious. As one is vic-

【原文】

曰：便吾器用，养吾武勇，发之如鸟击，如赴千仞之溪。

今国被患者，以重宝出聘，以爱子出质，以地界出割，得天下助卒。名为十万，其实不过数万尔。其兵来者，无不谓其将曰："无为天下先战。"其实不可得而战也。

量吾境内之民，无伍莫能正矣。经制十万之众，而王必能使之衣吾衣，食吾食。战不胜、守不固者，

【今译】

取胜。所以说，改进我军的武器装备，培养我军的勇敢精神，打起仗来就像猛禽捕食那样迅速凶狠，像积水从千仞高崖倾泻下来那样势不可挡。

现在国家如遭到入侵，就拿出大量的财宝到别国去求救，就让国君的子弟去当人质，就把本国的土地割让给别国，以求得别国的援军。而别国派出的援军往往号称十万，实际不过数万。而且出征之前，其国君必定嘱咐将领说："千万不要抢在他国之前出战。"其实是得不到他们的援助的。

估量一下我国的民众，没有不可以征发入伍的。但组织起了十万大军，朝廷就必须让他们穿上国家的衣、吃上国家的粮。如果仍然进攻不能取胜，防守不够坚固，那也不是民众之过，而是国家的内政

torious, ten will be victorious. As ten is victorious, hundreds of thousands will be victorious. Therefore, it is said: 'We improve our weapons and cultivate our fighting courage, and our troops setting forth will be as ferocious as birds of prey, and as powerful as the water rushing down from a thousand-fathom valley!'

Now a state that has been invaded grants a great deal of treasuries, sends its beloved sons out as hostages and cedes the land along the border for seeking troops under Heaven to its assistance. As for the foreign reinforcements, they are a hundred thousand in name, but only several tens of thousands in reality. When these troops come forth, none of their generals are not advised by their rulers, saying: 'Don't be the first to fight in any circumstance.' Indeed one is unable to have their assistance in battle.

In estimation of the population within our territories, no squads of five and ten cannot be conscripted. Commanding and controlling a host of a hundred thousand, the King must be able to have them wear our uniforms and eat our food.If they gain no victory in battle and are unable to make their defense impregnable, it is not the faults of our people for it is the consequence of

【原文】

非吾民之罪，内自致也。天下诸国助我战，犹良骥騄耳之駛，彼驽马鬐兴角逐，何能绍吾气哉！

吾用天下之用为用，吾制天下之制为制。修吾号令，明吾刑赏，使天下非农无所得食，非战无所得爵，使民扬臂争出农战，而天下无敌矣。故曰：发号出令，信行国内。

民言有可以胜敌者，毋许其空言，必试其能战也。视人之地而有之，分人之民而畜之，必能内有

【今译】

不善所造成的。天下诸侯给我们的援军，表面上像是飞驰的骏马，实际上却是竖着鬃毛追逐的劣马，这怎么能助长我军的士气呢！

我们要利用天下所有可以利用的东西，我们要把天下所有好的制度拿来作为我们自己的制度。整饬号令，严明赏罚，使所有不务农的人就得不到饭吃，无战功就得不到爵位，使民众争相从事农耕、投入战斗，我们就可以无敌于天下了。所以说，号令一旦发出，就要在国内得到确实的执行。

如果有人说他有破敌良策，不要轻信他的话，要在实战中检验他的实际能力。要想占有别国的土地、得到别国的人口，就必须接纳别国的人才。如

the internal affairs. When the feudal states under Heaven support and help us in battle, metaphorically it is as if in chasing the running legendary steeds, while actually they are worn-out old horses with their manes bristling. How can they boost our morale?

We should use all resources under Heaven for our own use and we should apply all institutions under Heaven to our own government. We should revise our commands and orders, and make our punishments and rewards clear, so that all the people under Heaven will have no food to eat without engaging in agriculture, nor ranks to be attained without devoting to military operations. If the people passionately vie with each other in engaging in agriculture and take part in the military operations, then under Heaven we are invincible. Therefore it is said: "When commands and orders are issued, their credibility will extend throughout the state."

If some people say they are able to defeat the enemy, their empty talks should not be allowed, and their abilities to fight must be tested. If one casts greedy eyes on other people's lands and occupy them, and divide up other rulers' subjects and nourish them, one must be able to ab-

【原文】

其贤者也。不能内有其贤而欲有天下，必覆军杀将。如此，虽战胜而国益弱，得地而国益贫，由国中之制弊矣。

【今译】

果不能接纳贤才，又想取得天下，那必然会损兵折将。这样，即使打了胜仗，国家也会日益削弱；得到了土地，国家也会越发贫困，这都是由于国家的制度存在弊病！

sorb and employ the Worthy. If one is unable to use the Worthy but want to possess All Under Heaven, the result will be certain to have one's armies destroyed and generals slain. Thereby even if one may be victorious in the military operations, the state will grow increasingly vulnerable. Even if one may occupy the lands, the state will be increasingly impoverished. All these are attributable to the malpractice of the state's institutions.

# 战威第四

【原文】

凡兵，有以道胜，有以威胜，有以力胜。讲武料敌，使敌之气失而师散，虽形全而不为之用，此道胜也。审法制，明赏罚，便器用，使民有必战之心，此威胜也。破军杀将，乘闉发机，溃众夺地，

【今译】

大凡用兵，有依靠谋略取胜的，有依靠威势取胜的，有依靠武力取胜的。研究韬略，分析敌情，使得敌人士气丧失而部队涣散，虽然编制完整却失去了战斗力，这就是靠谋略取胜。健全法制，严明赏罚，完善武器装备，使士兵有果敢战斗的决心，这就是靠威势取胜。攻破敌军杀其将帅，登上敌城扳动弩机，击溃敌众夺占土地，获胜凯旋而归，这就是靠武力取胜。君王懂得这些，这三种取胜的诀

# 4. Military Awesomeness

Generally in warfare there are some victories gained by *Dao* (Right Way), some by awesomeness and some by strength. Studies of the military situations and estimation of the enemy are made to cause the enemy's morale lost and his forces scattered so that even though the shape of his forces is complete, they are of no use. This is victory gained by *Dao* (Right Way). The laws and regulations are carefully examined, rewards and punishments are clearly performed, and weapons and equipment are improved so that the troops are determined to fight. This is victory gained by awesomeness. The enemy's army is penetrated and his generals are slain, the fortified walls sealed and the crossbows catapulted; the host of his army is overwhelmed and his territories are occupied. As soon as these successes have been made the troops return home. This is victory gained by strength. When kings and feu-

【原文】

成功乃返，此力胜也。王侯知此，以三胜者毕矣。

夫将之所以战者，民也；民之所以战者，气也。气实则斗，气夺则走。刑如未加，兵未接，而所以夺敌者五：一曰庙胜之论，二曰受命之论，三曰逾垠之论，四曰深沟高垒之论，五曰举陈加刑之论。此五者，先料敌而后动，是以击虚夺之也。

善用兵者，能夺人而不夺于人。夺者，心之机也。令者，一众心也。众不审，则数变；数变，则

【今译】

穷就完全掌握了。

将领能够打仗，靠的是士兵；士兵能够英勇作战，靠的是士气。士气饱满就能战斗，士气丧失就会逃走。如果战斗尚未开始，兵刃尚未交锋，就能够先机制敌的条件有五个：一是朝廷决策的正确，二是挑选和任命得力的将领，三是将领领兵外出能机断专行，四是构筑工事稳固坚实，五是列阵与进攻的战术得当。这五个条件，都要靠先分析敌情，然后采取行动，因此能击中对方弱点而使之丧失士气。

善于用兵的人，能够夺人士气而保持己方士气。夺人士气，是将领巧运匠心的结果。

号令，是用来统一全军意志的。很多将领不懂得如何发布号令，以至经常变更号令。号令多变，

dal lords understand these, the three ways to victory will be completely grasped by them.

Now the general able to fight depends upon the troops, and the troops able to fight depend upon the morale. When morale is high they will fight, and when lost they will retreat and scatter. Before encountering the enemy and the hand-to-hand fight, there are five means to defeat the enemy: The first is called discussing the policy-making to victory in the temple; the second, discussing the general receiving his mandate; the third, discussing the successful march crossing the borders; the fourth, discussing making the moats deep and ramparts high; the fifth, discussing raising and deploying the army and conquering the enemy. In these five ways first estimate the enemy and afterward move. This is to strike his weaknesses and conquer him.

Those adept in employing troops are able to take the initiative to seize men and not be seized by the others. Taking initiatives in one's own hands to seize others is the intelligence in one's mind. The orders issued are to unify the minds of the masses. If the masses are not understood, the orders will be changed frequently. Frequent changes will lead to the mistrust of the masses

【原文】

令虽出，众不信矣。故令之法，小过无更，小疑无申。故上无疑令，则众不二听；动无疑事，则众不二志。未有不信其心，而能得其力者；未有不得其力，而能致其死战者也。故国必有礼〔信〕亲爱之义，则可以饥易饱；国必有孝慈廉耻之俗，则可以死易生。古者率民，必先礼信而后爵禄，先廉耻而后刑罚，先亲爱而后律其身。

【今译】

即使下达，部众也不相信了。所以，发布命令的原则是：有小的差错也不要更改，有小的疑问也无须重新申明。所以，上级没有犹疑不定的命令，部下就不会无所适从；行动没有疑惑，部下就不会三心二意了。没有不得到百姓的信任而能使其自愿效力的；也没有未使百姓自愿效力而能使其拼死作战的。所以国家必须有崇礼守信、相亲相爱的风气，然后民众才能克服饥寒获得温饱；国家必须有子孝父慈懂得廉耻的风俗，民众才能挽救危亡求得生存。古时君王治理百姓，必定先讲求礼让信誉，然后才赐予爵位俸禄；先进行廉耻道德的教化，然后才实施刑罚惩治；先以仁爱之心爱护百姓，然后才用法律约束他们。

even though the orders are issued. Thus the way to issue orders is that no change should be made if there are slight suspicions. Therefore when the superiors have not issued doubtful orders, the masses will not be at a loss as to what the correct orders to obey. When the action is taken without any skeptical aspects the masses will not be of two minds in action. There has never been an instance where the sovereign was able to gain the people's strength without gaining their minds. It has never been the case that one was unable to realize their strength and yet attain their deaths in battle.

Therefore the state must promote the righteousness of rites, trust, kindness and love, and then it can exchange hunger for surfeit. The state must promote the customs of filial affection, parental love, honesty and shame, and then it can exchange death for life. The ancients who led the people were certain to place rites and trust in the first place and took the ranks and emoluments afterward. They regarded honesty and shame first and punishments afterward. They upheld kindred and love first, and then constrained themselves with laws and regulations.

**【原文】**

故战者必本乎率身以励众士，如心之使四支(肢)也。志不励，则士不死节；士不死节，则众不战。励士之道，民之生不可不厚也；爵列之等、死丧之礼，民之所营，不可不显也。必因民所生而制之，因民所营而显之，田禄之实，饮食之亲，乡里相劝，死丧相救，兵役相从，此民之所励也。使什伍如亲戚，卒伯如朋友，止如堵墙，动如风雨，车

**【今译】**

所以领兵作战的人，必须用自身的表率行为来激励部队，这样才能像大脑指挥四肢一样灵活自如。斗志没有激发出来，士兵就不会甘心为国捐躯；士兵不愿为国捐躯，军队就不能作战。激励士气的方法是：民众生活所需之物，不可不丰厚；爵位的等级、死者的抚恤，是民众所谋求的，不可不优厚。必须根据百姓生计的需求使其各得所需，必须根据百姓所最追求的东西使其得到满足。田地、俸禄的实惠，衣食的保障，乡里乡亲的互相鼓励，生死关头的互相救助，从军服役的相伴相随，这些都是可用来激励士气的重要因素。让同什同伍的士兵亲近如骨肉，让同卒同伯的士兵密切如朋友，这样，军队防御时就像铜墙铁壁，进攻时就像疾风骤雨，战

Thus the general who commands in the military operations must set an example for stimulation of all his officers as the brain controls the four limbs. If the fighting spirit is not stimulated the officers will not fight to the death. If the officers are not determined to fight to the death, the mass of troops cannot fight effectively in the military operations. It is the way to stimulate officers that the people's material welfare cannot but be plentiful. Ranks of nobility and pensions for families of the deceased cannot but be evident because the people have sought for it. It is imperative that the people's daily necessaries be guaranteed by the institutions and what the people have sought for be emphasized clearly. The substantial profits of the field fruits and salaries, the care for daily life of drinking and eating, the mutual assistance in neighborhood, the rescue to the life and death risks and comradeship cherished in the active service — these are what encourage the people. In the squads of five and ten their members will be as cohesive as relatives, and relationship between the company leader and its members will be as close as friends. When the troops encamp their defense will be as solid as the walls and when they move they will

【原文】

不结辙，士不旋踵，此本战之道也。

地所以养民也，城所以守地也，战所以守城也。故务耕者民不饥，务守者地不危，务战者城不围。三者，先王之本务。本务者，兵最急。故先王专于兵，有五焉：委积不多，则士不行；赏禄不厚，则民不劝；武士不选，则众不强；备用不便，则力不壮；刑赏不中，则众不畏。务此五者，静能守其所

【今译】

车有进无退，战士勇往直前，这些都是用兵作战的根本道理。

土地是用来养活百姓的，城池是用来保护土地的，战争是用来守卫城池的。所以，发展农业生产的国家，人民就不会挨饿；完善城防守备的国家，上地就没有危险；做好战争准备的国家，城池就不会被围困。这三件事是古代君王所注重的根本大事。根本大事中，战争是最要紧的事。所以古代君王专注于战争，尤其留意五个方面：钱粮积蓄不多，军队就不能行动；奖赏和俸禄不优厚，就无法号召百姓；武士不精选，部队战斗力就不强；武器装备不精良，军队的实力就不足；刑罚、赏赐不公正，士兵就不畏服。注意到这五个方面，防御就能坚不可

be as speedy as the wind and shower. The chariots will go forward without wheeling to the rear and the men will not turn about. This is the fundamental way to engage in military operations.

The nourishment of people depends upon the land, the protection of the land depends upon the fortified cities, and the defense of the cities depends upon fighting. Therefore if the state attaches great importance to cultivation, its people will not be hungry; if much attention is paid to defense, the land will not be in danger; if the fighting strength is emphasized, the cities will not be in a state of siege. These three were the basic concerns of the Former Kings, and among them military affairs were the most urgent. Thus the Former Kings focused on the five military affairs: When the supplies are not adequate, no troops will set out. When the rewards and salaries are not generous, the people will not be persuaded and encouraged. When the warriors are not selected, the host of the army will not be strong. When the weapons and equipment are not prepared, the fighting strength will not be great. When the punishments and rewards are not impartial, the masses will not respect and abide by the disciplines. If all these five are

**【原文】**

固，动能成其所欲。夫以居攻出，则居欲重，阵欲坚，发欲毕，斗欲齐。

王国富民，霸国富士，仅存之国富大夫，亡国富仓府。是谓上满下漏，患无所救。

故曰：举贤任能，不时日而事利；明法审令，不卜筮而事吉；贵功养劳，不祷祠而得福。又曰天

**【今译】**

摧，进攻能达到预期的目的。从防御转入进攻，要求防御要稳重，阵地要坚固，出击时要全力以赴，战斗中要协调一致。

称王于天下的国家，富足的是民众；称霸于诸侯的国家，富足的是有才能的人；勉强维持的国家，富足的是官吏；濒临灭亡的国家，富足的是国君的库府。这就是所谓的上面官府富足有余，下面百姓一贫如洗，一旦发生灾难就无法挽救了。

所以说：推举贤才任用能臣，不必挑选良辰吉日，也会事事顺利；严明、健全法令制度，不用求神占卜，也会事事吉祥；褒奖有功、勤劳的人，不须祭祀、祈祷，也会得到保佑和赐福。又说：天象

stressed, at rest the troops will be able to defend any place they secure, and in motion they will attain their objectives.

Now in turning the defensive to the offensive, the defense must be stable and formations solid. Launching offensive the troops must do their utmost, and in action they must be of one mind and well coordinated.

The state under a king's rule enriches the people, the state under a hegemon's domination enriches the officers, the state on the brink of survival enriches the high officials and the state about to perish enriches the ruler's storehouses. This is termed "the top is full while the bottom leaks." In such a case there will be no way to effect a rescue when a catastrophe befalls.

Therefore it is said that recommendations of the Worthy and appointments of the capable can be carried out without the time being propitious, and these affairs will still be advantageous. Making the laws clear and prudently issuing the orders without performing divination with the tortoise will still render fortune to the state. In esteem of those who have made achievements and in support of those who have made endeavors, blessings will be attained without praying. Fur-

【原文】

时不如地利，地利不如人和。圣人所贵，人事而已。

夫勤劳之师，将必先己。暑不张盖，寒不重衣，险必下步，军井成而后饮，军食熟而后饭，军垒成而后舍，劳佚必以身同之。如此，师虽久而不老不弊。

【今译】

时日，不及地利条件重要；地利条件，不及人心和睦重要。圣明的君主所重视的，不过是人的作用罢了。

能够吃苦耐劳的军队，将领必定能以身作则。暑热天气，将领不能独自躲在伞盖之下；寒冷天气，不要一个人裹得严严实实；道路陡峭之处，将领要下马与士兵走在一起；全军的水井挖成了以后，将领才能喝水；全军的饭食做好了以后，将领才能进食；全军的营寨搭好了以后，将领才能休息；劳苦与安逸一定要让自己与全体将士相同。这样，部队即使连续作战也不会士气低落、军心涣散，失去战斗力。

thermore, it is said: "The Heaven seasons are not as good as Earth advantages. The Earth advantages are not as good as human harmony." What the Sages treasure is human effort. That is all!

Now in the army sustainable with hardships the general must set himself as an example for his officers and men. In summer he does not set up a parasol; in winter he does not wear heavier clothes. On rugged ground he must dismount and walk. Only after the army's well is finished does he drink. Only after the army's food is cooked does he eat. Only after the army's ramparts are completed does he rest. He must personally share the comforts and hardships of the masses. Thus even though the army has engaged in military operations for a long time, it will be neither worn out nor exhausted.

# 攻权第五

【原文】

兵以静胜，国以专胜。力分者弱，心疑者背。夫力弱，故进退不豪，纵敌不禽(擒)。将吏士卒，动静一身，心既疑背，则计决而不动，动决而不禁。异口虚言，将无修容，卒无常试，发攻必衄。是谓

【今译】

军队沉稳镇静取得胜利，国家以集中统一取得胜利。力量分散，实力就会削弱；将领心存犹豫，士兵就会离心离德。实力削弱，军队前进、后退就没有气势，就会放走敌人而不能全歼。将领和士兵的动静，要像人的身体统一协调。将领狐疑不定，士兵离心离德，那么即使计划已确定，也不能采取行动；行动确定了，也无法给予约束。众说纷纭，满口虚言，将帅没有威严的仪容，士兵没有规范的举止，一旦出兵作战就必然受挫。这就叫一触即溃

# 5. Strategies of Attacking Cities

The military is victorious because of its steadfastness, and the state is victorious because of its unity. Divided strength leads to weakness and suspicions in the generals' minds lead to dissension and discord among the troops. Now when the strength is weak, the troops will not advance and withdraw boldly so that in pursuit they will let off the enemy instead of capturing him. Generals, officials, officers and soldiers should be a single body both in motion and at rest. But if the general's mind is already skeptical and the troops' morale is low, then even though a plan has been decided on they will not move. And when movement has been initiated they cannot be controlled. When empty talks are prevalent, and the general lacks stern measures,and the troops are not regularly trained, if they set out in action they will certainly be defeated.This is termed "Invalid and worn-out army" not worthy

【原文】

疾陵之兵，无足与斗。

将帅者，心也；群下者，支节也。其心动以诚，则支节必力；其心动以疑，则支节必背。夫将不心制，卒不节动，虽胜，幸胜也，非攻权也。

夫民无两畏也，畏我侮敌，畏敌侮我，见侮者败，立威者胜。凡将能其道者，吏畏其将也；吏畏其将者，民畏其吏也；民畏其吏者，敌畏其民也。是故知胜败之道者，必先知畏侮之权。

夫不爱说其心者，不我用也；不严畏其心者，

【今译】

的军队，这种军队是不堪一击的。

将领，就好比是心脏；士卒，就好比是四肢关节。决心坚定正确，四肢就必然坚强有力；决心迟疑不决，四肢就必然不听支配。将军不能像心脏那样果敢决断，士兵就不能像四肢那样灵活行动，即使取胜，也是侥幸而胜，不是靠谋略取胜。

士兵没有对敌我双方都心存畏惧的。畏惧自己的上级，就会藐视敌人；畏惧敌人，就会藐视自己的上级。被藐视的一方必败，树立威严的一方必胜。凡是将军能精通这个道理的，军吏就会畏惧他的将领；军吏畏惧他的将领，士兵就会畏惧他的军吏；士兵畏惧他的军吏，敌人就会畏惧我军的士兵。因此要懂得战争胜负的道理，必须先懂得畏惧与藐视的作用和策略。

不能用爱抚而使部下心悦诚服的，士兵就不会为我所用；不能以威严而使部下心悸畏服的，士兵

of a fighting force to contend with.

Now the commanding general is like the mind, and the troops are like the four limbs. When the decision in mind is sound, the limbs will be agile; when indecision arises in mind, the limbs will be hesitant. Now if the commanding general does not govern his mind the troops will not move as his limbs. Even though the troops gain victory, it will be one by chance, not through the sound strategies of attacking cities.

Now the people do not have two things they fear equally. Those who fear us despise the enemy, and those who fear the enemy despise us. The one who is despised will be defeated, and the one who is respected will be victorious. Generally when the generals excel at *Dao* (Right Way) the officials will fear their generals. When the officials fear their generals, the people will fear their officials. When the people fear their officials, the enemy will fear the people. Therefore those who understand the way to victory and defeat must first understand the tactics of the balancing of fear and contempt.

Now those who are not able to cause, with love and solicitude, their troops to cherish them and submit cannot be employed by me; those who are

【原文】

不我举也。爱在下顺，威在上立。爱故不二，威故不犯。故善将者，爱与威而已。

战不必胜，不可以言战；攻不必拔，不可以言攻。不然，虽刑赏不足信也。信在期前，事在未兆。故众已聚不虚散，兵已出不徒归，求敌若求亡子，击敌若救溺人。

分(囚)险者无战心，挑(佻)战者无全气，斗战

【今译】

就不会听我调遣。爱抚是为了使士兵顺从，树威是为了使将领获得尊敬。爱抚部下，士卒就会忠心不二；树立威信，士卒就不敢触犯将领的威严。所以所谓善于统兵，指的不过是爱抚部下和树立权威罢了。

作战没有必胜的把握，就不可轻言作战；攻城没有必克的把握，就不可轻言攻城。否则，即使施用刑罚、赏赐，也不足以取信全军了。要想使全军建立必胜的信念，就必须在战前做好一切准备工作；要想获得必胜的把握，就必须对将要发生的事情作出正确的判断和预测。因此军队一旦集中，就不会无缘无故地解散；军队一旦出动，就不会无功而返。追踪敌人要像寻找丢失的孩子那样志在必得，攻击敌人要像抢救溺水的人那样坚决果断。

陷入危险境地的军队，就没有战斗的决心；将领轻率出战，就不能保全高昂的士气；内部不团结

unable to cause, with awesomeness and severity, their troops to respect and fear them cannot direct the army for me. Love follows from below; awesomeness is established from above. Only by extending love to the troops will they not have divided minds. Only by establishing the generals' awesomeness will they not be violated. Therefore those who excel at employing the troops are adept in extending love and awesomeness. That is all.

If there is no assurance to win, one cannot lightly launch a battle. If there is no assurance to seize the cities, one cannot rashly attack them. Otherwise even though punishments and rewards are performed, no one will be convinced. Prestige must be established before the outbreak of war and preparations must be made before the first indications appear. Thus the masses once assembled will not disperse fruitlessly and the troops already set forth will not return empty-handed. One seeks the enemy as earnestly as he seeks his lost son, and one attacks the enemy as speedily as he rushes to save a drowning man.

When the troops are scattered to defend the different terrains, they will have no determination to fight. When the general indiscreetly

【原文】

者无胜兵。

凡挟义而战者，贵从我起；争私结怨，应不得已；怨结难起，待之贵后。故争必当待之，息必当备之。

兵有胜于朝廷，有胜于原野，有胜于市井。斗则失(得，服则失；)幸以不败，此不意彼惊惧而曲胜之也。曲胜，言非全也。非全胜者，无权名。

故明主战攻日，合鼓合〔角〕，节以兵刃，不求

【今译】

的军队，就不会有把握取得胜利。

凡是依仗正义进行的战争，贵在由我起兵；争夺私利而会结下怨恨的战争，应是出于不得已而应战；对于怨恨引起的战争，贵在等待时机、后发制人。所以兵争已起，必须等待战机；兵争停息，也须防备不测。

军队有的靠朝廷决策取胜，有的靠野战取胜，有的靠攻城取胜。敢于斗争才能有所收获，畏战屈服就会失败；侥幸而没打败仗，也是出人意料地由于敌人的惊慌恐惧而局部获胜。局部获胜，就不是完全的胜利。不是完全的胜利就谈不到权谋了。

所以英明的统帅在战争开始之际，能使全军行动服从统一的号令，武器装备整齐划一，不求强胜

challenges the enemy, the morale of all his troops will not be high. When the troops lack cohesion they will not be victorious.

Generally when the warfare is conducted on the basis of Righteousness, it is important to take a preemptive action. When the conflict is caused by personal animosities, military action will be taken only if it is unavoidable. When the confrontation is formed by hatred, one had better gain mastery by striking only after the enemy has struck. Hence if one takes military action he must wait for an opportune time and when the military action ceases one must keep alert.

Some armies gain victory in the court, some armies gain victory in the plains and fields, and some armies attain victory in the cities. Those who dare to fight will win and those who submit will be lost. If they are not defeated by fortune, it is at best a partial and lucky victory because of the unexpected scare and fear of the enemy. A partial and lucky victory is not a complete one, and this incomplete victory is without the general's authority.

Therefore on the day the enlightened sovereign launches an attack, he will make the drums and horns sounded orderly to command the troops in

【原文】

胜而胜也。兵有去备彻威而胜者，以其有法故也，有器用之早定也，其应敌也周，其总率也极。故五人而伍，十人而什，百人而卒，千人而率，万人而将，已用(周)已极。其朝死则朝代，暮死则暮代。权敌审将，而后举兵。

故凡集兵千里者旬日，百里者一日，必集敌境。

【今译】

利也会取得胜利了。军队也有故意解除戒备、表示怯弱而取胜的，那是因为主帅治军有方的缘故：武器装备早已安排停当，应敌计划早已严密周详，各级将领早已配备齐全。所以军队五人设一伍长，十人设一什长，百人设一卒长，千人设一率，万人设一将，战前已经筹划周密、编制完备。各级将领如有早上死去的，早上就有人接替；如有晚上死去的，晚上也有人接替。认真分析敌情，慎重选择将领，然后再出兵。

所以大凡集结部队，千里的路程期限为十天，百里的路程期限为一天，必须全部集中到敌国的边

a well-coordinated manner.Thus he will be victorious even though he does not deliberately seek victory. The army that abandons defense and abolishes awesomeness yet is able to win, because it has the best way to control the enemy. Furthermore, its victories are attributable to the earlier preparation of the weapons and equipment, and the detailed planning to meet the contingencies, and the well-established commanding system. Therefore the composition of the army's organization is as follows: For five men led by a squad leader, for ten men led by a lieutenant, for one hundred men led by a company captain, for one thousand men a battalion commander, and for ten thousand men a general.This military organization is already comprehensive and perfect. If a man dies in the morning another will replace him that morning, and if a man dies in the evening another will replace him that evening. Having analyzed the enemy and examined his generals, the enlightened sovereign can raise the army.

Thus generally when concentrating an army a thousand *li* away, ten days are required and when a hundred *li*, one day is required. The concentration area must be on the enemy's border.

【原文】

卒聚将至，深入其地，错绝其道。栖其大城大邑，使之登城逼危，男女数重，各逼地形，而攻要塞。据一城邑而数道绝，从而攻之。敌将帅不能信，吏卒不能和，刑有所不从者，则我败之矣。敌救未至，而一城已降。

津梁未发，要塞未修，城险未设，渠答未张，则虽有城无守矣。远堡未入，戍客未归，则虽有人

【今译】

境上。士兵会齐，将领到位，立即深入敌方腹地，切断交通要道，包围重要城市，迫使敌人困守孤城而陷于危险境地，把占领地的男女百姓组织起来，重重设防房屋配置，分别占据险要地形，向敌要塞发起攻击。占据一座城邑而能截断数条要道的，就要攻占这样的城邑。要使敌方的将领丧失威信，官兵失去和谐，虽然实施严刑峻法也不能迫使士兵服从命令，我们就可以击败敌人了。敌方援兵未到，城池已被攻下了。

渡口的桥梁没有拆毁，要塞的设施没有修筑完备，城市的关卡没有设立，各种障碍物没有设置，那么即使有城也无法可守了。外围的据点无人把守，

When the men are concentrated and the generals have arrived, they must penetrate to the enemy's depth and interdict his line of communications. They must encircle his big cities and big towns and ascend the walls to press the enemy into endangered positions. Furthermore several units of men and women will approach the difficult terrains and attack the strategic points. When a single city is occupied by the enemy and several roads connected to it are cut off, the troops should encircle and attack it immediately. When the enemy's commanding generals are not trusted by their subordinates and the officers and men are not in harmony, and the orders are not obeyed even though the punishments are imposed, we will be able to defeat the enemy. Before his reinforcements have arrived, a single one city will have already surrendered.

If the fords and bridges are not dismantled,the fortresses are not repaired, the dangerous points in the city walls are not fortified and iron caltrops are not set out, it will be defenseless even though the city is intact. If the remote strongholds are not manned and the border forces do not return, the fighting strength will be empty even though there are many men. If the

【原文】

无人矣。六畜未聚，五谷未收，财用未敛，则虽有资无资矣。夫城邑空虚而资尽者，我因其虚而攻之。《法》曰："独出独入，敌不接刃而致之。"此之谓也。

【今译】

外出的部队没有返回就位，那么即使有人也跟没人一样了。牲畜没有聚拢，庄稼没有收割，钱财没有敛取，那么即使有财物储备也跟没有财物储备一样了。对于这样防备空虚、物质财用匮乏的目标，我军应乘虚发起进攻。《兵法》上说："我军行动自由如入无人之境，敌人尚未及交锋就已被制服了。"指的就是这种情况啊。

six domesti animals have not yet assembled and the five grains not yet collected and properties not requisitioned, they will have no assets even though the resources are rich. Now the cities are on the brink of emptiness and the resources come to an end, we should take advantage of the weaknesses and attack them. The *Art of War* said: "They go out alone, they come in alone. Even before they encounter the enemy they have gained the victory." This is what is meant.

# 守权第六

【原文】

凡守者，进不郭围(圉)，退不亭障，以御战，非善者也。豪杰雄俊，坚甲利兵，劲弩强矢，尽在郭中，乃收窖廪，毁折而入保，令客气十百倍，而主之气不半焉。敌攻者，伤之甚也。然而世将弗能知。

夫守者，不失险者也。守法：城一丈，十人守

【今译】

凡是守城的军队，不能前出在城郭外围修筑防御设施，又不能退后在城边设置哨所和堡垒，来进行防御作战，这不是好的防守者。精锐部队、精良武器全部集中到城中，同时搜尽城外的所有粮食、财物，折毁城外的所有民居房屋，让所有的人都入守城中。这样就会使进攻者气焰嚣张，而使守军士气低落。敌军发动进攻，我军必然损失惨重。然而现在的将领不懂得这些道理。

进行防御作战，就不能放弃险要地形。守城的规则是：每一丈长的城墙，部署十人防守，勤杂炊

# 6. Strategies of Defending Cities

Generally when the defenders go forward and do not set up the positions within the outer walls of the cities and borderlands, and when they retreat and do not establish the watchtowers and barriers for the purpose of the defensive operations, they are not adept in defense. All the outstanding warriors and stalwarts, the sturdy armors and sharp weapons, and the powerful crossbows and strong arrows should be deployed within the outer walls of the cities. Meanwhile the grains stored in the granaries should be collected and houses outside outer walls dismantled so that the suburbanites may enter the cities to strengthen the defense. This will compel the attackers to make ten or one hundred times the effort, while the defenders will not make half of theirs. When the enemy attacks a lot of casualties will be inflicted upon him. However, the contemporary generals do not understand this.

Now the defenders should not abandon the

【原文】

之，工食不与焉。出者不守，守者不出。一而当十，十而当百，百而当千，千而当万。故为城郭者，非妄费于民聚土壤也，诚为守也。千丈之城，则万人之守，池深而广，城坚而厚，士民备，薪食给，弩坚矢强，矛戟称之，此守法也。

攻者不下十余万之众，其有必救之军者，则有必守之城；无必救之军者，则无必守之城。若彼

【今译】

事人员不算在内。出击的部队不负责防守，防守的部队不负责出击。这样一人可以抵敌十人，十人可以抵敌百人，百人可以抵敌千人，千人可以抵敌万人。所以建城筑郭，并非随意耗费民财民力堆积土壤，而要确实为防御做准备。有一千丈长的城墙，就要部署一万人来驻守。护城河要挖得又深又宽，城墙要筑得又坚固又厚实，守城的部队和百姓做好准备，粮草供应充足，各种武器装备优良合用，这才是防守的法则。

攻城的敌方军队不下十余万人，如有可靠的援军，就有固守的城市；没有可靠的援军，就没有固守的城市。如果城池坚固而援军可靠，那么全城的

key points in the difficult terrains. The method of defending cities is that each ten feet of the city walls should be defended by ten men — artisans and cooks being not included. Those who go out to fight do not defend the city and those who defend the city do not go out to fight. One is able to withstand ten, ten withstand one hundred, one hundred withstand one thousand, and one thousand withstand ten thousand. Therefore establishment of the fortified outer walls of the city does not waste the people's resources to pile up earth. It is truly for defense. If the walls are ten thousand feet long they should be defended by ten thousand men. The moats should be deep and wide and the walls solid and thick. The officers and men should be in combat readiness. The supplies of food and firewood should be adequate, and crossbows powerful and arrows strong, and both spears and halberds sharp. This is the method of defense.

When attackers are more than one hundred thousand and when the outside reinforcements of the defenders can certainly come to the rescue, it is a city that must be defended. When there are no outside reinforcements, it is not a city that must be defended. If the city walls are

【原文】

〔城〕坚而救诚，则愚夫蠢妇无不蔽城尽资血城者。期年之城，守余于攻者，救余于守者。若彼城坚而救不诚，则愚夫蠢妇无不守陴而泣下，此人之常情也。遂发其窖廪救抚，则亦不能止矣。必鼓其豪杰雄俊，坚甲利兵，劲弩强矢并于前，分历(幺麽)毁瘠者并于后。

十万之军顿于城下，救必开之，守必出之。据出要塞，但救其后，无绝其粮道，中外相应。此救

【今译】

男女老少就没有不为守城而竭尽财力以至血染城头的。能坚守一年的城市，是因为防御的力量大于进攻的力量，救援的力量又大于防御的力量。城市虽然坚固，援军却靠不住，那么全城的男女老少就没有不守着城墙垛口而哭泣的，这是人之常情啊。即使打开仓库发放粮物来安抚众心，也不能制止这种绝望的情绪。必须动员精壮军民，装备最精良的武器，全部配置在第一线，以老幼病弱者作为后援，方可坚守。

当十万敌军顿兵城下，救援部队一定要撕开包围圈，守城部队一定要主动出击。援军抢占险要地形，只支援守军的后方，使其粮道不致断绝，使城中与城外保持联系。这样似救非救、制造假象，就可改变敌人的部署，我则等待可乘之机。敌把精锐

solid and the reinforcements certain, the broad masses including foolish men,and silly women will devote to defense with all their resources and even shed blood on the walls. For a city to withstand the siege for one year, the strength of the defenders should exceed that of the attackers and the strength of the reinforcements exceed that of the defenders. If the walls are solid but the reinforcements are not certain, then the broad masses including the foolish men and silly women will defend the parapets, but they will sob. This is what is normal and natural in human emotion. Even though the granaries are opened and grains given to relieve and pacify them, their passion cannot be stopped. The valiant warriors and stalwarts with sturdy armors and sharp weapons, powerful crossbows and strong arrows must be deployed and encouraged to exert themselves to defend the city in the front and the young, weak and invalid to exert themselves to defend the city in the rear.

When the enemy's one hundred thousand forces encamp beneath the city walls, the outside reinforcements must break his encirclement and defenders set out to occupy the key points. The reinforcements will take action in the enemy's

【原文】

而示之不诚，则倒敌而待之者也。后其壮，前其老，彼敌无前，守不得而止矣。此守权之谓也。

【今译】

部署到后面（打援），把老弱部署到前面（围城），那么敌军前面的部队实力就削弱了，这时守军就不可消极等待（而应主动出击）了。这就是守城的谋略。

rear but not cut off his line of supplies. The troops outside and those inside the city will respond to each other. Thus this rescue will demonstrate as a half-hearted commitment, and the enemy will be puzzled to reverse his deployment so that we can wait for an opportunity to strike. He will put the strong and valiant force in the rear, and the old and weak one in the front. Then the enemy will not be able to advance nor be able to stop the defenders from breaking out. This is what is meant by "strategies of defending the cities".

# 十二陵第七

【原文】

威在于不变；惠在于因时；机在于应事；战在于治气；攻在于意表；守在于外饰；无过在于度数；无困在于豫备；慎在于畏小；智在于治大；除害在于敢断；得众在于下人。

悔在于任疑；孽在于屠戮；偏在于多私；不祥在于恶闻己过；不度在于竭民财；不明在于受间；

【今译】

树立威严在于不轻易变更决定；施人恩惠在于选择适当的时机；机谋在于适应事物的变化；作战在于鼓励士气；进攻在于出人意表；防守在于伪装掩饰；不犯错误在于考虑周密；不陷入困境在于预有准备；谨慎在于能警惕蛛丝马迹；明智在于能处理大事；清除祸害在于果敢决断；取得人心在于能尊重别人。

后悔在于狐疑不决；罪孽在于肆意杀戮；办事不公在于私心太重；不吉利在于不愿听到对自己的批评；入不敷出在于耗尽民财；不明事理在于受人离间；劳而无功在于轻举妄动；固执浅陋在于疏远

# 7. Twelve Disciplines

Awesomeness lies in making no change.Favor lies in an opportune time. Subtlety lies in adapting to the changing affairs. Military operations lie in boosting the morale. Attack lies in unexpected surprise. Defense lies in external camouflage. Not committing mistake lies in precaution. Not encountering difficulty lies in preparedness. Prudence lies in fearing any slight errors. Wisdom lies in controlling the large and key points. Eliminating harm lies in being decisive. Winning the masses lies in deferring to other men.

Regret lies in trusting what is doubtful. Evil lies in wanton slaughter. Prejudice lies in too much selfishness. Inauspicious events arise from detesting to hear about one's own errors.Extravagance lies in exhausting people's resources. Confusing right and wrong arises from discords sown by others. Working hard but to no avail arises from acting rashly. Established bad habits

【原文】

不实在于轻发；固陋在于离贤；祸在于好利；害在于亲小人；亡在于无所守；危在于无号令。

【今译】

了有才能的人；招祸在于贪财好利；受害在于亲近小人；丧失土地在于不设防；危险在于没有严明的号令。

lie in estrangement from the Worthy.Misfortune lies in coveting profits. Harm lies in drawing the mean persons near. Losing territory lies in lacking defense at any place. Danger lies in lacking strict and clear commands and orders.

# 武议第八

【原文】

凡兵，不攻无过之城，不杀无罪之人。夫杀人之父兄，利人之货财，臣妾人之子女，此皆盗也。故兵者，所以诛暴乱、禁不义也。兵之所加者，农不离其田业，贾不离其肆宅，士大夫不离其官府，由其武议在于一人，故兵不血刃而天下亲焉。

万乘农战，千乘救守，百乘事养。农战不外索

【今译】

凡是用兵，不应攻打无罪过的城市，不应杀害无罪过的人。残杀别人的父兄，掠夺别人的财富，奴役别人的子女，这些都是强盗的行为呵。所以战争，是用来讨伐暴乱，禁止不义行为的。军队所到之处，应使农民不离开其田地，商人不离开其店铺，士大夫不离开其官府，这是由于国君英明正确的军事决策，所以不经流血战斗就可以使天下归服。

拥有万乘兵车的大国，应致力于农耕征战；拥有千乘兵车的中等国家，应努力自守自救；拥有百乘兵车的小国，应实现生产自给。致力于农耕征战，可以不必寻求别国的权势；实行自守自救，就不必

# 8. Discussion on Conducting Warfare

Generally the army does not attack the cities that have not committed offense, nor kill the innocent people. Now those who have murdered others' fathers and elder brothers, those who have plundered others' properties, and those who have enslaved others' sons and daughters are brutal robbers. For this reason launching warfare is an act killing the brutal and stopping the unrighteous. Wherever the army encamps,the peasants do not leave their farms, the merchants do not leave their stores, and the high officials and nobles do not leave their offices. For the decision-making of the military operations depends upon the enlightened sovereign, the army is able to win victory without shedding blood and gain the support of All Under Heaven.

A large state of ten thousand *sheng* (the basic unit for chariots, one *sheng* consisting of one chariot, four horses, three armored horsemen and seventy-two infantrymen) is engaged in the

【原文】

权，救守不外索助，事养不外索资。

夫出不足战、入不足守者，治之以市。市者，所以外(给)战守也。万乘无千乘之助，必有百乘之市。

凡诛赏者，所以明武也。杀一人而三军震者，杀之；杀一人而万人喜者，赏之。杀之贵大，赏之

【今译】

乞求别国的援助；实现生产自给，就不必向别国乞讨借债。

如果国家的财政既不足以支撑进攻作战，又不足以应付防御作战，那就应该加强对市场的管理。市场的税收是可以用来支付战争费用的重要财源。万乘之国宁可没有千乘之国的援助，也必须具有百乘之国那样的市场收入。

凡使用刑罚，都是为树立军威的。诛杀一人而能使三军震动的，就杀掉他；诛杀一人而能使万人振奋的，就杀掉他。杀人关键在于杀掉有罪的大人

combination of farm cultivation and military operations. A medium state of one thousand *sheng* is engaged in self-aid and self-defense operations. A small state of one hundred *sheng* is engaged in the self-reliance activities. The state engaged in the combination of farm cultivation and military operations will not seek outside influence. The state engaged in self-aid and self-defense will not seek outside assistance. And the state engaged in self-reliance activities will not seek loans from outside. Now when the resources of a state are not adequate to support the offensive operations, nor maintain the defensive operations, the solution is to improve the control of the market and trade. It is the market that can provide the financial support to maintain both offensive and defensive operations. The state of ten thousand *sheng* without assistance from the state of one thousand *sheng* must develop the market as the state of one hundred *sheng* does.

Generally the executions are performed for the purpose of making military awesomeness conspicuous. If you kill one man and the Three Armies are shocked, kill him. If you reward one man and ten thousand men are pleased, reward him. Death penalty tends to punish the great

【原文】

贵小。当杀而虽贵重必杀之，是刑上究也；赏及牛童马圉者，是赏下流也。夫能刑上究、赏下流，此将之武也，故人主重将。

夫将，提鼓挥枹，临难决战，接兵角刃。鼓之而当，则赏功立名；鼓之而不当，则身死国亡。是存亡安危，在于枹端，奈何无重将也！夫提鼓挥枹，接兵角刃，君以武事成功者，臣以为非难也。

【今译】

物，赏赐关键在于赏赐有功的小人物。应该杀的，即使身份高贵、地位重要，也一定要杀掉，这就是刑罚能够制裁上层人物；赏赐应该使放牛养马的人也有份，这就是奖赏包括了下层人物。能做到对有罪的大人物绳之以法，对有功的小人物给予奖励，这才能体现出将领的威严。所以，国君很重视将领的作用。

将领击鼓发令，在危难之际与敌进行决战。在两军兵刃相交之时，将领指挥得当，就能立功成名；指挥失误，就会身死国灭。因此个人与国家的生死安危，全在于将领指挥得是否正确，怎么能不重视将领的作用呢！将领上阵指挥，双方展开厮杀，君主以武力成就大功，我认为这并不是一件难事。

personages and reward tends to encourage the unimportant persons. If someone should be killed, then even though his position is noble and important, he must be executed. This is the penalty to be performed to the top. When rewards are bestowed on cowherds and stable boys, this is award down to the lowest. Now punishments can be performed up to the top and rewards bestowed down to the lowest. This is the general's awesome power. Therefore the sovereign attaches great importance to generals.

Now the general takes up drum and brandishes drumsticks, he commands his army to fight a decisive battle at the critical juncture. In the hand-to-hand combat with clashing blades, if the general makes proper drum beating to command and win victory, he will be rewarded for his achievements and his fame will be established. If not, he will die and the state will perish. For this reason survival and extinction, safety and danger all lie at the end of drumsticks!How can one not value the generals? Now when his general carries drum and wields drumsticks to command the hand-to-hand combat with clashing blades, the sovereign will make achievements by the military operations. I do not think this is difficult.

【原文】

古人曰：“无蒙冲而攻，无渠答而守，是为无善之军。”视无见，听无闻，由国无市也。夫市也者，百货之官也。市贱卖贵，以限士人。人食粟一斗，马食粟(菽)三斗，人有饥色，马有瘠形，何也？市所出，而官无主也。夫提天下之节制，而无百货之官，无谓其能战也。起兵，直使甲胄生虮者，必为吾所效用也。鸷鸟逐雀，有袭人之怀、入人之室

【今译】

古人说：“没有蒙冲而攻城，没有铁蒺藜而守城，就不是善攻善守的军队。”（部队缺乏必要的装备，就如同）人眼不见物、耳不闻声，这都是由于国家没有管理好市场的缘故。所谓市场，是百货流通、集散的地方。国家应该在物价便宜的时候买进，在物价昂贵的时候卖出，以防止商人操纵物价、牟取暴利。每人每天不过吃一斗口粮，每匹马每天也不过吃三斗豆料，但人却饿得面黄饥瘦，马也饿得瘦骨嶙峋，这是什么缘故呢？是因为市场有利润，官府却没有管理好啊。统领着一国的军队，却没有设立管理市场流通的机构，就不能保证其军队真有战斗力。出征作战，直到士兵的铠甲头盔中都生出了虱子，也必定要令其听从我的指挥。这就像被猛禽追逐的小鸟，有时撞入人的怀中，有时钻进人家的房子里，这并不是出于它的本性，而是后面有令它恐惧的东西啊。

The ancients said: "Attacking without assault vehicles, defending without barriers such as the iron caltrops, this is what is meant by an army that does not have excellent and complete equipment." And without the equipment, men will see nothing with their eyes and hear nothing with their ears. This is because there is no control of the market. Now for market is a place to control the general merchandise, the state should buy in goods when the price is low and sell out when it is high so as to restrict the nobles and merchants to seek exorbitant profits. People eat one *dou* (one *dou* is equal to 1,870 milliliters) of grain and horses eat three *dou* of beans, so why is it the people have a famished look and the horses have sunken shape? The markets have goods to deliver, but the office lacks a controller. Now if one commands the army under Heaven but does not control the general merchandise, it cannot be referred to as "being able to conduct military operations." As the troops have been raised and retained in service till their armors and helmets are spawned with lice, they will be certain to be the men whom we can employ. This is like a bird of prey chasing a sparrow that flies

【原文】

者，非出生，后有惮也。

太公望年七十，屠牛朝歌，卖食盟津，过七年（十）余而主不听，人人之谓狂夫也。及遇文王，则提三万之众，一战而天下定。非武议，安得此合也。故曰："良马有策，远道可致；贤士有合，大道可明。"

武王伐纣，师渡盟津，右旄左钺，死士三百，战士三万。纣之陈亿万，飞廉、恶来，身先戟斧，陈开百里。武王不罢士民，兵不血刃，而〔克〕商

【今译】

姜太公七十岁时，在朝歌宰牛，在孟津卖食物。过了七十岁，君主还是不任用他，人人都说他是疯子。等到他遇到周文王受到了重用，率领三万军队，只经一次决战就平定了天下。如果没有国君的正确决策，姜太公哪会有这样的机会呢？所以说："好马得鞭策，才能至远方；贤人遇明君，高见可彰明。"

周武王讨伐商纣王，率军队渡过孟津，右手执白旄，左手举黄钺，有敢死之士三百人，士兵共三万人。商纣王陈兵数十万，将领飞廉、恶来身先士卒，不避戟斧，军阵绵延有数百里之长。周武王没

into somebody's bosom or enters somebody's room. This is not because the sparrow is willing to cast away its life, but because there is something to fear in its back.

When Tai Gong was seventy years old, he butchered cattle in Chao Ge and peddled food in Meng Jin. When he was more than seventy years old, the sovereign did not yet listen to him, and the people called him a mad fellow. Later, he met King Wen and then he commanded a host of thirty thousand men and with one battle to settle down All Under Heaven. Without the king's military strategies how could he gain such an opportunity? Therefore it is said: 'If a good horse has a whip, a distant road can be traversed. If a worthy man has an opportunity, the great doctrine of governance can be illuminated.'

When King Wu attacked King Zhou and his army forded the Yellow River at Meng Jin, he held a pennant in his right hand and an axe of punishment in his left hand. There were three hundred warriors committed to die and thirty thousand fighting men under his command. King Zhou's formations composed of several hundred thousand men with Fei Lian and E Lai carrying spear and axe in forefront, and their frontline

【原文】

诛纣，无祥异也，人事修不修而然也。今世将考孤虚，占城(咸)池，合龟兆，视吉凶，观星辰风云之变，欲以成胜立功，臣以为难。

夫将者，上不制于天，下不制于地，中不制于人。故兵者，凶器也；争者，逆德也；将者，死官也。故不得已而用之。无天于上，无地于下，无主

【今译】

有使士兵百姓疲劳，也没有让武器沾上鲜血，就战胜了敌军，诛杀了纣王，这与发生祥瑞灾异无关，只是由于人事的善与不善造成的。现在的将领只知道考究时辰，判定方位，对照龟甲，判断凶吉，观察星辰风云的变化，想借此获得胜利建立功名，臣下以为那是难以如愿的。

统率军队的将领，上不受制于天，下不受制于地，中不受制于人。武器，是杀人的凶器；战争，是违背道德的行为；将领，是掌握生杀的官吏。所以只有在不得已的时候才能使用。（一旦使用）就应该上不顾忌天，下不顾忌地，后不顾忌国君，前不顾忌敌人。将领一人全权统率军队，就会像虎狼

extended one hundred li. King Wu did not tire out his officers and men. He won victory without shedding blood and conquered the Shang Dynasty and killed King Zhou. There was nothing auspicious nor abnormal, it was merely something to do with the question of whether personnel affairs could be best handled or not. Now the contemporary generals investigate the ominous and propitious bearings, divine about Yan Chi, interpret full and disastrous days in accord with tortoise augury, look for the auspicious and ominous, observe the changes of planets, constellations and winds — wanting to thereby win the battle and their honor. I think this is very difficult.

Generally a general is not controlled by Heaven above, nor governed by Earth below,nor controlled by men in the middle. Thus weapons are evil tools. Conflict is contrary to virtue. A general is the death official who holds power over men's life. Hence all these can be employed only when it is unavoidable. When they are employed, there will be no Heaven above, no Earth below, no sovereign in rear, and no enemy in front. When the troops are as cohesive as a man, they will be as violent as wolves and

【原文】

于后，无敌于前。一人之兵，如狼如虎，如风如雨，如雷如霆，震震冥冥，天下皆惊。

胜兵似水。夫水，至柔弱者也，然所触，丘陵必为之崩。无异也，性专而触诚也。今以莫邪之利，犀兕之坚，三军之众，有所奇正，则天下莫当其战矣。故曰：举贤用能，不时日而事利；明法审令，不卜筮而获吉；贵功养劳，不祷祠而得福。又曰：天时不如地利，地利不如人和。古之圣人，谨人事

【今译】

一样凶猛，像暴风雨一样迅疾，像雷霆一样突然，声威赫赫，神秘莫测，天下的人都为之震惊。

打胜仗的军队就像流水一样。水是最柔弱的东西，但它所冲击的地方，山陵也会崩塌。这没有别的原因，只是由于水性专一而冲击持久。如今凭借着莫邪般锋利的兵器，使用犀牛皮革制成的坚硬甲衣，三军将士运用奇正多变的谋略，那么普天之下就无人能抵挡它的进攻了。所以说：推举贤才任用能人，不择良辰吉日也会事事顺利；健全法制严明号令，不用占卜问卦也会事事吉祥；尊崇有功、勤劳之人，不用祭祀祈祷也会得到神的保佑。又说：天象时辰不如地理条件重要，地理条件不如人事和

tigers,as speedy as wind and rain, and as overwhelming as thunder and lightning. It is so shocking and darkening that All Under Heaven is surprised.

The victorious army is like water. Now water is very soft and weak, but when it collides with hills, the hills will be certain to collapse for no other reason than its nature is concentrated and its attack is totally committed. Now if weapons are sharp as the famous Mo Ye swords and armors are as tough as rhinoceros hide, the host of the Three Armies with the unorthodox and orthodox tactics will be invincible in military operations. Therefore it is said: "Recommend the Worthy and appoint the capable. Do not choose the auspicious day and the affairs can be successful. Laws and regulations must be clear, and orders and commands prudent. Do not divine with the tortoise shell and the affairs can be auspicious. Respect those who have made achievements and well treat those who have worked hard. Do not make prayer and fortune can be obtained." It is also said that seasons of Heaven were not as good as Advantages of Earth, and Advantages of Earth were not as good as human harmony. Anciently the Sages honored the hu-

【原文】

而已。

吴起与秦战，舍不平陇亩，朴樕盖之，以蔽霜露。如此何也？不自高人故也。乞人之死不索尊，竭人之力不责礼。故古者，甲胄之士不拜，示人无己烦也。夫烦人而欲乞其死、竭其力，自古至今未尝闻矣。

将受命之日忘其家，张军宿野忘其亲，援枹而鼓忘其身。吴起临战，左右进剑。起曰："将专主

【今译】

睦重要。古代的圣贤，只是能谨慎处理好人事罢了。

吴起领兵与秦国作战，就睡在未加平整的田埂上，只用小树枝来遮蔽霜露。为什么要这样做呢？为的是表示不自以为高人一等。要求部下献身就不必苛求对自己毕恭毕敬，要求部下尽力就不必讲究繁文缛节。所以古时候身穿盔甲的将士不行跪拜礼，就是向人表示不必用繁琐的礼节来增添麻烦。用礼节来麻烦别人而又要求人家为你舍生忘死、竭尽全力，这样的事从古至今也不曾听说过。

将领从接受国君命令之日起就要忘记自己的家室，出兵启程宿营野外就要忘记自己的双亲，挥槌击鼓指挥作战时就要忘记自己的安危。吴起在临战之前，手下人送上宝剑。吴起说："将领的专职是发号施令。在危急关头作出决策，指挥军队作战，

man effort. That is all.

When Wu Zi fought Qin in battle, he encamped on the rugged farmland without flattening it and covered with saplings at the top to resist frost and dew. Why did he act like this? This is because he did not think highly of himself. If you beg men to die, you should not ask them to pay much respect to you. If you want men to exert themselves to do something you should not be overcritical about ritual. Therefore, anciently the officers wearing armors and helmets did not bow, showing people that one should not be troubled by any unnecessary and over-elaborate formalities. Now to annoy the people and yet demand them to die or exhaust their strength, from ancient times until today, has never been heard of.

On the day a commanding general is mandated, he must forget his family. When the troops set forth and encamp in the field, he must forget his parents. When he wields the drumsticks to beat the drum, he must forget himself. When Wu Zi approached the time for battle, his aides offered their swords. Wu Zi said: "A commanding general is totally committed to standards and drums to command. At the juncture of approach-

【原文】

旗鼓尔。临难决疑，挥兵指刃，此将事也。一剑之任，非将事也。”三军成行，一舍而后，成三舍。三舍之余，如决川源。望敌在前，因其所长而用之，敌白者垩之，赤者赭之。

吴起与秦战，未合，一夫不胜其勇，前获双首而还。吴起立斩之。军吏谏曰：“此材士也，不可斩。”起曰：“材士则是矣，非吾令也。”斩之。

【今译】

这才是将领的事。至于手拿利剑与敌格斗，那可不是将领的事。”三军整队行军，日行三十里，三天走九十里。九十里之后，部队就要像决堤的江河一样势不可挡。望见敌军在前方，要根据其特点而采取相应的对策。如果敌人用白色标记，我军也用白色标记（来迷惑敌人）；如果敌人用红色标记，我军也用红色标记（来欺骗敌人）。

吴起率军与秦国作战，两军尚未交锋，有一骁勇之士控制不住自己的杀敌情绪，径自冲向前去，斩获两个敌军的首级后归阵。吴起立即下令将其斩首。军吏劝说道：“这是勇士啊，不能杀。”吴起说：“勇士倒是勇士，但没有遵守我的命令。”还是杀了他。

ing hardships, it is the duty of a general to determine the doubtful things, to command the troops and to direct the weapons — bearing a single sword, that is not a general's affair."

When the Three Armies were marching in columns, they marched thirty *li* per day and ninety *li* in three days. After ninety *li* was traversed the momentum of the marching was irresistible like rushing water unblocked from the source of a river. Seeing the enemy deployed in front, they took advantage of the enemy's characteristics. When the enemy's markings were white, they used whiteness. When his markings were red, they used redness.

Wu Zi fought Qin in battle. Before contact one man could not resist the temptation to exhibit his courage and went forth to attack and returned with two enemy's heads. Wu Zi wanted to execute him immediately. An army commander remonstrated, saying: "This is a skilled warrior, you should not execute him.' Wu Zi said: 'Of course, he is a skilled warrior, but he did not follow my order." Then he was executed.

# 将理第九

【原文】

凡将，理官也，万物之主也，不私于一人。夫能无移(私)于一人，故万物至而制之，万物至而命之。

君子不救囚于五步之外；虽钩矢射之，弗追也。故善审囚之情，不待箠楚，而囚之情可毕矣。笞人之背，灼人之胁，束人之指，而讯囚之情，虽国士，有不胜其酷而自诬矣。

【今译】

凡是将领，又都是执法者，各种军务都由他来掌管，不对任何人徇私情。能做到不对任何人徇私情，所以各种军务到他那里都能得到公正的处理，各种军务到他那里都能听其安排。

君子不会不经当面审讯而随便赦免囚犯；（同时又能像齐桓公对待管仲那样）即使有发箭射中身上带钩的怨仇，也不予追究。所以善于审案的人，不必等待动用刑具，犯人的案情就可全部掌握了。鞭打犯人的脊背、烧灼犯人的两肋、捆夹犯人的手指，以此来逼问犯人的口供，即使英雄好汉也会经不住这样的酷刑，而被屈打成招的。

# 9. The General as a Law Official

Generally a general is an officer of the law. He is an arbitrator in the multitude of cases and does not practice favoritism for anyone.Since he is not partial to anyone, he is able to control the numerous cases and handle them correctly.

A man of noble character will make investigation in the closest contact with the prisoner not beyond a five-pace distance.Even though there is an old personal grudge that someone has hit his hooked belt with an arrow,he will not look into it. Therefore one who excels at trial of prisoners will not rely on the flogging with thorn branches and can obtain a complete understanding of the prisoners 'situations. If you whip a person 's back, brand his ribs, and pinch his fingers in order to investigate a criminal case,even though he is a strong warrior he cannot bear this cruelty but will self-confess to false charges under torture.

There is a saying in our age: "Those who have

【原文】

今世谚云：“千金不死，百金不刑。”试听臣之言、行臣之术，虽有尧舜之智，不能开一言；虽有万金，不能用一铢。

今夫决狱，小圄不下十数，中圄不下百数，大圄不下千数。十人联百人之事，百人联千人之事，千人联万人之事。所联之者，亲戚兄弟也，其次婚姻也，其次知识故人也。是农无不离其田业，贾无不离其肆宅，士大夫无不离官府。如此关联良民，

【今译】

如今世上有谚语说：“千金可以免死，百金可以免刑。”如果能听取我的意见，实行我的办法，即使有尧舜那样的智慧，也无法说上一句通融的话；即使有家财万贯，也无法用上一铢钱来行贿。

如今审理案件，小的监狱不下几十人，中等监狱不下几百人，大的监狱不下几千人。十个人的事牵连上百人，百人的事牵连上千人，千人的事牵连上万人。所牵连的人，首先是父母兄弟，其次是婚姻亲家，再次是熟人朋友。这样一来，务农的被迫离开田地，经商的被迫离开店铺，做官的被迫离开官府，（都被各种各样的案件牵连进去了）。如此牵

one thousand pieces of gold but committed severe crimes can get rid of death penalty, and those who have one hundred pieces of gold but committed ordinary crimes can get rid of corporeal punishments." I beg you to listen to my advice and put my technique in practice,then even a person with the wisdom of Yao or Shun will not be able to speak a word for himself, nor one with one thousand pieces of gold be able to use a bit of gold to bribe for escaping punishments.

Today those in prison waiting for judgment are numerous. In small jails there are no less than several tens; in medium-sized jails no less than several hundred, and in large prisons no less than several thousand. Ten men connect with one hundred men in their affairs, one hundred men drag in one thousand, and one thousand men entangle ten thousand. Those who are involved in affairs are parents and brothers;next the relatives by marriage, and next those who are acquaintances and old friends. Thus all the peasants leave their farms, all the merchants depart from their stores, and all the high officials and nobles leave their offices. To such an extent the good people have all been entangled, and it is the true picture of the imprisonments. The *Art of*

**【原文】**

皆囚之情也。《兵法》曰："十万之师出，日费千金。"今良民十万而联于囚(囹)圄，上不能省，臣以为危也。

**【今译】**

涉无辜，就是目前狱中的真实情况啊。《兵法》上说："十万人的军队出征，一天的费用需要千金。"如今有十万无辜的百姓被牵连入狱，而君主却不能明察，我认为这是很危险的。

*War* said: "When an army of one hundred thousand men goes forth, its daily expense is as tremendous as one thousand pieces of gold." Now when one hundred thousand good people are involved and imprisoned, yet the sovereign is not able to perceive the situation — I think it is dangerous.

# 原官第十

【原文】

官者，事之所主，为治之本也。制者，职分四民，治之分也。贵爵富禄，必称，尊卑之体也。好善罚恶，正比法，会计民之具也。均井地〔分〕，节赋敛，取与之度也。程工人，备器用，匠工之功也。

【今译】

设置官员，作为各种事务的主宰，是治理国家的根本。建立官制，按照职掌分管士、农、工、商四类人，是治国分工的需要。显贵的爵位、丰厚的俸禄，必须与官位相称，这是区别尊贵卑贱的基础。奖励善良惩罚邪恶，整顿考察人口财产和官吏政绩的“比法”，这是正确考核官员能力的凭据。土地分配平均合理，征收赋税有所节制，这是经济收支的准则。规定工人的生产定额，准备好各种生产用具，这是管理工匠的官员的职责。划分地域，设立关卡，

# 10. The Source of Offices

Bureaucratic offices are means to control affairs and the foundation of governance. Bureaucratic institution divides the people into four groups by profession, and this division of professions is made for the purpose of governance. Honor, rank, fortune and salaries must be appropriately determined for they are the embodiment of nobility and humbleness. The good must be encouraged, and the evil punished. The statistic regulations must be rectified to improve the implements of accounting people's properties. The equitable distribution of land must be made to the people, and taxation must be readjusted and reduced so that taking from and giving to the people will be in an appropriate manner. The production quota of artisans must be fixed and the implements prepared in order to improve the efficiency of artisans. Defense area must be divided and strategic points manned in order to eliminate oddities and stop licentiousness.

【原文】

分地塞要，殄怪禁淫之事也。

守法稽断，臣下之节也。明法稽验，主上之操也。明主守，等轻重，臣主之权也。明赏赉，严诛责，止奸之术也。审开塞，守一道，为政之要也。下达上通，至聪之听也。知国有无之数，用其仂也。知彼弱者，强之体也。知彼动者，静之决也。官分文武，惟王之二术也。

俎豆同制，天子之会也。游说开(间)谍无自入，

【今译】

这是禁绝怪异奢侈物品流通买卖的措施。

恪守法度，调查决断，是下面臣子的职责。申明法度，考察检验，是上面君主的职责。明确各个部门主管的事务，衡量各种事情的轻重缓急，这是君主和臣子各司其职的关键。赏赐要公开，处罚要严厉，这是制止奸邪恶行的有效手段。弄清如何兴利除弊，坚持既定的耕战之道，这是治理国家的要务。上情下达，下情上通，就可使上下信息的交流达到最畅通的程度。掌握国家的财政情况，就可只用其多余的部分（而避免超支）。知道对方存在的弱点，是我方得以强大的基础。知道对方动荡的原因，是我方得以保持安定的重要因素。官职划分文武，是王者治国的两种手段。

俎、豆等礼器统一规格，这是天子朝会诸侯的要求。说客、间谍无法打入，这是端正言论的办法。

Abiding by the laws and investigating affairs and making decisions are the responsibilities of the subordinates.

Ordaining laws and supervising their enforcement are functions of the sovereign. Making duties clear on their posts and differentiating between what is important and what is unimportant in state affairs are the roles of ministers and the sovereign. Making rewards impartial and punishments strict are methods to stop evil. Examining ways to promote what is beneficial and prohibit what is harmful and adhering to the the unique principle of combination of agriculture and warfare are essentials to government. When information from below reaches to high and information from high penetrates the low, the unimpeded exchange of information will be the best way to find out about the overall situations. By knowing the financial status of the state, you can use the surplus. Knowing the weaknesses of others is the basis on which the strength can be built up. Knowing the cause of others' disturbance is the way to calm the turbulence. Offices are divided into the civil and the military, and only the sovereign exercises power over both.

The ceremonial utensils are all registered

【原文】

正议之术也。诸侯有谨天子之礼，君民继世，承王之命也。更造(号)易常，违王明德，故礼得以伐也。

官无事治，上无庆赏，民无狱讼，国无商贾，何王之至！明举上达，在王垂听也。

【今译】

诸侯要谨守天子规定的礼法，倘若有立为国君、父死子继的，都必须接受周王的册封。更换名号，改变常法，是违背了周王的德政，所以按照礼法可以对其进行讨伐。

官府无事可办，国君不用奖赏，百姓没有要打的官司，国内无（外来的）商贩，王政实行得何等尽善尽美啊！我将这些明智的措施陈述给大王，就看大王是否肯垂听了。

for the Son of Heaven's convocation. When roving persuaders and spies find no way to enter, this is the method to rectify speeches and opinions. The feudal states have honored the rites set forth by the Son of Heaven, and rulers and their people — generation after generation — continue to acknowledge the king's mandate to rule. If someone changes the ritual status and traditional institution in contradiction with the king's illustrious Virtue, the king can in the name of rites attack him.

Officials without affairs to administer, the sovereign without ranks and rewards to bestow, the people without criminal lawsuits to present, and the state without merchants and traders — how perfect the king's rule! What I have so clearly suggested should be heeded by Your Majesty.

# 治本第十一

【原文】

凡治人者何？曰：非五谷无以充腹，非丝麻无以盖形，故充腹有粒，盖形有缕。

夫在芸耨，妻在机杼，民无二事，则有储蓄。夫无雕文刻镂之事，女无绣饰纂组之作。木器液，金器腥。圣人饮于土，食于土，故埏埴以为器，天下无费。

今也，金木之性不寒而衣绣饰，马牛之性食草饮水而给菽粟。是治失其本，而宜设之制也。春夏

【今译】

治理百姓靠什么呢？回答是：没有五谷杂粮就不能填饱肚子，没有丝帛麻布就不能遮盖身体，所以充饥要有粮食，遮体要有布帛。

丈夫从事耕种，妻子从事纺织，百姓不做别的事，就会有所积蓄。男子没有绘画雕琢的差事，女子没有刺绣织锦的劳役。木制器皿容易渗漏，金属器皿会有腥气。古时圣人因为喝的水来自土中，吃的粮食也来自土中，所以将粘土放到模子里做出各种器皿，天下便没有什么浪费。

如今，金属和木质器皿本性是不怕冷的，却给它们披裹上刺绣锦缎；牛马的本性是吃草喝水，却要喂它大豆稻谷。这样治国就丧失了立国的根本，应该为此建立必要的制度。春夏季节男子都到田里

# 11. Foundation of Administration

Generally what is the means to administer people? The reply is that without the five grains you have nothing to fill their stomachs; without silk and hemp, nothing to cover their bodies. Therefore when stomachs are filled with grains and bodies covered with textile, and when husbands engage in farming and wives in weaving without doing other jobs, there will be goods accumulated in the storehouses.

Men should not engrave nor make decorative carving, and women should not embroider nor do decorative stitching. Wooden utensils tend to have water infiltrated and metal vessels tend to have smelling of fish. The Sages drink from earthen cups and eat from earthen bowls.Since the earthenware is made of molded clay,there will be no waste under Heaven.

At present people think the nature of metal and wood can resist cold and yet decorative embroideries are put on the metal and wooden

【原文】

夫出于南亩，秋冬女练布帛，则民不困。今短褐不蔽形，糟糠不充腹，失其治也。古者，土无肥硗，人无勤惰，古人何得，而今人何失邪？耕有不终亩，织有日断机，而奈何寒饥！盖古治之行，今治之止也。

夫谓治者，使民无私也。民无私，则天下为一

【今译】

耕种，秋冬季节女子都在家里纺织，那么百姓就不会贫困了。现在百姓穿麻布短衣遮不住身体，吃酒糟谷糠填不饱肚子，是因为丧失了治国的根本。古时候，土地的肥沃与贫瘠（与今天比）没有什么不同，百姓的勤勉和懒惰（与今天比）也没有什么两样，但古人为什么丰衣足食，而今人为什么缺吃少穿呢？如今耕田的不能完成其耕作，织布的时常要停下其织机，这怎么能应付寒冷和饥饿！这都是因为古时治国之本得以实行，今天治国之本却得不到实行。

治国之道，是要使百姓没有私心；没有私心，天下就成为一家，就不会只为个人的小家去耕作织

articles. The nature of horse and cattle is to eat grass and drink water and yet beans and grains are given to feed them. This is administering which has lost its foundation, and it would be appropriate to formulate regulations to control it. When men go out to plow farmland in spring and summer, and women dye and weave cloth and silk in autumn and winter, the people will not be in poverty. Now short clothes do not cover their bodies nor bad foodstuffs fill their stomachs. This is lacking in the foundation of administration. Anciently fertility and sterility of land were not different from those of today's land, and diligence and laziness of the ancient men were not different from those of today's men. Why the ancients attained ample food and clothes? Why people are lacking in food and clothes at present? The men do not finish their plowing in fields and women frequently stop their shuttles, so how could they not suffer from cold and hunger? This is because the foundation of administration in antiquity was put in practice and that of the present administration is not put in practice.

Now it is said that good administration is to cause people to have no selfish interests. When

【原文】

家，而无私耕私织。共寒其寒，共饥其饥。故如有子十人，不加一饭；有子一人，不损一饭。焉有喧呼酖酒以败善类乎！民相轻佻，则欲心与(兴)，争夺之患起矣。横生于一夫，则民私饭有储食，私用有储财。民一犯禁，而拘以刑治，乌有以为人上也。善政执其制，使民无私。为下不敢私，则无为非者矣。反本缘理，出乎一道，则欲心去，争夺止，图

【今译】

布。大家都把别人的寒冷当做自己的寒冷，把别人的饥饿当做自己的饥饿。所以即使一家有十个孩子，也不会增加其父母一口饭的负担；一家只有一个孩子，也不会减少其父母一口饭的负担。这样人们哪会还有吵吵嚷嚷、酗酒闹事、败坏良家子弟的事呢！百姓之间轻薄放浪，贪欲之心就会萌生，你争我夺的祸乱就由此而起。君主一人违背了这种无私原则，那么百姓也会为自家有饭吃而储备粮食，为自家有钱用而储备财物。百姓一旦为私利而触犯刑律，就加以拘捕用刑法治罪，这哪里还有在人之上做君主的资格。清明的政治是要采取措施，使百姓消除私心。百姓不敢追逐私利，那么就没有为非作歹的了。使百姓返归耕织的本业，遵循无私的法则，国家坚持这样一贯的治国之道，百姓的贪欲心就会除去，争夺就会停止，监狱就会空闲，乡间民家粮食充足，

people have no selfish interests, All Under Heaven will become a family. Without private plowing and private weaving, they will suffer from cold together and experience hunger together. Thus if the parents have ten sons they will not have the expense of even an extra bowl of rice, while if they have one son their expenses will not be reduced by even one bowl. How could these families indulge in boisterous and drunken feasts to corrupt public morals? If people are frivolous and unrestrained, their selfish desire will expand and the misfortune of competition for seizing things will arise. If perversity begins with one ruler, people will store food for their private meals and accumulate fortune for their private expenditure. If people commit one single offense, you arrest and punish them for controlling them, how is one acting as the ruler of the people?

Those who are adept in governing adhere to regulations and cause people not to be selfish. When people below have no selfish interests, they will not commit evil. Returning to the foundation of plowing and weaving, and following the reason of unselfishness, people will get rid of their selfish desires. Then competition for seizing

【原文】

囷空，野充粟多，安民怀远，外无天下之难，内无暴乱之事，治之至也。

苍苍之天，莫知其极。帝王之君，谁为法则？往事不可及，来世不可待，求己者也。

所谓天子者四焉，一曰神明，二曰垂光，三曰洪叙，四曰无敌。此天子之事也。

野物不为牺牲，杂学不为通儒。

今说者曰："百里之海，不能饮一夫；三尺之泉，足以止三军渴。"臣谓"欲生于无度，邪生于无

【今译】

人民安居乐业，远方的人民也来归顺，外面没有敌国的入侵，内部没有暴乱之事发生，国家的治理就达到了最完美的境界了。

苍芒的天空，无法知道它的终极。创立帝王之业的君主，谁可以作为效法的楷模？过去的时代不可追及，未来的时代不可等待，只有要求自己去努力创造。

能够称得上天子的，有四个标准：一是神圣英明，智慧超群；二是垂示光华，普降恩泽；三是上下有序，赏罚严明；四是英武果敢，天下无敌。这是天子应该做到的事。

野外的动物不可作为祭祀的供品，庞杂的学问不能算是博学通儒。

现在游说的人说："百里宽的大海，不够一个贪得无厌的人喝；三尺深的小泉，却足够三军上下解除干渴。"我认为私欲产生于没有节制，邪恶产生于没有禁令。治国的最高境界是随心所欲，无为而

things will be stopped, prisons will be empty and fields full and grains ample. People will live in peace and the distant tribes will show their allegiance. When there is no external disaster under Heaven nor rebellious affair at home, it is the perfection of administration.

The blue sky — no one knows its extremity! Of the ancient Five Emperors and Three Kings who is the example we should follow? The past ages cannot be regained and the future ages cannot be awaited. Seek them in yourself.

There are four qualities for one referred to as the Son of Heaven: The first is called "spiritual enlightenment"; the second, "brilliance of bestowing bounties"; the third, "vast discourse"; and the fourth, "being without enemies." These are the aspects of the Son of Heaven.

Wild animals are not used for sacrifice offerings; men of miscellaneous knowledge are not learned scholars.

Today's persuader says: "A hundred *li* of the sea is not sufficient for a man to drink; a spring three feet deep is enough to quench the thirst of the Three Armies." I say: "Desire comes from extravagance and evil comes from lacking prohibitions." The best administration is to inspire

【原文】

禁”。太上神化，其次因物，其下在于无夺民时，无损民财。夫禁必以武而成，赏必以文而成。

【今译】

治，自然天成。其次是根据客观情况，因地制宜，因事利导。再次是不误农时，不竭民财。要禁止的事情必须靠法律等强制手段才能实现，要鼓励的事情必须靠教化劝导的方式才能成功。

people; the next relies on circumstances; the lowest relies on not depriving people of the agricultural seasons and not taking away people's properties. Now prohibitions must be performed by the military and rewards must be performed by the civil.

# 战权第十二

【原文】

《兵法》曰："千人而成权，万人而成武。"权先加人者，敌不力交；武先加人者，敌无威接。故兵贵先，胜于此则胜彼矣，弗胜于此则弗胜彼矣。

凡我往则彼来，彼来则我往，相为胜败，此战

【今译】

《兵法》上说："千人的军队可用权谋取胜，万人的军队可用武力取胜。"抢先对敌使用谋略，敌军就无法施展能力来应战；抢先对敌使用武力，敌军就失去了与我对抗的军威士气。所以用兵贵在先发制人，善于运用这一原则，就能战胜敌人；不善于运用这一原则，就不能战胜敌人。

我方去进攻敌方，敌方必然要反击；敌方来进攻我方，我方也必然要反击。不是我方胜敌，就是敌方胜我。这是战争的规律啊。精明专一在于将领出神入化、用兵如神，掌握战争的权谋在于将领对战争规律的洞悉。我方有用兵的意图和实力要伪装

# 12. Combat Tactics

The *Art of War* said: "A force of one thousand men relies on combat tactics. An army of ten thousand men relies on military strength.When the force imposes combat tactics on the opponent first, the enemy will be unable to exert all his strength to compete. When the army imposes military strength upon the opponent first,the enemy will be lacking in morale to fight."Thus the military values being first. One who has a good command of this principle will win victory over the enemy, and one who does not have will be lost to the enemy.

Generally when we go and attack the enemy will come and counterattack, and when he comes and attacks we will go and counterattack. The outcome is either our victory with the enemy's defeat or his victory with our defeat. This is the rule of warfare. Now accurate assessment and excellent command lie in outstanding intelligent foresight. Combat tactics lie in grasping the

【原文】

之理然也。夫精诚在乎神明，战楹(权)在乎道之所极。有者无之，无者有之，安所信之。

先王之所传闻者，任正去诈，存其慈顺，决无留刑。

故知道者，必先图不知止之败，恶在乎必往有功。轻进而求战，敌复图止，我往而敌制胜矣。故《兵法》曰："求而从之，见而加之，主人不敢当而陵之，必丧其权。"

凡夺者无气，恐者不可守，败者无人，兵无道

【今译】

成没有，我方没有用兵的意图和实力要伪装成有，敌人又怎么能弄清我方的真实情况。

前代的君王留下了这样的训戒：任用正直的人，远离奸诈的人，对仁慈恭顺的人要安抚，对邪恶之徒决不姑息迁就。

所以懂得用兵之道的人，必然事先考虑到轻率出兵只进不止会招致失败，又怎能指望只要进攻就必然能取胜。轻兵冒进、盲目求战，敌人已做好了防御的准备，我军还要去进攻，制胜权就掌握在敌方手中了。所以《兵法》上说："寻求决战而穷追不舍，发现敌人就轻易冒进，守方假意示弱，攻方气势陵人，就必然丧失作战的主动权。"

凡失去主动的军队就没有士气，军心恐惧就守不住阵地，溃败逃跑就没有战斗力，这是因为用兵不得法的缘故。进攻的决心已定而没有疑惑不清的

law of warfare. When one has something but demonstrates to have nothing, when one has nothing but demonstrates to have something,how can the opponent trust the posture?

What is said about the Former Kings is that they entrusted the upright and honest persons and dismissed the crafty and evil persons, and they protected the benevolent and docile persons and relentlessly executed those who should be executed without alleviation of punishments.

Thus those who understand the way to employ the troops will certainly plan against defeats which arise from not knowing where to stop. Why must one always advance to be successful? If we rashly advance to seek engagement with the enemy in battle and go forth when the enemy has already prepared his defense,then the enemy will have the initiative in his hands to control victory. Therefore the *Art of War* said: "If the enemy seeks to fight us, pursue him. When you see the enemy, attack him. When the defenders are not able to withstand the attackers and yet launch an offensive, the initiative in defense will certainly be lost."

Generally those who have been deprived of

【原文】

也。意往而不疑则从之，夺敌而无败(前)则加之，明视而高居则威之，兵道极矣。

其言无谨，偷矣；其陵犯无节，被(破)矣。水溃雷击，三军乱矣。必安其危，去其患，以智决之。高之以廊庙之谕(论)，重之以受命之论，锐之以逾垠之论，则敌国可不战而服。

【今译】

情况就坚决发起进攻，使敌丧失士气而我士气空前高涨就立即与敌交战，掌握了各方面情况而占据优势地位就以威势慑服敌人，这才是用兵之道的极致。

讲话不谨慎就会泄露军事机密，进攻无节制就会招致败绩，（犯了这样的错误）就会像洪水决堤、迅雷击物一样，使三军陷入混乱。一定要切实消除危险，排除隐患，用智谋来决策。朝廷的谋略高明、正确，对将领的选拔和任用慎之又慎，使进攻的作战行动锐不可当，那么敌军就会不战而降服了。

the initiatives are without morale. Those who have been frightened are unable to defend positions. Those who have suffered defeats are without the capable men. All these cases are attributable to lacking in good command of employing troops. When you are determined to fight and there is no suspicion, take action. When the enemy's morale has been blunt and he dares not advance, attack him. When you clearly see the overall situation and your encampment is at heights, impose awesomeness on the enemy into submission. This is the best way to employ the troops.

Those who are unguarded in their discussions can be overheard. Those who press hard to attack without limitation will be defeated. If men are as impatient as rushing water and lightning strike, the Three Armies will be in turmoil. You must settle those in danger, eliminate their worries, and decide matters through wisdom. Be superior to the enemy through discussions in the court; be serious through discussions on conferring the mandate of command; arouse their fighting spirit through discussions of crossing the enemy's borders. Then the enemy state can be forced into submission without fighting.

# 重刑令第十三

【原文】

将自千人以上，有战而北，守而降，离地逃众，命曰“国贼”。身戮家残，去其籍，发其坟墓，暴其骨于市，男女公于官。自百人已上，有战而北，守而降，离地逃众，命曰“军贼”。身死家残，男女公于官。

【今译】

统兵千人以上的将领，有进攻而败走、防守而投降、擅离战场弃军逃跑的，称之为“国贼”。要斩首抄家，削去他的官籍，发掘他的祖坟，把尸骨暴露在街市之上示众，男女亲属充当官府的奴婢。统兵百人以上的军吏，有进攻而败北、防守而投降、擅离战场弃军逃跑的，称之为“军贼”。要斩首抄家，男女亲属充当官府奴婢。

使全军将士对内畏惧重刑，对外则可蔑视敌人。

# 13. Orders for Severe Punishments

If a general commanding more than one thousand men retreats from battle, surrenders his defenses, or abandons his positions and deserts his troops, he is termed a state traitor. He should be decapitated, his houses searched and properties confiscated, his name abolished from the registers, his ancestral graves broken open,his bones exposed in the marketplace, and his male and female family members pressed into government servitude. If a commander of more than one hundred men retreats from battle,surrenders his defenses, or abandons his positions and deserts his troops, he is termed an army traitor. He should be executed, his houses searched and properties confiscated, his name abolished from the registers, and his male and female family members pressed into government servitude.

If you cause the people to fear severe punishments within the state, then outside the state they will take the enemy lightly.Therefore the Former

【原文】

使民内畏重刑，则外轻敌。故先王明制度于前，重威刑于后。刑重则内畏，内畏则外坚矣。

【今译】

所以古代的君主首先明确各种制度法令，然后对违反制度法令的人给予严惩。严刑重罚，将士就会对内畏惧；对内畏惧，就会对外坚强了。

Kings made the regulations and orders clear before making their awesomeness and punishments severe. When punishments are severe, then the people will fear them within the state. When they are fear ful within the state, then they will be staunch outside it.

# 伍制令第十四

【原文】

军中之制，五人为伍，伍相保也；十人为什，什相保也；五十人为属，属相保也；百人为闾，闾相保也。伍有干令犯禁者，揭之，免于罪；知而弗揭，全伍有诛。什有干令犯禁者，揭之，免于罪；知而弗揭，全什有诛。属有干令犯禁者，揭之，免于

【今译】

军中的制度，五人编为一伍，同伍的人互相担保；十人编为一什，同什的人互相担保；五十人编为一属，同属的人互相担保；百人编为一闾，同闾的人互相担保。一伍之中有人触犯了法令，伍内其他人揭发他，可以免罪；知情而不揭发，全伍都受处罚。一什之中有人触犯了法令，什内其他人揭发他，可以免罪；知情而不揭发，全什都受处罚。一属之中有人触犯了法令，属内其他人揭发他，可以免罪；知情而不揭发，全属都受处罚。一闾之中有

# 14. Orders for the Squads of Five

In the army the regulations for organization are as follows: Five men comprise a squad of five, with all members being mutual bondsmen for each other. Ten men comprise a double squad of ten, with all members being mutual bondsmen for each other. Fifty men comprise a platoon, with all members being mutual bondsmen for each other. One hundred men comprise a company, with all members being mutual bondsmen for each other. When one member of the squad of five violates an order or commits an offense, if others expose it, their punishments will be pardoned. If they know about it but do not expose it the whole squad of five will be punished. When one member of a double squad of ten violates an order or commits an offense, if others expose it, their punishments will be pardoned. If they know about it but do not expose it, the whole double squad of ten will be punished. When one member of a platoon violates

【原文】

罪；知而弗揭，全属有诛。闾有干令犯禁者，揭之，免于罪；知而弗揭，全闾有诛。

吏自什长以上，至左右将，上下皆相保也。有干令犯禁者，揭之，免于罪；知而弗揭者，皆与同罪。

夫什伍相结，上下相联，无有不得之奸，无有不揭之罪。父不得以私其子，兄不得以私其弟，而况国人！聚舍同食，乌能以干令相私者哉！

【今译】

人触犯了法令，闾内其他人揭发他，可以免罪；知情而不揭发，全闾都受处罚。

将吏自什长以上，直至左军主将、右军主将，上下级之间实行连保。有触犯法令的，其他将吏揭发他，可以免罪；知情而不揭发，连保的将吏皆与犯法者同罪。

什伍有连保，上下有连坐，就没有捉不到的坏人，就没有揭发不出来的罪行。这样，父亲就不敢偏袒他的儿子，兄长就不敢偏袒他的弟弟，更何况没有亲属关系的平民百姓！在军中被编在一起，同吃同住，怎么敢甘冒犯禁之险相互袒护呢！

an order or commits an offense, if others expose it, their punishments will be pardoned. If they know about it but do not expose it the whole platoon will be punished. When one member of a company violates an order or commits an offense, if others expose it, their punishments will be pardoned. If they know about it but do not expose it the whole company will be punished.

All the officers — from the double squad of ten up to the generals of the left and right, superiors and inferiors — are mutual bondsmen for each other. When someone violates an order or commits an offense, those who expose it will be spared from punishments, while those who know about it but do not expose it will share the same offense.

Now when squads of five and double squads of ten are mutually bonded and the superiors and inferiors linked, no evil cannot be discovered and no offense cannot be exposed. Fathers will not be able to conceal their sons and elder brothers will not be able to cover for their younger brothers. How much less so will be the people of the state? Will they living and eating together be able to violate orders and shield each other?

# 分塞令第十五

【原文】

中军，左、右、前、后军，皆有地分，方之以行垣，而无通其交往。将有分地，帅有分地，伯有分地，皆营其沟洫，而明其塞令。

使非百人，无得通。非其百人而入者，伯诛之；

【今译】

中军、左军、右军、前军、后军，都有划分的营地，四周筑起围墙，不准互相往来。将有划定的营地，帅有划定的营地，伯有划定的营地，都修筑各自区域的沟壕，而申明营地的禁令。

假使不是本百的人不得通行。不是本闾的人进

# 15. Orders for Division of Encampment Garrison

The Central, Left, Right, Forward and Rear armies all have their encampments. Each army's encampments are surrounded by separate walls respectively and no passage and association among them are allowed. The general has his encampment, the regimental commander has his encampment, and the battalion commander also has his encampment. Around the encampment trenches and ditches are constructed and garrison orders are made clear to block one who is not a member of the company of one hundred.

Should someone who is not a member of the company of one hundred enter, the battalion commander will execute him. If the battalion commander does not execute the transgressor,he will share the same offense.

Along the crisscrossing roads in the encampments a watchtower is set up at intervals of one hundred and twenty paces each to measure the movement of the men and distance of the terrain.

**【原文】**

伯不诛，与之同罪。

军中纵横之道，百有二十步而立一府柱，量人与地，柱道相望，禁行清道。非将吏之符节，不得通行。采薪刍牧者，皆成行伍；不成行伍者，不得通行。吏属无节，士无伍者，横门诛之。逾分干地者，诛之。故内无干令犯禁，则外无不获之奸。

**【今译】**

入本闾的营地，伯长有权诛杀他；若伯长不予诛杀，就与犯禁者同罪。

军营中纵横交错的道路上，每隔一百二十步树立一个瞭望台，根据营中的人数和地形，使岗哨能监视各条道路，禁绝随意通行，以肃清道路。没有将吏的符节作凭证，不得通行。外出打柴、放牧的人员，都要整队出行；不整队的，不得通行。将吏的亲随没有符节的，士兵没有整队的，在营门口一经发现，就地处决。逾越营区进入别人营区者，都要诛杀。所以内部没有触犯禁令的人，外部就没有抓不到的奸细。

The watchtower should be within sight of each other. Haphazard passengers are prohibited and roads are clear. If a soldier does not have the token or tally issued by a general or other commanding officers, he cannot pass.Firewood collectors, fodder seekers and animal herds all should move in orderly formations. If not in orderly formation, they are not allowed to pass. If the attendants of a general or commanding officer have no tally, if the soldiers move in disorder, the guards at crossing gates should execute them. Those who transgress the encampment and commit offense should be executed. Thus within the army no man will violate orders nor commit offense, then without there will not be any spy that is not caught.

# 束武令第十六

【原文】

束武之令曰：五人为伍，共一符，收于将吏之所。亡伍而得伍，当之；得伍而不亡，有赏；亡伍不得伍，身死家残。亡长得长，当之；得长不亡，有赏；亡长不得长，身死家残，复战得首长，除之。亡将得将，当之；得将不亡，有赏；亡将不得将，

【今译】

《束武令》上规定：五人编成一伍，共签一份五人连保凭证，收存在将吏之处。伤亡了同伍之人，同时斩获了敌方伍中的人，功罪相抵；斩获了敌方伍中的人，己方没有伤亡，给予奖赏；伤亡了同伍的人，却没有斩获敌方伍中的人，伍中其他人处死，其家抄灭。伤亡了己方的军官，斩获了敌方的军官，功罪相抵；斩获敌方的军官，己方军官没有伤亡，给予奖赏；伤亡了己方的军官，却没有斩获敌方的军官，下属本人处死，其家抄灭。如果再战斩获敌方高级军官，可以免罪。伤亡了己方的将帅，同时斩获了敌方的将帅，功罪相抵；斩获敌方将帅，而

# 16. Orders for Binding the Squads of Five

The orders that bind the squads of five state: Five men comprise the squad of five. They collectively have a tally which is under the custody of the headquarters of a general or a commanding officer. If in battle they lose men but capture or kill an equivalent number of the enemy, their gains can balance the losses. If they capture or kill members of an enemy squad without losing anyone themselves, they will be rewarded. If they lose members without capturing or killing an equal number of the enemy, they will be executed and their houses searched and properties confiscated. If they lose a squad leader but capture or kill an enemy squad leader, their gains can balance the losses. If they capture or kill an enemy squad leader without losing anyone themselves, they will be rewarded. If they lose a squad leader without capturing or killing an enemy squad leader, they will be executed and their houses searched and properties confiscated.

【原文】

坐离地遁逃之法。

战诛之法曰：什长得诛十人，伯长得诛什长，千人之将得诛百人之长，万人之将得诛千人之将，左、右将军得诛万人之将，大将军无不得诛。

【今译】

己方将帅无伤亡，给予奖赏；伤亡了己方的将帅，却没有斩获敌方的将帅，就按临阵脱逃论罪。

《战诛法》上规定：什长可以诛杀属下的十个人，伯长可以诛杀属下的什长，统兵千人的将领可以诛杀属下的伯长，统兵万人的将领可以诛杀属下的千人之将，左军主将、右军主将可以诛杀属下的万人之将，大将军没有不能诛杀的人。

However, if they rejoin the battle and capture or kill a higher enemy officer, they will be spared from punishments. If in battle they lose a general but capture or kill an enemy general, their gains can balance the losses. If they capture or kill an enemy general without losing their own, they will be rewarded. If they lose a general without capturing or killing an enemy general, they will be punished according to the Law of Abandoning Their Positions and Deserting Their Troops.

*The Law for Battlefield Executions* states:The leader of a double squad of ten can execute the other nine. A company commander can execute the double squad leaders. The general of one thousand men can execute company commanders. The general of ten thousand men can execute the generals of one thousand men. The generals of the Armies of the Left and Right can execute the generals of ten thousand men. The Grand General has no one he cannot execute.

# 经卒令第十七

【原文】

经卒者，以经令分之，为三分焉：左军苍旗，卒戴苍羽；右军白旗，卒戴白羽；中军黄旗，卒戴黄羽。

卒有五章：前一行苍章，次二行赤章，次三行黄章，次四行白章，次五行黑章。次以经卒，亡章者有诛。前一五行置章于首，次二五行置章于项，次三五行置章于胸，次四五行置章于腹，次五五行

【今译】

编组士兵，就是按编队条令把部队分为三部分：左军打青色旗帜，士兵戴青色羽毛；右军打白色旗帜，士兵戴白色羽毛；中军打黄色旗帜，士兵戴黄色羽毛。

士兵佩戴五色徽章：第一行佩戴青色徽章，第二行佩戴红色徽章，第三行佩戴黄色徽章，第四行佩戴白色徽章，第五行佩戴黑色徽章。按此次序编队，遗失徽章的，要给予处罚。第一组五行的士兵把徽章佩戴在头上，第二组五行把徽章佩戴在颈上，第三组五行把徽章佩戴在胸前，第四组五行把徽章

# 17. Orders for the Battle Formations of the Troops

The battle formations of the troops are divided into three segments of armies according to the Orders for the Battle Formations of the Troops. They are: The Army of the Left will have green flags, and the troops will wear green feathers. The Army of the Right will have white flags, and the troops will wear white feathers.The Central Army will have yellow flags and the troops will wear yellow feathers.

The troops have five emblems. The front row will have green emblems, the second row red emblems, the third row yellow emblems, the fourth row white emblems, and the fifth row black emblems. As the troops are organized into the battle formations, any one who loses his emblem will be executed. The first five rows place their emblems on their heads, the next five on their necks, the next five on their chests, the next five on their stomachs and the last five on

【原文】

置章于腰。

如此，卒无非其吏，吏无非其卒。见非而不诰(诘)，见乱而不禁，其罪如之。鼓行交斗，则前行进为犯难，后行进(退)为辱众，逾五行而前者有赏，逾五行而后者有诛；所以知进退先后，吏卒之功也。故曰：“鼓之，前如雷霆，动如风雨，莫敢当其前，莫敢蹑其后。”言有经也。

【今译】

佩戴在腹部，第五组五行把徽章佩戴在腰间。

这样一来，士兵就不会错认他的官长，官长也不会错认他的士兵。官长发现不属于自己单位的士兵而不加盘问，发现行列错乱而不加禁止，他的罪过就与违禁者相同。擂鼓前进两军厮杀之际，超越同行向前是敢于冒险，落后同行退缩就是给大家丢脸。超过同一五行而前进的有赏，落后同一五行而退缩的处罚。这样就能看出部下的进退先后的情况，知道有谁该立功了。所以说：“擂鼓麾兵，前进如同雷霆般迅疾，行动像暴风骤雨一样猛烈，没有人胆敢在前面阻挡，也没有人胆敢在后面追赶。”指的就是部队编队列阵有方啊。

their waists.

Thus no soldier will not be recognized by his officer and no officer will not be recognized by his soldiers. If someone sees a case where it is incorrect but does not dare to inquire about it,or sees confusion but does not manage to stop it,the crime will be similar to that of the offender.

When drums roll for engagement in battle, one who goes forward ahead of his row is not afraid of danger; one who retreats from his row is a disgrace to the troops. Those who venture forward past the five rows will be rewarded; those who race past the five rows to the rear will be executed. By this means it can be known the advancing and retreating, moving to the fore and rear are achievements of the commanders and troops. Therefore it is said: "If you beat the drums and they advance like a thunderclap, they move like wind and rain, no one will dare to oppose you to the fore, no one will dare to follow to the rear." This speaks about having battle formations.

# 勒卒令第十八

【原文】

金、鼓、铃、旗，四者各有法。鼓之则进，重鼓则击。金之则止，重金则退。铃，传令也。旗，麾之左则左，麾之右则右。奇兵则反是。

一鼓一击而左，一鼓一击而右。一步一鼓，步鼓也。十步一鼓，趋鼓也。音不绝，骛鼓也。商，

【今译】

金、鼓、铃、旗，这四种指挥工具各有各的用法。击鼓就前进，再次击鼓就发起攻击；鸣金就停止战斗，再次鸣金就后退。铃是用来传达命令的。旗帜向左挥动部队就向左运动，向右挥动部队就向右运动。使用奇兵的指挥信号与此正好相反。

有时一通鼓是命令部队向左冲击，有时一通鼓是命令部队向右冲击。走一步击一声鼓，是慢步前进的信号；走十步击一声鼓，是快步前进的信号；

# 18. Orders for Restraining the Troops

Gongs, drums, bells and flags are four command implements having their methods of employment respectively. When the drums are rolled the troops should advance; when the drums are rolled again, they should attack. When the gongs are sounded, they should stop; when the gongs are struck again, they should withdraw. Bells are employed for transmitting orders. When the flags indicate to the left, the troops should go left. When the flags indicate to the right, they should go right. However when unorthodox units are employed these command signals will be changed otherwise.

Beat the drums once and the army goes left; beat them again and it goes to the right. If for each stop there is one beat, this is the pace beat.If for ten steps there is one beat, this is the quickstep beat. If the sound is unbroken, this is the racing beat. The shang note is that of the general's drum. The jiao note is that of a regimental commander's

【原文】

将鼓也。角，帅鼓也。小鼓，伯鼓也。三鼓同，则将、帅、伯其心一也。奇兵则反是。

鼓失次者有诛，讙哗者有诛。不听金、鼓、铃、旗而动者有诛。

百人而教战，教成，合之千人；千人教成，合之万人；万人教成，会之于三军。三军之众，有分有合，为大战之法，教成，试之以阅。

方亦胜，圆亦胜，错邪亦胜，临险亦胜。敌在

【今译】

鼓声不绝，是跑步前进的信号。发出商音的，是万人之将使用的鼓；发出角音的，是千人之帅使用的鼓；发音细小的，是伯长使用的鼓。三种鼓音一同响起，表示将、帅、伯意图一致。使用奇兵的指挥信号正好与此相反。

击鼓不按规定的要受处罚。喧哗吵闹的要受处罚。不听从金、鼓、铃、旗发出的号令而擅自行动的，要受处罚。

以百人为单位进行作战训练，练成后，再以千人为单位进行演练；千人练成后，再以万人为单位进行合练；万人练成后，再集合全军进行合练。三军将士能分散，也能集中，这是大规模作战的训练方法。练成以后，举行校阅来检查效果。

方阵能取胜，圆阵能取胜，错综复杂的地形能

drum. The small drum is that of a company commander. When the three drums are sounded together, the generals, regimental commanders, and company commanders are all of one mind. However when unorthodox units are employed these command signals will be changed otherwise.

If the drummer fails to beat, he will be executed. One who sets up clamor will be executed. Those who disobey the gongs, drums, bells and flags and move by themselves will be executed.

When one hundred men are taught the combat methods, on completion of this instruction they will unite with other companies to comprise one thousand men. When the instruction of one thousand men is finished, they will unite with other regiments to comprise ten thousand men. When the instruction of the armies of ten thousand is completed, these armies will assemble into the Three Armies. The multitude of the Three Armies can divide and unite, and this is a method to engage in large-scale operations. Upon completion of the instruction, they will be tested with military exercises.

The square formation leads to their victory; the circular formation also leads to their victory;

【原文】

山，缘而从之；敌在渊，没而从之。求敌若求亡子，从之无疑，故能败敌而制其命。

夫蚤决先敌(定)，若计不先定，虑不蚤决，则进退不定，疑生必败。故正兵贵先，奇兵贵后，或先或后，制敌者也。

世将不知法者，专命而行，先击而勇，无不败

【今译】

取胜，面临险要之地也能取胜。敌人在山上，就登山追击它；敌人在深渊，就下水追击它。追歼敌人就像寻找丢失的孩子那样迫切，全力追击毫不迟疑，所以能打败敌人、制其死命。

(采取重大的作战行动)应及早谋划、定下计策，如果计策不预先制订，疑虑不预先解决，部队的行动就会进退不定，这种游疑的态度只能导致战争的失败。所以使用正兵，贵在先发制人；使用奇兵，贵在后发制人。无论先发制人还是后发制人，都要根据实际情况去制服敌人。

现在的将领中有不懂兵法的人，独断专行，以抢先进攻为勇敢，这样没有不失败的。出兵时本来

the complicated terrain also leads to their victory; if they face a dangerous situation,victory will be at their hands too. When the enemy is high up in the mountains, they will climb up after him. When the enemy is in the depths, they will plunge in after him. They seek the enemy as if searching for their lost son, and they follow him without hesitation. Hence they are able to defeat the enemy and his fate is doomed.

Now decision-making must be early and planning must be in advance. If planning is not determined in advance and intentions are not decided early, advance or withdrawal of the troops will be uncertain. When doubts arise defeat will be certain. Therefore orthodox units attach great importance to being first;unorthodox units attach great importance to being afterward. To determine whether being first or being afterward is aimed at controlling the enemy.

Contemporary generals who have not known this method act arbitrarily and try to be the first to exhibit their courage alone. There are none who will not be defeated. On raising an army they are not skeptical about what is doubtful; in

【原文】

者也。其举有疑而不疑，其往有信而不信，其致有迟疾而不迟疾。是三者，战之累也。

【今译】

有疑问却不以为疑，进攻时本来情况明了却又犹豫不决，在战斗中当快不快、当慢又不慢。这三种情况，都是不利于作战的。

advancing they are lacking in confidence in what is trusted; in fighting their actions are neither quick nor slow when there should be quick advance or slow movement. These are three hindrances in battle.

# 将令第十九

【原文】

将军受命，君必先谋于庙，行令于廷，君身以斧钺授将，曰："左、右、中军皆有分职，若逾分而上请者死。军无二令，二令者诛，留令者诛，失令者诛。"

将军告曰："出国门之外，期日中，设营表，

【今译】

将军接受任命，君主一定要先在庙堂上谋划好，然后在朝廷上发布命令。君主亲自将斧钺授予将领，并宣布："左、中、右三军，都有各自的职责，如有越职向上请示者处死。军中不允许有两种命令，擅自发布命令者处死，截留命令者处死，贻误命令者处死。"

将军接受任命后宣布说："出国都城门之外，

# 19. Orders for the General

When the commanding general is going to receive the mandate, the sovereign must first make planning in the temple, then declares the order in the court. The sovereign personally bestows the axe of punishment on the general, saying: "The Left, Right, and Central armies have their separate responsibilities. If anyone oversteps the bounds of his responsibilities to seek the instructions of higher ranks, he shall be put to death. Within the army no order is issued by other than one source. Anyone who issues order without authorization shall be executed. Anyone who withholds an order from implementation shall be executed. Anyone who disobeys an order shall be executed."

The commanding general states: "To those about to depart from the gates of the state capital, the time for assembling is set as midday. A gnomon will be set up and placed at the gate of the encampment. In the expected assembling

【原文】

置辕门。期之，如过时，则坐法。”

将军入营，即闭门清道。有敢行者诛，有敢高言者诛，有敢不从令者诛。

【今译】

限定中午设立军营，在军营门口设置计时表柱等待，如有过时不报到者，即按军法处置。”

将军进入军营后，立即关闭营门，肃清道路。有敢随意行走者处死，有敢高声喧哗者处死，有敢不服从命令者处死。

those who arrive past the deadline shall be put to military discipline."

When the commanding general has entered the encampment, he closes the gate and has the roads cleared. Those who dare to walk through them will be executed. Those who dare to set up clamor will be executed. Those who dare to disobey an order will be executed.

# 踵军令第二十

【原文】

所谓踵军者，去大军百里，期于会地，为三日熟食，前军而行。为战，合之表，合表乃起。踵军飨士，使为之战势，是谓趋战者也。

兴军者，前踵军而行，合表乃起。去大军一倍

【今译】

所谓踵军(前卫部队)，通常距离大部队约百里，按期到达会合地点，准备好三天的干粮，先于大部队出发。要预先规定好行动的信号，接到信号后就开始行动。踵军采取行动之前，应犒赏士卒，进入临战状态，这就是所谓的进入战斗的方法。

兴军(在踵军前面行动的部队)，要先于踵军出发，接到信号后就开始行动。其距大部队有比踵军远一倍的路程，距踵军有百里之遥，并按期到达会

# 20. Orders for the Vanguard

What is termed "the vanguard" moves off from the main body of the armies about one hundred *li* and reaches the assembly area as scheduled. It carries a three-day supply of cooked food. It moves in front of the main body of the armies. Pennants of the prearranged command signal are made for the military operations.When the command signal is coincided and the pennants are raised, it will take action. Pending the military action the vanguard should feast its troops and exert itself to form a combat momentum. They are referred to as "attacking the enemy's positions."

The advance detachment moves in front of the vanguard. When the command signal is coincided and the pennants for battle are raised, it will take action. The advance detachment moves off from the main body double the vanguard's distance, i.e. one hundred *li* ahead of the vanguard. It reaches the assembly area as scheduled.The

【原文】

其道，去踵军百里，期于会地。为六日熟食，使为战备。

分卒据要害，战利则追北，按兵而趋之。

踵军遇有还者，诛之。所谓诸将之兵在四奇之内者胜也。

兵有什伍，有分有合，豫为之职，守要塞关梁而分居之。战，合表起，即皆会也。大军为计日之食，起，战具无不及也。令行而起，不如令者有诛。

凡称分塞者，四境之内，当兴军、踵军既行，

【今译】

合地点。兴军应预备好六天的干粮，并做好战斗准备。

分卒（在兴军前面行动的小分队），要据守各处重要地点，战斗顺利就追击败逃的敌军，否则按兵不动，做好攻击敌人的准备。

踵军若遇到逃兵就处罚他们。每个将领所率之兵都能按踵军、兴军、分卒、大军四个部分来部署和指挥，就能取得战争的胜利。

军队有什伍的编制，有时分散有时集中，要预先确定各自的任务，并扼守要塞、关卡、桥梁，实施分区驻防。遇有战事，见到信号就开始行动，立即按规定会合。大部队按预计天数准备干粮，出发时，各种战具都要带齐。命令一经下达就要立即出发，不按命令行动者要严惩。

凡是担任分散据守要塞任务的部队，部署在四境之内，当兴军、踵军出发之后，就负责使四境之

advance detachment carries a six-day supply of cooked food and must be in a state of combat readiness. The advancing party occupies the strategic points. When they are victorious in battle, they will pursue the retreating enemy. When they come to a halt, they should be prepared to press the enemy's positions.

If the vanguard encounters anyone who has turned back, they should execute him. What are termed the "armies of the various generals," consisting of four forces (main body, vanguard, advance detachment and advancing party) will gain victory through their orchestrated military operations.

The army has its squads of ten and five, and the tactics of dividing and reuniting. Their duties are assigned beforehand. The designated units should occupy the strategic points, passes, and bridges respectively. When the command signal is coincided and the pennant is raised, they should all assemble. The main body of the armies moves with a fixed daily ration and their combat implements are all complete. If anyone disobeys the order, he will be executed.

Generally what is referred to as "the division of encampment garrison" is dispersed within

【原文】

则四境之民无得行者。奉王之命，授持符节，名为顺职之吏。非顺职之吏而行者，诛之。战，合表起，顺职之吏乃行，用以相参。故欲战，先安内也。

【今译】

内的百姓不得随便通行。身负国王之命、手持符节的人，称为执行特殊使命的官吏。非此官吏而擅自通行的，就要受处罚。战斗信号发出，部队出发以后，执行特殊使命的官吏才开始行动，其任务是检查境内的情况。所以要取得战场上的胜利，必须先使国内的秩序安定。

the four borders of the state. When the advance detachment and vanguard have already set out, the people within the borders are not allowed to move about. Those who have received the king's orders and have been authorized to carry tallies and tokens are called "officers performing special duties." Officers who are not performing special duties and move about arbitrarily should be executed. When the pennant is raised for engagement in battle, the officers performing special duties will travel about and be employed to participate in planning military affairs. Therefore one who wants to launch warfare must first secure the interior.

# 兵教上第二十一

【原文】

兵之教令，分营居陈，有非令而进退者，加犯教之罪。前行者，前行教之；后行者，后行教之；左行者，左行教之；右行者，右行教之。教举五人，其甲首有赏；弗教，如犯教之罪。罗地者，自揭其伍。伍内互揭之，免其罪。

凡伍临陈，若一人有不进死于敌，则教者如犯

【今译】

军队的训练条令规定，在划分的营区或布列的阵势中，有不按军令前进后退者，就以违反训练条令论罪。前行的士兵，由前行的教官负责训练；后行的士兵，由后行的教官负责训练；左行的士兵，由左行的教官负责训练；右行的士兵，由右行的教官负责训练。训练好一行五人，做教官的伍长有赏赐。教官没训练好，以违反训练条令论罪。不能参加训练的人，自己在伍内说明原因，伍内其他人为其作证，可以免除他的罪过。

一伍士兵上了战场，如有一人不前行与敌拼死

# 21. Military Instructions I

According to military instructions, army encampment is divided and training formations are established. Those who advance or retreat not in accord with orders will be punished for the crime of violating the instructions. The front lines are instructed by the commander of the front lines; the rear lines by the commander of the rear lines; the lines to the left are instructed by the commander of the left lines; the lines to the right by the commander of the right lines. When the training of the squad of five is successfully completed, the squad leader will be rewarded. If the training is not successful, he will commit a crime as if violating the instructions. If anyone is absent in training for sickness and reports to the squad leader, and all the other members of the squad confirm it, he will be spared from punishments.

Generally if the squad of five approaches to the battle front, if anyone of the squad dare not

【原文】

法者之罪。凡什保什，若亡一人，而九人不尽死于敌，则教者如犯法者之罪。自什已上至于裨将，有不若法者，则教者如犯法者之罪。凡明刑罚，正劝赏，必在乎兵教之法。

将异其旗，卒异其章。左军章左肩，右军章右肩，中军章胸前，书其章曰："某甲某士。"前后章各五行，尊章置首上，其次差降之。

【今译】

搏斗，那么教官就与犯法者同罪。一什之内的十人互相连保，如果伤亡一人，而其他九人不与敌人拼死作战，那么教官就与犯法者同罪。自什长以上直到副将，有不遵守法令者，那么教官就与犯法者同罪。凡是能严明刑罚、公平奖赏的，一定靠的是遵守部队训练的条令。

将领使用不同的旗帜，士兵佩戴不同的徽章。左军的徽章戴在左肩，右军的徽章戴在右肩，中军的徽章戴在胸前，在徽章上写明单位和姓名。部队按照前后五行的顺序，佩戴五种不同颜色的徽章，第一行把徽章戴在头上，其余各行依次降低佩戴的位置。

fight the enemy to the death, the instructor will be punished as if he had committed a crime of violating the law. In general the double squad of ten must guarantee the safety of all the ten members. If anyone is killed in action and the remaining nine men dare not fight the enemy to the death, the instructor will be punished as if he had committed a crime of violating the law. From the leader of the double squad of ten up to the low-ranking general, anyone who does not abide by the law will be punished as if he had committed a crime of violating the law. Generally one who is able to make punishments clear and rewards impartial rests with the enforcement of the law of military instructions.

Generals have different flags, and companies have different emblems. The soldiers of the Left Army wear emblems on their left shoulders;the soldiers of the Right Army wear emblems on their right shoulders; the soldiers of the Central Army wear emblems on their chests. Each emblem indicates one's unit and one's name. From front to rear there are troops of five rows in order. The first row places the emblems on their heads, the others accordingly place the emblems lower and lower.

The leader of the squad of five instructs the

【原文】

伍长教其四人，以板为鼓，以瓦为金，以竿为旗，击鼓而进，低旗则趋，击金而退，麾而左之，麾而右之，金鼓俱击而坐。伍长教成，合之什长。什长教成，合之卒长。卒长教成，合之伯长。伯长教成，合之兵尉。兵尉教成，合之裨将。裨将教成，合之大将。大将教之，陈于中野，置大表三，百步

【今译】

伍长训练其所属的四人时，以木板为鼓，以瓦为金，以竿为旗。击鼓表示前进，旗帜低斜表示快速前进，鸣金表示后退，旗指向左表示向左运动，旗指向右表示向右行动，金鼓齐鸣表示原地跪坐。伍长训练好之后，集合起来由什长训练。什长训练好之后，集合起来由伯长训练。伯长训练好之后，集合起来由兵尉训练。兵尉训练好之后，集合起来由副将训练。副将训练好之后，集合起来由大将训练。大将训练时，在旷野中列阵，设立大旗竿三根，每隔百步树一根。列阵完毕，在距第一根旗竿百步

other four men to use a board as a drum, a tile as a gong, and a branch as a flag. When he beats the drum they advance; when he lowers the flag they race; when he strikes the gong they retreat; when his flag points to the left, they go to the left; when his flag points to the right, they go to the right; when gong and drum are struck together they sit down. When the leaders of squads of five have completed instructing their squads,they should be assembled to receive instructions by the leader of the double squad of ten. When the leaders of double squads of ten have completed instructing, they should be assembled to receive instructions by platoon leaders. When platoon leaders have completed instructing, they should be assembled to receive instructions by company commanders. When company commanders have completed instructing, they should be assembled to receive instructions by army commandants. When army commandants have completed instructing, they should be assembled to receive instructions by lower-grading generals. When lower-grading generals have completed instructing, they should be assembled to receive instructions by the Grand General. When the Grand General has completed instructing, the

**【原文】**

而一。既陈，去表百步而决，百步而趋，百步而骛。习战以成其节，乃为之赏法(罚)。

自尉吏而下尽有旗，战胜得旗者，各视其所得之爵，以明赏劝之心。战胜在乎立威，立威在乎戮力，戮力在乎正罚。正罚者，所以明赏也。

令民背国门之限，决死生之分，教之死而不疑

**【今译】**

之处开始前进，在距第二根旗竿百步之处开始快步前进，在距第三根旗竿百步之处开始跑步前进。经反复演练，掌握各种动作要领。然后视演练情况进行赏罚。

从兵尉以下的各级军官都有旗帜，凡是胜敌获得敌人旗帜的，分别按照所缴获的旗帜赏赐爵位，以此彰明国君奖赏激励有功将士的意图。作战取胜靠的是树立军威，树立军威靠的是将士尽力，将士尽力靠的是刑罚严正。刑罚严正，也是突出奖赏的办法。

使士兵远离国土，在生死关头作出抉择，训练

troops should be deployed into formations in the field. There are three big poles erected at an interval of one hundred paces. When the formations are already established, the troops set out to fight at a distance of one hundred paces from the first pole, advance at a distance of one hundred paces from the second pole, and race at a distance of one hundred paces from the third pole. The exercises are repeated so as to fix an appropriate tempo in battle. Afterward, rewards and punishments should be performed.

From the commandants down, every officer has a flag. Those who have gained victory and have captured the enemy's flags will be rewarded in accord with the ranks of the captured flags. Thereby the intentions for stimulating the hearts of the troops with rewards are very clear. To win victory lies in establishing awesomeness. To establish awesomeness lies in uniting strength. To unite strength lies in impartial punishments. The purpose of impartial punishments is to make rewards clear.

If the troops are offered to depart from the border gates to take part in a life-and-death battle and instructed to fight to the death without

【原文】

者，有以也。令守者必固，战者必斗；奸谋不作，奸民不语；令行无变，兵行无猜；轻者若霆，奋敌若惊。举功别德，明如白黑；令民从上令，如四支(肢)应心也。

前军绝行乱陈，破坚如溃者，有以也。此之谓兵教，所以开封疆，守社稷，除患害，成武德也。

【今译】

他们战死而毫不犹豫，是有道理的。使防御的部队守必坚固，进攻的部队战必敢斗；阴谋诡计无从发生，奸诈之人不敢胡言乱语；命令发布后不随意更改，部队行动没有疑虑；进攻迅猛若雷霆，冲锋杀敌若惊马。这些靠的都是评功论德，清楚准确像黑白一样分明；士兵服从上级的命令，像心脏支配四肢一样自如。

前锋部队冲垮敌人队伍打乱敌人阵形，攻破敌人坚固的阵地如同洪水决堤一样不可阻挡，这是有道理的。所以说军队的训练，是开拓疆土、保卫国家、消除祸患、成就武德的重要手段。

hesitation, there is a reason. Training and instructions have caused the defenders to definitely be solid; those engaged in battle to inevitably fight; conspiracy not to crop up; those involved in conspiracy not to speak; orders to be effected without any changes; the troops to advance without doubt; the light units to move like a thunderclap and charge the enemy like a startled horse. Promote those of merit; distinguish those of virtue; make their distinctions as clear as black and white. Cause the troops to obey the orders of their superiors just as the four limbs respond to the mind.

If the forward troops break up the enemy's ranks, disrupt his formations, and crack his strong positions like overwhelming flood, there is a reason. This is what is referred to as "military instructions." Their purposes are pioneering frontiers, defending the state, eliminating disaster and harm, and achieving Military Virtue.

# 兵教下第二十二

【原文】

臣闻人君有必胜之道，故能并兼广大，以一其制度，则威加天下。有十二焉：一曰连刑，谓同罪保伍也；二曰地禁，谓禁止行道，以网外奸也；三曰全车，谓甲首相附，三五相同，以结其联也；四曰开塞，谓分地以限，各死其职而坚守也；五曰分

【今译】

臣下听说君主掌握了必胜之道，就能兼并列国，扩大疆域，统一制度，进而统治天下。其方法有十二条：一是连刑，即一人犯法，全伍连坐；二是地禁，即军营中禁止在道路上随意通行，以便捕捉外来的奸细；三是全车，即战车上的甲士互相配合协同，各伍之间互相协作有序，构成密切的联系；四是开塞，即划分防区，各部队誓死尽职，坚守阵地；五是分限，即营地内左右互相警戒，前后互相照应，

# 22. Military Instructions II

I have heard that if a sovereign has had a good grasp of the methods to inevitably gain victory, he would annex vast territories and unify the ordinances and regulations, and impose his awesomeness on All Under Heaven. There are twelve points of the methods: The first is called "connected punishment" and refers to the method of joint liability in committing a crime for all members of the squad of five. The second, "area restrictions," refers to prohibiting traffic on the roads in order to ensnare the external spies. The third, "preserving chariots," refers to the chariot commanders and infantry leaders mutually dependent, the three officers in the chariots and squads of five being cohesive to bind them together. The fourth, "opening and stopping," refers to dividing the area with boundaries and loyally assuming each one's garrison duty, and securely defending his positions. The fifth, "demarking boundaries,"refers to the left and right

【原文】

限，谓左右相禁，前后相待，垣车为固，以逆以止也；六曰号别，谓前列务进，以别其后者，不得争先登不次也；七曰五章，谓彰明行列，始卒不乱也；八曰全曲，谓曲折相从，皆有分部也；九曰金鼓，谓兴有功，致有德也；十曰陈车，谓接连前矛，马冒其目也；十一曰死士，谓众军之中有材力者，乘于战车，前后纵横，出奇制敌也；十二曰力卒，谓

【今译】

并用战车环绕以为屏障，以便于御敌和宿营；六是号别，即前行应奋力前进，与后列拉开距离，后列不得抢先冒进，以免扰乱阵形次序；七是五章，即用徽章来区别行列，自始至终保持队列不乱；八是全曲，即部队行进中要保持连贯，保证所属战斗单位的完整；九是金鼓，即激励将士杀敌立功，以成就武德；十是阵车，即战车前后连接成阵，遮蔽马的双目，以免惊驰；十一是死士，即从各部挑选勇敢强健、武艺高超的士兵，乘着战车，在阵地的前后左右纵横驰骋，伺机出奇制胜；十二是力卒，即

keeping alert for each other,the front and rear awaiting each other, and a circular array of chariots creating a solid defense in order to oppose the enemy and make the encampment secure.The sixth, "commanders are distinguished," refers to the forward rows striving to advance so as to keep a distance from the rear rows, which are not able to contend for being the first to ascend nor overstep their positions. The seventh, "five emblems," refers to distinguishing the rows with different color emblems so that they will keep in order from beginning to end. The eighth, "preserving units,"refers to units breaking up and following each other, each having their designated sections. The ninth, "gongs and drums," refers to stimulating the troops to make achievements and forcing them to respect Military Virtue. The tenth, "arraying the chariots," refers to connecting the chariot arrays with the forward troops, and blindfolding the horses' eyes with hoods. The eleventh, "warriors of death," refers to selecting the talented and brave from among the masses of the army to ride in chariots. They race forward and back, across and about, using unorthodox tactics to control the enemy. The twelfth, "strong soldiers," refers to the

【原文】

经旗全曲，不麾不动也。

此十二者教成，犯令不舍。兵弱能强之，主卑能尊之，令弊能起之，民流能亲之，人众能治之，地大能守之。国车不出于阃，组甲不出于橐，而威服天下矣。

兵有五致：为将忘家，逾垠忘亲，指敌忘身，必死则生，急胜为下。百人被刃，陷行乱陈；千人

【今译】

选用强健有力的勇士掌管军旗，以约束全军，没有将领的号令不得擅自行动。

这十二个方面的训练完成后，再有违犯条令者，严惩不贷。（如能做到这些，）弱小的军队能够强大，卑微的君主能够尊显，废弛的法令能够振兴，流散的百姓能够归附，人口众多也能治理得很好，土地辽阔也能守卫得住。国都中的战车不必驶出郭门，收藏起来的铠甲不必取出甲套，就能以声威慑服天下了。

用兵作战要做到五条：受命为将就要忘掉家室；出国作战就要忘掉父母；临阵杀敌就要忘掉自己；只有抱定必死的决心，才能绝处逢生；心浮气躁，急于取胜，则是下策。百人死战，可以冲入敌群，

stalwarts' handling the flags to regulate the units. Without their brandishing of flags to indicate an order, the units will not move. When instructions about these twelve points have been successfully taught,anyone in violation of these instructions will not be pardoned. If the army is weak they will be able to make it strong. If the sovereign is unpopular, they will be able to honor him. If the ordinances are lax, they will be able to revitalize them. If the people migrate, they will be able to gain their allegiance. If the populace is numerous, they will be able to govern them. If the land is vast, they will be able to defend it. When the state chariots have not departed from the border gates and the helmets and armors have not been taken out of their storage bags, your awesomeness will cause All Under Heaven into submission.

There are five demands for the army: For the generals they should forget their families; for those crossing the borders they should forget their parents; for those fighting the enemy they should forget their own lives in battle; for those determining to fight to the death they will survive; for those seeking a hasty victory it is inferior tactics. When one hundred men are will-

【原文】

被刃，擒敌杀将；万人被刃，横行天下。

武王问太公望曰："吾欲少间而极用人之要。"望对曰："赏如山，罚如溪。太上无过，其次补过。使人无得私语，诸罚而请不罚者死，诸赏而请不赏者死。"

伐国必因其变。示之财以观其穷，示之弊以观其病，上乖者下离，若此之类，是伐之因也。

【今译】

扰乱敌阵；千人死战，可以打败敌军，杀死敌将；万人死战，可以所向披靡，天下无敌。

周武王问太公望说："我想在很短的时间里洞悉用人的要诀。"太公望回答说："赏赐要像山峰那样高，惩罚要像溪水那样深。最好是赏罚没有差错，其次是有了差错赶紧补救。应该使属下不得随意议论赏罚问题，凡是有罪当罚而请求不罚者处死，凡是有功当赏而请求不赏者处死。"

讨伐敌国，必须利用它内部的变故。观察它的财政情况，看它是否贫困；观察它国内的弊政，看它有何危机；其上层专横暴虐，下层必定离心离德。如出现这样的情况，都是讨伐敌国时可利用的因素。

ing to suffer the pain of a blade, they will be able to break in the enemy's formations and disrupt his positions. When one thousand men are willing to suffer the pain of a blade, they will be able to capture the enemy and kill his generals. When ten thousand men are willing to suffer the pain of a blade, they will be able to traverse All Under Heaven at will.

King Wu of Zhou said to Tai Gong Wang: "I want to spend a short time to grasp the key points of how to employ persons." Wang replied: "Your rewards should be like mountains, your punishments like valleys. The best is to commit no fault; the next best is to correct the fault. No one is allowed to make irresponsible remarks. If someone should be punished, execute anyone who requests that he be spared. If someone should be rewarded, execute anyone who requests that he not be rewarded. If you attack a state you must take advantage of its internal changes. Demonstrate assets in order to observe its poverty. Demonstrate weaknesses in order to observe its malpractices. If the sovereign is immoral and the people disaffected, in cases such as these one you have a basis for attack."

Generally when you are going to raise an

**【原文】**

凡兴师，必审内外之权，以计其去。兵有备阙，粮食有余不足，校所出入之路，然后兴师伐乱，必能入之。

地大而城小者，必先收其地；城大而地窄者，必先攻其城；地广而人寡者，则绝其阨；地狭而人众者，则筑大堙以临之。无丧其利，无夺其时，宽其政，夷其业，救其弊，则足以施天下。

今战国相攻，大伐有德。自伍而两，自两而师，

**【今译】**

凡兴兵作战，必须详细考察权衡内外形势，以此来决定军队的去就进退。看看军队是否做好了准备，粮草是否充足够用，计划好出兵和返回的路线，然后起兵讨伐暴乱，就一定能攻破敌国。

敌国地域广阔而城郭卑小，必须先占领广大的土地；城郭高大而地域狭小，必须先攻打其城市；其地域辽阔而人口稀少，就要控制其险要关塞；地域狭小而人口众多，就要筑起土山以居高临敌。不要损害当地百姓的利益，不要耽误百姓的农时，要放宽原有的政策，使百姓安居乐业，要革除原有的弊政，这样就足以施恩于天下了。

如今好战之国互相攻伐，大举进攻有德政的国家。军队从伍到两，从两到师，不能统一号令。通

army, you must first investigate and weigh the internal and external postures. You must know whether the army is prepared or not, whether the supply of food is adequate or not. You must examine the routes for advancing and returning. Thereafter when you raise the army to attack the rebellious you will be certain to enter the state. If the territory is vast but the city small, you must first occupy the land. If the city is large but the territory is narrow, you must first attack the city. If the territory is vast but the populace few, you should isolate the strategic points. If the territory is confined but the population in great numbers, you should pile up a great earth hump to overlook and attack them. Do not harm the people's profits; do not seize the agricultural seasons. Be magnanimous to their government officials. Stabilize the people's occupations. Take remedial measures to rectify their malpractices. Thereby it is sufficient for you to bestow favor on All Under Heaven.

Today warring states attack each other. Those that launch large-scale offensives against the state of virtue, from the squad of five to platoon, from platoon to army, do not unify their commands and cause the shaking of the army's morale.

【原文】

不一其令。率俾民心不定，徒尚骄侈，谋患辩讼，吏究其事，累且败也。日暮路远，还有挫气；师老将贪，争掠易败。

凡将轻、垒卑、众动，可攻也；将重、垒高、众惧，可围也。凡围，必开其小利，使渐夷弱，则节吝有不食者矣。众夜击者，惊也；众避事者，离

【今译】

常使得士兵人心不定，养成骄横奢侈的风气，惹事生非、争吵不断，军官忙于处理这些事情，徒耗精力，导致作战的失败。（事先不做好计划，以至）日暮天昏，征途却遥远无尽头，返回又会挫伤部队的士气；军队疲惫不堪，将领贪得无厌，争抢掠夺财物，往往轻易致败。

凡是将领轻率、营垒低矮、军心动摇的敌人，就可以对其发动进攻；对于将领持重、营垒高大、士兵心存戒备的敌人，可以采取围困的方式。凡是

They incline to arrogance and extravagance and provoke disputes in endless quarrels. Their commanders taking trouble to investigate disputes are exhausted, and the chances of winning a battle are bungled. When the sun has set the roads remain long; when the troops come back their morale will be dampened. When the troops are worn out, their generals covet for personal achievements and soldiers contend for plundering, they can be defeated easily.

Generally if generals are indiscreet, fortified works low, and troops unstable, they can be attacked. If generals are discreet, fortified works high and troops frightened, they can be besieged.In general the siege must open a small gap to give them a gleam of hope so as to weaken them in an incremental process, and at last no matter how they save on food they will be hunger-stricken without food. If the troops fight each other at night, they will be terrified. If the troops shirk their duties, they will be in dissension and discord. If they just wait for others to come and rescue them, and when the date for battle arrives they will be tense with worried frown, and they will be losing confidence and morale.

【原文】

也；待人之救，期战而蹙，皆心失而伤气也。伤气败军，曲谋败国。

【今译】

围困敌人，一定要留给敌人一线希望，使其逐渐消耗（而不至作困兽之斗），敌人再节省，也有吃不上饭的时候。敌人夜间自相攻击，是惊恐的表现；敌人推辞差事，是离心离德的表现；等待他人的救援，约定战期却又忧心重重，都是丧失信心、士气不振的表现。损伤士气会使军队失败，错误的策略会使国家遭殃。

When the morale is lost, the army will be defeated. When the strategic plan is erroneous, the state will be defeated.

# 兵令上第二十三

【原文】

兵者，凶器也；争者，逆德也。事必有本，故王者伐暴乱、本仁义焉。战国则以立威抗敌相图，而不能废兵也。

兵者，以武为植，以文为种；武为表，文为里。能审此二者，知胜败矣。文所以视利害、辨安危；武所以犯强敌、力攻守也。

专一则胜，离散则败。陈以密则固，锋以疏则达。卒畏将甚于敌者胜，卒畏敌甚于将者败。所以

【今译】

兵器，是杀人的凶器；争夺，是违反道德的行为。万事万物必有其根本，所以推行王政者讨伐暴乱，以仁义为根本。争战之国却以树立声威、抗衡敌国而互相攻伐，所以不能废弃战争。

用兵作战，要以武力为枝干，以文略为根基；武力是外在表现，文略才是本质。能弄清这二者的关系，就能把握战争的胜败了。文略，是用来观察利害、辨别安危的；武力，是用来对抗强敌、奋力攻守的。

意志统一就能取胜，离心离德就会失败。布阵严密就能稳固，前锋稀疏才能机动灵活。士兵畏惧

# 23. Military Orders I

Weapons are inauspicious implements.Conflict is contrary to Virtue. All affairs must have their foundation. Hence a true king attacks the rebellious on the basis of Benevolence and Righteousness. Warring states want to establish their awesomeness so that they will resist their opponents and plot against each other. Thus warfare cannot be ended.

One who conducts warfare will take the military as its support pillar, and the civil as its good foundation. The military is surface, the civil substance. The one who is able to understand the relation between these two will foresee victory or defeat in battle. The civil is used to observe advantage and harm, and make distinction between safety and danger. The military is used to assault the strong enemy and do utmost to attack and defend.

Unity of will leads to victory. Dissension and discord lead to defeat. If formations are tight,

【原文】

知胜败者，称将于敌也。敌与将，犹权衡焉。

安静则治，暴疾则乱。出卒陈兵有常令，行伍疏数有常法，先后之次有适宜。常令者，非追北袭邑攸用也。前后不次，则失也。乱先后，斩之。

常陈皆向敌，有内向，有外向，有立陈，有坐

【今译】

将吏超过敌人的军队就能得胜利，士兵畏惧敌人超过将吏的军队就会遭失败。用以预知胜负的办法，就是比较士兵畏敌还是畏将。用比较畏敌与畏将的办法预测胜负，就像用秤称物一样准确。

镇定冷静就能井然有序，暴戾急躁就会乱成一团。出兵列阵有规定的条令，队列疏密有规定的法则，先后次序有适宜的排列。规定的条令不是用来追歼逃敌、袭击敌城的。阵形中前后次序紊乱，就会导致失利，所以对扰乱队列次序的人要处死。

一般的阵法都是面向敌方摆设的。但阵中的士兵有的面向阵里，有的面向阵外，有的站立在阵中，

they will be solid. If vanguard troops are deployed in dispersal, they will be convenient for maneuvering. If soldiers fear their generals far more than the enemy, they will gain victory.If soldiers fear the enemy far more than their generals, they will be defeated. Thus if you want to know who will be victorious, who defeated,compare the generals to the enemy. The comparison of the enemy with the generals is like weighing something in the nicest scales.When the generals are calm, the troops will be under control. When they are rash, the troops will be in confusion.

When troops are about to set off and formations to be deployed, they have the standing orders. When formations keep the dispersal and density of the lines and squads of five, they have standing methods. Arraying the rows from front to rear has its congruousness and appropriateness. The standing orders are not used to pursue a fleeing enemy and attack cities.If the front and rear rows are disordered, the troops will be defeated. Anyone who disrupts the order of the front and rear rows will be decapitated.

Normal deployment of formations is always facing toward the enemy. There are also internally oriented formations, externally oriented formati-

【原文】

陈。夫内向，所以顾中也；外向，所以备外也。立陈，所以行也；坐陈，所以止也。立坐之陈，相参进止，将在其中。坐之兵剑斧，立之兵戟弩，将亦居中。

善御敌者，正兵先合，而后扼之。此必胜之术也。

陈之斧钺，饰之旗章，有功必赏，犯令必死。存亡死生，在枹之端。虽天下有善兵者，莫能御此

【今译】

有的跪坐在阵中。面向里的士兵是保卫中军安全的，面向外的士兵是为防备敌人袭击的。站立的士兵是准备发起冲锋的，跪坐的士兵是用来稳住阵脚的。阵中士兵有立有坐，相互配合，就能使攻击敌人与稳定内部两相兼顾，将领则居中指挥。跪坐的士兵使用的兵器是剑和斧，站立的士兵使用的兵器是戟和弩，将领总是位于军阵的中央。

善于克敌制胜的将领，先以正兵与敌交战，然后出奇兵制敌于死地。这是必胜的战法。

布阵时陈列执法的斧钺，给官兵配饰各色旗帜徽章，有功者必给予奖赏，犯法者必给予严惩。官

ons, standing formations and sitting formations. Now the internally oriented formations care for safeguarding the center; the externally oriented formations provide strength to meet threats from outside; the standing formations are convenient to move; the sitting formations provide means for encampment.Mixed formations — with some soldiers standing,others sitting — respond to each other in accord with the need to move or encamp, with the general being in the middle. The seated soldiers are equipped with swords and axes,and the standing soldiers with spear-tipped halberds and crossbows, with the general also being in the middle.

Those adept in resisting the enemy first join battle with the orthodox units, then dispatch the unorthodox units to hit him hard. This is the tactics for certain victory.

When formations are deployed, axes of punishments will be arrayed, and flags and emblems for the troops displayed. Anyone who makes achievement shall be rewarded; anyone who disobeys an order shall be executed. survival or extinction of the state and life or death of soldiers lie in the tip of the general's drumsticks. Even those

【原文】

矣。

矢射未交，长刃未接，前噪者谓之虚，后噪者谓之实，不噪者谓之秘。虚、实、秘者，兵之体也。

【今译】

兵的生死存亡，都由将领指挥用的鼓槌来决定。这样，即使天下有善于用兵的人，也无法战胜这支部队。

敌我双方的弓箭尚未对射，兵刃尚未交锋，敌方前军喧哗鼓噪是虚弱的表现，后军喧哗鼓噪是有实力的表现，前后都不喧哗鼓噪是其有意隐蔽自己实力和意图的表现。虚、实、秘，是军阵中的三种状态。

under Heaven adept in conducting warfare will not be able to resist them.

When arrows have not yet been shot, when long blades have not yet clashed, those in front yelling out are termed "empty," those in rear yelling out are termed "substantial," and all ranks not yelling out are termed "secretive." "Empty," "substantial," and "secretive" are the characteristics of warfare.

# 兵令下第二十四

【原文】

诸去大军为前御之备者，边县列候，各相去三五里。闻大军为前御之备，战则皆禁行，所以安内也。

内卒出戍，令将吏授旗鼓戈甲。发日，后将吏及出县封界者，以坐后戍法。兵戍边一岁，遂亡不

【今译】

大部队行动之前被派遣到前沿地区担任防御、警戒任务的部队，应在边境县邑设立哨所，各哨所之间相距三五里地。一得到主力出动的消息，立即加强边境的防御、警戒工作。一旦战事发动，边境地区就一律禁止通行，目的是保证国内的安定。

内地士兵去守卫边疆，要求将领或军吏授予他们军旗、战鼓、武器和铠甲。出发之后，如有迟于将吏离开县境者，按“后戍法”处罚。士兵守卫边疆满一年，不等到接替的人到来就擅自离开岗位的，

# 24. Military Orders II

Detachments are sent from the main body of the army to undertake forward defense missions. They should set up outposts in border counties and their outposts should keep a distance of three to five *li* each other. Hearing that the main body has set off, they should step up preparations for forward defense. In wartime, they should prohibit all movement in order to provide security to the state.

When the troops are about to depart from the interior to perform border duty, their general or commanding officer should be ordered to render them flags, drums, dagger-axes and armors. On the day of setting off, anyone who arrives after the general or commanding officer has gone out beyond the county border, shall be punished by the Law of Late Arrival for Border Duty. When a soldier has served the border duty for one year but left without waiting for his relief, he shall be punished as a deserter. If his parents and wife

【原文】

候代者，法比亡军。父母妻子知之，与同罪；弗知，赦之。卒后将吏而至大将所一日，父母妻子尽同罪。卒逃归至家一日，父母妻子弗捕执及不言，亦同罪。

诸战而亡其将吏者，及将吏弃卒独北者，尽斩之。前吏弃其卒而北，后吏能斩之而夺其卒者，赏。

军无功者，戍三岁。

三军大战，若大将死，而从吏五百人已上不能死敌者，斩；大将左右近卒，在陈中者，皆斩；余

【今译】

应同逃兵一样治罪。父母妻子知情的，与其同罪；不知情的，免罪。士兵在将吏之后到达大将所在地，迟到一日，其父母妻子都与其同罪。士兵逃跑回家哪怕只呆一天，其父母妻子既不拘捕送官，也不报告的，也与其同罪。

凡是作战中擅自离开将吏的士兵，以及将吏丢弃部队独自逃跑的，都应斩首。前面的将吏丢弃部队而逃跑，后面的将吏如能将其处决并夺取其属下士兵的，给予奖赏。

在军中久不建功的人，罚他戍守边疆三年。

三军大战，倘若大将战死，其属下统兵五百人以上的将吏，不能与敌死战的，处死；大将身边的

know about it, they will share the offense with him. If they do not know about it, pardon them.If a soldier reaches the headquarters of the Grand General a day after his general or commanding officer, his parents and wife shall share the offense with him. If a soldier shuns his duty to go home even only for one day, and his parents and wife do not seize him and hand him over to the office nor report it, they shall also share the offense with him.

In battle any soldier who escapes from his general or commanding officer, and the general or commanding officer who deserts his troops to flee by himself, shall all be decapitated. If an officer in front abandons his troops and flee, any officer to the rear who is able to behead him and take his troops over will be rewarded.

Anyone among such troops who makes no achievement within the army must undertake a three-year tour of duty on the border.

If the Three Armies launch large-scale operations and the Grand General dies, his subordinate officers commanding more than five hundred men who are not able to fight the enemy to the death should be decapitated, and the soldiers protecting and attending to the Grand General in

【原文】

士卒有军功者，夺一级；无军功者，戍三岁。

战亡伍人，及伍人战死不得其尸，同伍尽夺其功；得其尸，罪皆赦。

军之利害，在国之名实。今名在官，而实在家，官不得其实，家不得其名。聚卒为军，有空名而无实，外不足以御敌，内不足以守国。此军之所以不给，将之所以夺威也。

臣以谓卒逃归者，同舍伍人及吏罚入粮为饶，

【今译】

近卫士卒，在军阵中的全部处死；其余士兵有军功的，削爵位一级；没有军功的，罚戍边三年。

战斗中伍内有人逃亡，以及伍内有人战死而不能夺回其尸体的，同伍的人都要剥夺军功；能够夺回死者尸体的，都赦免其罪。

军队的利害所系，在于国家登册的名额与军中的实际人数是否相符。如今名字虽然在官府的簿籍上，但本人实际呆在家里，这样官府得不到实际兵员，而其家里也没有他的名籍。征集士卒组成军队，只有空名而无实际兵员，对外不足以抵御敌人，对内不足以维护国家安定。这就是军队不能满员，将领丧失威望的原因啊。

臣下认为，士兵逃亡回家，与其同舍的伍人及军吏都要交纳粮食以赎罪，名义上叫做军实，实际

battle should be beheaded without exception. The remaining officers and men who have had military merits will be demoted by one grade. Those who have had no merits must be on border duty for three years.

If anyone of the squad of five deserts in battle and members of the squad die in action but their bodies are not recovered, all the merits of the squad should be deprived. If the bodies are recovered, all the squad members should be pardoned.

The gains and losses of the army lie in the registered strength of the state being in conformity to its real strength. Today those who nominally have registered in the state roll stay at home in reality. Thus the state does not acquire its real strength. Meanwhile the hometown has not registered those staying at home. When soldiers are assembled to form an army but it has an empty name without real strength, the army cannot afford to resist the enemy from outside and defend the state at home. This is the way in which the strength of army becomes inadequate, in which the general's awesomeness is deprived.

I believe that when a soldier deserts to go

【原文】

名为军实，是有一军之名，而有二实之出。国内空虚，自竭民岁，曷以免奔北之祸乎！

今以法止逃归、禁亡军，是兵之一胜也。什伍相联，及战斗，则卒吏相救，是兵之二胜也。将能立威，卒能节制，号令明信，攻守皆得，是兵之三胜也。

臣闻古之善用兵者，能杀卒之半，其次杀其十

【今译】

上是空有一个士兵的名额，下面却要交两份军粮。结果造成国内库府空虚，百姓存粮枯竭，靠什么来避免军队失败的祸患呢！

现在若能用法令制止士兵逃跑回家，禁绝士兵离开军队的现象，这就是用兵取胜的第一个条件。军中什伍之内互相连保，在战斗中，士兵与军官就会互相救助，这是用兵取胜的第二个条件。将领能树立声威，士兵能服从节制，号令明确坚定，进攻防御策略运用得当，这是用兵取胜的第三个条件。

臣下听说，古代善于用兵的人，能使半数的士兵甘愿战死，其次使十分之三的士兵甘愿战死，其

home, his colleagues of the squad of five and commanding officer shall be fined to present their food to enrich the ration storage. For all the name of military rations, this is nominally a single man at front only to consume two rations. Thus the resources of the state become empty, and people have exhausted their storage of food naturally. How can the catastrophe of defeat be avoided?

Now making laws to prevent soldiers in battle from going home and prohibiting desertion of the troops are the first military victory. Combining the double squad of ten with the squad of five in joint responsibility and making mutual assistance between officers and soldiers in battle are the second military victory.If the general is able to establish awesomeness,if the soldiers are able to follow the ordinances and regulations, if the orders and commands are clear and firm and the tactics of attacking and defending are appropriate and effective, these are the third military victory.

I have heard that anciently those who were adept in employing troops could bear to kill half of their officers and soldiers. The next could bear to kill thirty percent and the lowest ten

【原文】

三，其下杀其十一。能杀其半者，威加海内；杀十三者，力加诸侯；杀十一者，令行士卒。

故曰：百万之众不用命，不如万人之斗也；万人之斗〔不用命〕，不如百人之奋也。赏如日月，信如四时，令如斧钺，制如干将，士卒不用命者，未之有也。

【今译】

下能使十分之一的士兵甘愿战死。能使一半士兵甘愿战死的，其威势可以慑服天下；能使十分之三士兵甘愿战死的，其武力可以征服诸侯；能使十分之一士兵甘愿战死的，其号令可以在部下中畅通无阻。

所以说：百万人的军队不听命效力，还不如万人的军队英勇战斗；万人的军队不听命效力，还不如百人的军队奋不顾身。赏赐如日月般光明正大，守信如四时交替般准确，命令如斧钺般威严，决断如干将般锐利，若还有士兵不拼死效命的，那是不可能的事情。

percent. The awesomeness of one who could sacrifice half of his troops is established within the Four Seas. The strength of one who could sacrifice thirty percent could be applied to the feudal states. The orders of one who could sacrifice ten percent would be followed among his officers and soldiers.

Therefore, it is said that a mass of one million who do not implement orders is not as good as ten thousand men who fight. Ten thousand men who fight but do not follow orders are not as good as one hundred men who are aroused to fight desperately.

When rewards are as clear as the sun and moon and as credible as the four seasons, when orders are as strict as an axe of punishments and as sharp as the famous sword Gan Jiang, it has never been heard that there were officers and soldiers not implementing orders!

**图书在版编目(CIP)数据**

吴子 司马法 尉缭子/王式金,黄朴民,任力校;
潘嘉玢译 .—北京:军事科学出版社,2004.11
(大中华文库)
ISBN 7-80137-721-4

Ⅰ.吴… Ⅱ.①王… ②黄… ③任… ④潘…
Ⅲ.兵法-中国-古代-汉、英 Ⅳ.E892.2

中国版本图书馆 CIP 数据核字(2004)第 121508 号

**责任编辑**:潘宏 王显臣
**审 校**:马欣来 梁良兴

大中华文库
**吴子 司马法 尉缭子**
潘嘉玢 译

**出版者**:
军事科学出版社
(北京市海淀区青龙桥军事科学出版社 邮政编码:100091)

**制版、排版者**:
恒基佳业科技有限公司(北京市海淀区)

**印制者**:深圳市佳信达印务有限公司

开本:960×640 1/16(精装) 印张:25 印数:1-3000 册
2005 年第 1 版第 1 次印刷
(汉英对照)ISBN 7-80137-721-4/E·486
定价:46.80 元

---